Praise for I THOUGHT WE'D NEVER SPEAK AGAIN

"*I Thought We'd Never Speak Again* is a gift for anyone who needs inspiration, courage, and guidance in making peace with troubled relationships. Davis's powerful stories teach us that by bridging the separations between us, we heal what is broken within us. I recommend this book with my whole heart. It changed my life."

> —Charlotte Sophia Kasl, Ph.D., author of *Finding Joy,*
> *If the Buddha Dated, If the Buddha Married*

"Laura Davis has a real knack for putting her finger on the pulse of what people are struggling with and what they need to hear. With this groundbreaking book on reconciliation, she has done it again. With grace and clarity she brings us a critical message: that making peace in our own lives and in the larger world needs to be first and foremost on both our personal and national agenda."

> —Marilyn Van Derbur, former Miss America
> and National Speaker for Children's Rights

"As we hunger for authentic expressions of peace and reconciliation, Laura Davis has given us a true gift. She offers pathways for us to let go of pain, bitterness, fear, and even hatred. She presents a continuum of reconciliation that goes far beyond simple answers and allows for the individual needs and cultural context of the involved parties. Davis eloquently presents her message that attaining peace in our lives and in the larger world must first be anchored within our own personal journey of healing. Few authors have addressed the issues of forgiveness and reconciliation with such clarity, compassion, and sensitivity."

> —Mark Umbreit, Ph.D., founding director,
> Center for Restorative Justice and Peacemaking,
> University of Minnesota, School of Social Work

"With prodigious love and wisdom, Laura Davis teaches us new ways to view and resolve a wide array of ruptured relationships so that we can come out whole, perhaps for the first time. She describes excruciating struggles to find love and self after interpersonal fractures ranging from painful misunderstandings to criminal assaults to ethnic wars. Ms. Davis shows us ways to reconcile with our own fear and pain and rage, if not always with our adversaries. *I Thought We'd Never Speak Again* is a gift of the heart, full of wisdom, courage, and hope. I highly recommend it."
> —David C. Hall, M.D., family psychiatrist and author of *Stop Arguing and Start Understanding: Eight Steps to Solving Family Conflicts*

"Leave it to Laura Davis, who opened a whole generation with *The Courage to Heal*, to once again give us what we need—a book about how we come home to each other and ourselves. I want to buy this for everyone I know. And Davis has presented this healing with such compassion, clarity, warmth, and good, solid prose that this book is unbeatable. No one can turn from its truth."
> —Natalie Goldberg, author of *Thunder and Lightning* and *The Essential Writer's Notebook*

"Laura Davis understands that in order to deeply touch the human heart, you must touch it with relevant story. It is a rare adult who has not come to know the bitter pain of estranged, bruised, or broken relationships. Davis provides a vehicle for giving those stories voice, never glossing the pain or suggesting panacea, but masterfully stitching them together and offering to us all a counterpane of comfort, a harbinger of hope."
> —Dave Gustafson, M.A., R.C.C., Canadian pioneer in victim-offender reconciliation and restorative justice

"If you have been hurt in a relationship and have unresolved pain, I encourage you to READ THIS BOOK. If you are a therapist or are in a position of nurturing the emotional well-being of others, I encourage you to READ THIS BOOK. Whether your relationships are fraught with resentments or filled with love, this is a book not to be missed!"
> —Robin Casarjian, author of *Forgiveness: A Bold Choice for a Peaceful Heart*; director of the Lionheart Foundation; sponsor of the National Emotional Literacy Project for Prisoners and Youth-at-Risk

"Anybody who has given up on the possibility of reconciliation should read this book. Davis builds a web of hope that human beings can indeed move on, even when relationships have been painful and very destructive."
> —Ron Kraybill, professor, Conflict Transformation Program, Eastern Mennonite University

"This positive yet realistic guide to repairing broken relationships is a pleasure to read. It is filled with the compelling stories of real people weighing the risks and benefits of reconnecting with estranged loved ones before it is too late. They do so in a remarkable variety of ways, some with cautious trepidation, others with relieved abandon. Laura Davis leads the pack, courageously modeling her own experience of reconciliation with her mother, after years of painful separation. *I Thought We'd Never Speak Again* inspires a deep understanding that, although they can be hurtful, relationships are crucial to our human experience. I strongly recommend this book."
> —Esther Giller, president and director, Sidran Traumatic Stress Foundation

"The best books offer readers the tools they need to become better people. This one will surely inspire many to say, 'I still care about you; let's try again.' "
> —Mariah Burton Nelson, author of *The Unburdened Heart: Five Keys to Forgiveness and Freedom*

"With warmth, humor, and sensitivity, Laura Davis teaches us personal and practical truths about healing painful, broken relationships. She does not offer simplistic answers or tell us that there is only one way to reconcile. Her book is a tremendous gift, and will change the way we think about reconciliation in our personal lives, in the criminal justice process, and in the greater world."
> —Greg D. Richardson, Restorative Justice Institute

"In order to practice nonviolence and peacemaking, we must first understand the principles of forgiveness and reconciliation. Laura Davis illuminates the suffering and losses that keep us isolated from each other, as well as the steps required to mend broken relationships. Her book gives us the courage and hope we need to confront the fears that keep us from living full and healthy lives."
> —Dot Walsh, Global Peace Coordinator and Peace Chaplain, The Peace Abbey

"*I Thought We'd Never Speak Again* will be useful to anyone who wants to use dialogue and reconciliation as a healing path. Davis's narratives reveal the complexity of personal transformation and the challenges of reconciliation with individuals who have caused great harm. Persons seeking such transformation need boundaries, time, and most of all choices, and Davis's book shows us that there are multiple doors through which even the most damaged and estranged individuals can find a healing path toward reconciliation."
  —Gordon Bazemore, Ph.D., director, Community Justice Institute,
    Florida Atlantic University

"A most helpful and practical book about finding the stepping-stones of releasing the past and healing the hole in our hearts so we can move on in our lives."
  —Gerald Jampolsky, M.D., author of *Forgiveness:*
    The Greatest Healer of All

"This is a book of enormous personal and social significance for a society steeped in conflict and alienation. It is a deeply moving and spiritually uplifting work that you will want to give to family, friends, and colleagues alike."
  —Donald T. Saposnek, Ph.D., family therapist and author of
    Mediating Child Custody Disputes

"*I Thought We'd Never Speak Again* is an impressive, deep, and thorough guide to relationship healing. It is filled with insights, tools, and a wide variety of poignant stories that help readers figure out whether, when, and how to reconcile troubled relationships. Laura Davis writes with heart and soul and offers a path to self-love, compassion for others, community, and inner peace."
  —Wendy Maltz, M.S.W., author of *The Sexual Healing Journey*

"Congratulations, Laura! You have taken an in-depth look at a timely and difficult subject. This book will be an inspiration to all those who read it."
  —Dr. Eileen R. Borris, psychologist and founder of *Peace Initiatives*

I THOUGHT WE'D NEVER SPEAK AGAIN

ALSO BY LAURA DAVIS

The Courage to Heal (with Ellen Bass)

The Courage to Heal Workbook

Allies in Healing

Beginning to Heal (with Ellen Bass)

Becoming the Parent You Want to Be (with Janis Keyser)

I THOUGHT WE'D NEVER SPEAK AGAIN

The Road from Estrangement to Reconciliation

LAURA DAVIS

HarperCollins*Publishers*

HarperCollins books may be purchased for educational, business, or sales promotional use. For information, please write to: Special Markets Department, HarperCollins Publishers Inc., 10 East 53rd Street, New York, NY 10022.

FIRST EDITION

Designed by Laura Lindgren and Celia Fuller

Printed on acid-free paper

Library of Congress Cataloging-in-Publication Data

Davis, Laura.
I thought we'd never speak again : the road from estrangement to reconciliation / Laura Davis.
p.   cm.
Includes index
ISBN 0-06-019762-5
1. Interpersonal conflict.   2. Interpersonal communication.   3. Reconciliation.
I. Title.
HM1121 .D38   2002
158.2—dc21   2001026479

02   03   04   05   06   CG/RRD   10 9 8 7 6 5 4 3 2

To my mother, Temme Davis, for her courage, persistence, and love

and to my father, Abram Davis, a remarkable man
March 2, 1919–August 17, 2000

I will permit no man to narrow and degrade my soul by making me hate him.

—BOOKER T. WASHINGTON

Nothing will ever be attempted, if all possible objections must be first overcome.

—DR. SAMUEL JOHNSON

Hope is an orientation of the spirit. It is not the conviction that things will turn out well, but the certainty that something makes sense, regardless of how it turns out.

—VÁCLAV HAVEL

CONTENTS

That Happens Unilaterally · The Trouble with Pseudo-Forgiveness · Resolution Is Possible Without Forgiveness · *Vicki Malloy: Rebuilding a Relationship with My Perpetrator* · Are Some Things Unforgivable? · A Personal Decision

PART FIVE

FINDING PEACE

CHAPTER 10

When Reconciliation Is Impossible: The Task of Letting Go / 295

Accepting That the Relationship Is Over · Letting Go When You Don't Know Why the Relationship Ended · *Peggy O'Neill: It's in Her Hands Now* · Letting Go Is a Process · *Helen Meyers: I Can't Force Him to Open the Door* · Leaving the Porch Light On · *Pam Leeds: Compassion from Afar* · The Opposite of Estrangement

CHAPTER 11

When We Meet Again: The Benefits of Reconciliation / 311

Enjoying the Pleasures of Recovered Love · Reweaving the Web of Community · Reconciliation Leads to Peace · Reconciliation Rekindles Optimism · *A Deep Sense of Peace*

ACKNOWLEDGMENTS

First and foremost, I thank the hundred-plus men and women who entrusted me with their deeply personal stories. Although I could not include all the stories they shared with me, their experiences, struggles, and triumphs deepened my understanding of reconciliation. Their courage and generosity infuse this book.

There are two women in particular without whom this book would not exist. It was over lunch in Sara Friedlander's kitchen that the idea for this book was conceived. Throughout the two years it has taken me to complete it, her warmth, encouragement, hand-holding, humor, psychological savvy, superb line-editing, and complete belief in this project have sustained me.

Ellen Bass, with whom I have traveled many roads, has also been integral to the successful completion of this book. Ellen edited the manuscript and did an impeccable job, twice. She stood as a beacon of light at every turning point I faced along the way. She taught me about "fishing for stories," patiently argued her point of view when she thought I was wrong, and gave me a quiet place to work one weekend when I really needed it. I can't wait for her next book so I can return the favor.

I would also like to thank my stalwart readers: Michele Cooper, Lauren Crux, Abe Davis, Temme Davis, Susan Frankel, Julie Free-stone, Michael Gillen, Evelyn Hall, Donna Jenson, Nancy London, Robin Moulds, Nona Olivia, Keith Rand, Bryan Rawles, Muriel

Salmansohn, Ziesel Saunders, Leslie Smith, Darren Starwynn, Hank Vogler, and Karen Zelin for wading through an incredibly long manuscript and sharing their thoughtful, honest feedback.

For encouraging me to pursue this dream, I am grateful to all of the folks who came to my "help Laura think about her work" party: Yona Adams, Karyn Bristol, Carla Carstens, Cliff Friedlander, Sara Friedlander, Jim Greiner, Evelyn Hall, Janis Keyser, Jan Landry, Judy Phillips, Barbara Schatan, Leslie Smith, Nancy Stucker, and Karen Zelin.

For introducing me to people to interview, thanks to Yona Adams, David Calof, Temme Davis, Melodye Feldman, Molly Fisk, Terry Fletcher, Thom Harrigan, Fran Henry, Gus Kaufman, Jan Landry, David Lerman, Marc Levy, Mike Lew, Bill McBride, Steve Nawojczyk, Hina Pendle, Marty Price, Suzette Southfox, Marty Spiegel, Carol Sullivan, Joan Tabachnick, and Armand Volkas.

For help with the proposal: Ellen Bass, Charlotte Kasl, and Jennifer Meyer.

I commend Sigrid Hvolboll, for answering my mail and continuing to lighten my load.

Janet Goldstein, for the conversation that inspired the book's thematic structure.

Charlotte Raymond, my agent, for good humor, loyalty, and belief in this project. She also came up with the title.

Trena Keating, my first editor, for sticking to her guns and helping me hone this book to a manageable size.

Toni Sciarra, my second editor, for joining this project midstream with grace and enthusiasm. And to her assistant, Nicholas Darrell, for handling all those details.

Kapo Ng, for a beautiful cover.

Susan Weinberg, Carrie Freimuth, Christine Caruso, Patti Kelly, Abby Kunath, Diane Burrowes, Jennifer Swihart, and Christopher McKerrow, for collaborative genius in getting the word out.

Beth Silfin, for going over this book with a legal, fine-tooth comb.

The folks at the Tariq Khamisa Foundation, for being generous and always helpful.

In my personal life, I'd like to thank:

My mother, Temme Davis, for going the distance and letting me tell our story.

Nona Olivia, for twenty-five years of laughter and friendship. I've learned a lot from our estrangement and reconciliation. Thanks for encouraging me to pursue this project when I thought I should be off doing something else.

Karen Zelin, for twenty-plus years of friendship, sisterhood, and ongoing support. You're the best, most loyal friend I could hope for. I'm thrilled we reconciled and get to share our daily lives again.

Susan Frankel, for pursuing our reconciliation and making our friendship better the second time around.

Natalie Devora, for renewing our friendship and accepting my apology with an open heart.

Janet Gellman, for forgiving me not just once, but twice.

Evelyn Hall, for hypnotherapy, massages, women's creativity circles, and being a generous friend.

Mary O'Neill, Denny de Harne, Yosi Kliger, Ellen Bass, Janet Bryer, and Lisa Condon for supporting our family, loving our kids, and stepping in with childcare in a pinch.

Yona Adams and Adam Rose, for consistent support, great food, and friendship when I was under the crunch of deadlines.

Nancy London, for wisdom, good humor, and daily sustenance as we walked parallel paths, laboring to bring books to completion.

Donna Jenson, for clear thinking, humor, and intelligence.

Bob Stahl, for his warm heart and our dialogue about honesty.

Roberta Rutkin, for her belief in reconciliation and in this book, and for continuing to stay in touch.

Lisa Kolbeck, Betty Lou Sturm, Tara Sheltz, Stacie Wright, and Khalisa Herman of Little School and Kathy and Marty Newman and Rosalee Schelstraete of Family Network Preschool for excellence in childcare—for giving Lizzy safe places to play, create, imagine, and "be Dorothy." Also to Darwin Hunt, Martha Intersimone, and Lisa Foster-Mackeonis and the folks at Santa Cruz Montessori school, for giving Eli a great place to learn and thrive.

Kofi Busia, Maya Lev, and the other teachers at Yoga Center Santa Cruz, for helping me stay sane, centered, and in my body, despite long hours at the computer.

Virginia Mayer, for compassion, acupuncture, and herbs when I was staying up late to work on this book.

Linda Buckman, the shopping sherpa, for helping me look my best.

Lee Keyser-Allen and John Tracy, for keeping my computer up and running.

Ophelia Balderrama, for being herself and for nursing Abe with complete love and dedication.

Karyn Bristol, my partner, for continuing to pursue her own dreams while giving me the space to realize mine.

And to my children, Bryan, Eli, and Lizzy, for keeping me grounded and always reminding me what matters most.

P.S. I also thank the dozens of people in our community who came forward and helped us when our house burned just weeks before this book was due. You know who you are. And also our pit bull, Tyson, for saving our lives.

Author's Note

Some of the people I interviewed for this book wanted their real names used. Others preferred the use of a pseudonym. I have respected their wishes, but have chosen not to indicate when real names or pseudonyms are being used. In some cases, identifying details have been changed to further protect people's privacy.

When an interviewee is identified only by a first name, it means that person appears only once. Use of first and last names indicates a more in-depth story or a person whose experiences are discussed more than one time.

A SPECIAL PREFACE TO THE FIRST EDITION

There are those who are trying
to set fire to the world
We are in danger.
There is time only to work slowly,
There is no time not to love.

—DEENA METZGER, "SONG"*

As this book was going to press, four American planes were hijacked and used as missiles against the World Trade Center and the Pentagon, forever changing our consciousness as a nation. We learned that we are vulnerable to the same kind of violence and devastation that ravages much of the rest of the world. As we struggle with our grief, fear, and anger, many of us are feeling a new sense of kinship with others who have suffered around the globe. Suddenly, in the most horrible way possible, we have become inextricably linked to our larger human family.

As we learn to live in a world that has profoundly changed, it is natural to feel afraid and powerless. Yet each of us has a sphere of personal influence in which we can enact our highest values. We can

---

*From "Song," published in *Looking for the Faces of God*, © 1993 by Deena Metzger. Used by permission of the author.

strengthen bonds with our loved ones, build networks of support in our communities, and work to create a more just and peaceful world. Taking positive action is not only essential for the survival of our optimism, it is vital to our very future.

The book you are holding in your hands is about people making peace in very difficult circumstances. In these pages, war veterans return to Vietnam, children of Holocaust survivors meet with children of Nazis, and Palestinian and Israeli girls learn to listen to one another. Ordinary people rebuild relationships with the fathers, mothers, children, and friends they thought they'd never speak to again.

The events of September 11 have reminded us that people are precious and that we have only a short time to love each other. May these stories of hope inspire you to build peace and understanding in the world—one relationship at a time.

Laura Davis
SEPTEMBER 18, 2001

The Path of Reconciliation

It is not impossibilities which fill us with the deepest despair, but possibilities which we have failed to realize.

—ROBERT MALLETT, DEPUTY SECRETARY,
U.S. DEPARTMENT OF COMMERCE

When we lose a relationship that has been precious to us, the fabric of life is torn. Whether the end comes suddenly in an explosion, inevitably after a long, painful struggle, or by simply petering out, we feel a sense of loss. Even when our predominant feeling is relief at no longer being engaged in struggle, there is still an empty place where the other person used to be. As one woman put it, "When I was estranged from my father, it was like having a rotten tooth. It gnawed at me all the time."

This book is about relationships that have been torn apart—and the many paths to reconciling them. Whether we are dealing with a brother we no longer speak to, an adult child we wish we knew, a parent we long to make peace with, a friendship gone sour, or an enemy we have been taught to hate and fear, there is a path that we can use to repair—or make peace with—relationships that have been painfully estranged.

What Enables Reconciliation to Occur?

I began my research hoping to pinpoint the steps people need to take in order to transform blame, alienation, and bitterness into compassion, acceptance, and love. Early on, I discovered that there are no hard-and-fast rules about reconciliation. No matter how much I tried, I could not delineate an orderly series of stages that would lead to rapprochement. In fact, every time I thought I had pinned down some essential truth about reconciliation, an exception would appear.

I began with several working assumptions. I believed that reconciliation necessitated taking things slowly, so people could gradually ease back into trusting. But then I talked to Linnie Smith, who, after a ten-minute phone call, reembraced her brother wholly and completely. I assumed that reconciliation could only occur when people talked openly about the differences that had torn them apart, only to find numerous examples of people who found their way back to each other not by discussing the past but by carefully avoiding potential minefields. In families where incest and other heinous crimes occurred, I presumed that reconciliation could only occur if the perpetrator took responsibility for what he or she had done. Then I talked to Kathleen Ryan, who made peace with parents who continue to deny that she was ever abused.

Again and again, my assumptions about reconciliation were shot down, to be replaced by a growing sense of respect and admiration for the diversity of strategies people use to make peace with relationships that once seemed irreconcilable. It became clear that there was no objective lens through which I could judge the progress of someone's reconciliation—that the only measure of success was the emotional integrity of the solution for the people involved.

What I consistently observed in people who had achieved satisfying levels of reconciliation was a particular constellation of inner qualities: it was the maturity, autonomy, discernment, courage, determination, honesty, compassion, humility, and accountability that one or both people brought to the table that determined the depth and quality of their reconciliation. These themes, which overlap and influence each other, manifest in an amazing variety—depending on the people and circumstances involved.

The Reconciliation Continuum

The reconciliation continuum presented here encompasses four possible outcomes. The first—the most coveted and the hardest to achieve—is reconciliation that is deep and transformative, in which intimacy is established (or reestablished), past hurts are resolved, and both people experience closeness, satisfaction, and renewed growth in the relationship. The second outcome, which is far more common, is a relationship in which one person changes his or her frame of reference and expectations, so that the perception of the relationship—and its possibilities—opens up *whether or not the other person makes significant changes*. In the third, much about the relationship remains unresolved and ambivalent feelings persist, yet both people "agree to disagree" and establish ground rules that enable them to have a limited but cordial relationship. The final outcome is realizing that no viable relationship is possible with the other person, and that our only option is to find resolution within ourselves. Although this alternative is not the one that most people would choose, it too can bring peace.

Reconciliation stories are always works-in-progress. Frequently when I asked people to review their stories, months after our initial interview, they informed me that the ending had already changed. We often achieve one level of reconciliation—figuring out how to have a limited, social relationship, for instance—only to have things shift later, enabling a deeper connection. Other times, there are reversals; a setback undermines the tentative trust that has been built, and relations drift back toward estrangement.

With human relationships, nothing is ever final. We cannot be sure how things will end until both people are dead. There are always surprises, unexpected twists, moments of grace, and at times, unfathomable tragedies. If we approach reconciliation with an intention to stay open and see what is possible, there are few limits to what might happen.

Big Reconciliations, Little Reconciliations

This book is filled with stories of everyday estrangements and reconciliations: friends who stopped speaking over a misunderstanding at the movies, siblings who fought over a will, children who made peace with parents they hadn't spoken to in years.

Mixed with these stories are more dramatic tales: victims of drunk drivers facing the people whose actions devastated their lives, children of Holocaust survivors meeting with children of Nazis, Palestinian and Israeli teenagers learning to get along. These stories are deeply inspiring and demonstrate that the principles of reconciliation are consistent whether we are dealing with family members or the larger world.

I have also included stories where attempts at reconciliation led to small, positive changes rather than major transformations. Wendy Richter, a woman I interviewed, had one such experience. When I sent her a copy of her story for her to review, she e-mailed back:

> So many times it is the phenomenal recoveries, the great emotional stories, the magnificent changes that are told. But each of us can only make a few such breakthroughs in our lives. However, the rest of the time we shouldn't experience the failure to be miraculous as a failure. Even a few tiny steps forward represent progress.

Telling Both Sides of the Story

This is an extremely subjective book. I interviewed more than one hundred people about their experiences of estrangement and reconciliation, and in most cases, I spoke with only one of the people involved in the relationship.

I made no attempt to tell both sides of the story, to be fair, or to objectively portray reality. I chose not to question the veracity of people's stories, the accuracy of their memories, or the process they went through in seeking reconciliation. Yet despite the fact that each person was free to tell the story as he or she wanted it to be told, all of these stories reflect compassion, humility, and a sincere desire to make things right. No one I spoke to was looking for retribution or vengeance. On the contrary, people were extremely careful to ensure that sharing their stories would *further* the reconciliations in their lives. No one wanted to endanger fragile relationships they had worked so hard to rebuild. Nor did I.

How I Came to Write This Book

Fifteen years ago, when Ellen Bass and I began writing The Courage to Heal, *I interviewed more than one hundred women who had been sexually abused. I sat with them for long hours in their living rooms as they poured out stories of humiliation, brutality, betrayal, and cruelty. I listened to their grief, anger, anguish, and incredible determination to fight back and survive. I cried with them. I raged with them. I understood them. For I was a survivor, too.*

For ten years of my life, the fact that I had been sexually abused was the principle around which I organized my existence. It was as if my whole life had sprung from that one bitter seed.

During this period I was alienated from my mother's side of the family. My rule was simple: if you believed me, you were in; if you didn't, you were out. In my polarized world, there were good people (mostly, those who had been hurt like me) and bad people (the pedophiles, nonprotective parents, and those who didn't believe me). I surrounded myself with people who supported me; I found safety in a culture of my peers.

My relationship with my mother was particularly affected. It had been rocky; now it was a shambles. She was devastated by my revelations, furious at my public exposure of our family, and rendered powerless by her inability to shift the course of events. I, on the other hand, felt betrayed, self-righteous, and angry. Although I longed to be close to her, I wanted to do so only on my terms. If she wasn't going to believe me, I wanted nothing to do with her.

There things stood—at an impasse—for years. I grieved for my mother and my lost relatives, certain we would never speak again.

Fortunately, that prognosis was wrong. Slowly, then with gathering momentum, the walls gave way. Not in a dramatic turn of events, where I recanted or my family believed me, but because I was able to change my perspective and so were they.

As the healing process began to bear fruit, sexual abuse stopped being the center of my life. In my midthirties, I met my life partner, helped raise a teenage stepson, and had two babies of my own. My life, once filled with angry rebellion, was softened by the daily routines of domestic life. I grew into a person my relatives could recognize, respond to, respect. I relaxed my expectations of them, accepted their limitations, and learned to appreciate their unique gifts. I stopped putting them on the spot and began swapping recipes instead. I sent out birth announcements and photographs; I made long-distance phone calls and small talk. With small, measured steps, and with conscious intent, we gradually wove our way back into each other's lives. And I couldn't help but ask myself, "How could such a reconciliation be possible?"

The Role of Memory in Reconciliation

Our potential for reconciliation is inextricably linked to the way we remember our lives. Yet no two people, sharing the same experience, will ever remember it in exactly the same way. Early in my research, I spoke with Rachel Thomas about her estrangement and reconciliation with her sister Vivian. Rachel related their story powerfully and with conviction, although she readily acknowledged that her grasp on dates and sequences was spotty. When I wrote up the story and showed it to her, Rachel assured me that it accurately represented the truth of her experience.

Several months later, Vivian came to town and agreed to meet me as well. When we sat down to talk, I asked her the same questions I had asked Rachel, and heard a completely different, often contradictory, story. Both Rachel and Vivian had strong emotional memories of the culminating event that had "been the last straw," yet each sister remembered an entirely different event. Although Rachel and Vivian agreed that the big rift between them had occurred in the wake of their mother's death, from that point on, their stories diverged completely. In fact, when they sat down later to compare notes about each other's versions of "the truth," neither Rachel nor Vivian had any memory of the central event her sister had recounted!

I was amazed at how few similarities their stories held, and how many erroneous (and often damaging) assumptions the sisters had made about each other. Yet beneath their conflicting accounts, the emotional reality of their stories resonated with a similar truth. As one of the sisters said later, "Even though the events are murky, the feelings we each had were real." Both sisters felt judged and criticized, and both acknowledged feeling judgmental and critical, yet neither had the skills necessary to bridge the divergent paths their lives were taking. These common threads wove their disparate stories together.

If I had the opportunity to interview the other "half" of each estranged pair in this book, I am convinced that many of the results would be similar. Each of us builds our life story around shared events that are experienced differently depending on who we were, how old we were, how much power we had when an event occurred, and manifold other factors.

Novelist Lynne Sharon Schwartz once wrote, "Memory is a story we make up from snatches of the past." Memory is not a photographic rendering of our history; it is a collage of images, feelings, perspectives, and fragments that we piece together to form a coherent perception of our past. We create stories about our lives, and as we tell those stories to ourselves—and to others—they become embedded in our sense of personal history. We claim that history and use it to make sense of our lives. Whether or not it corresponds to anyone else's version of the same events, it becomes an integral part of our own self-identity. As the poet Anne Sexton once said, "It doesn't matter who my father was; it matters who I remember he was."

Even within individuals, memory is not fixed. If you had asked me to tell you my life story when I was twenty or thirty or forty, you would have heard three different versions of "my life." With each new decade, I would have emphasized different themes, starred different players, and focused on different struggles.

It is this very phenomenon that enables many reconciliations to occur. Old hurts, which seemed huge and insurmountable at one time, often recede to the back burner after a number of years. As we gather new experiences in life, we frequently view the old ones from a different perspective. When we are open to the changing landscape, our lives can expand in ways that previously seemed impossible.

The Power of Reconciliation

Throughout this book, you will meet ordinary people who responded to difficult relationships with resourcefulness and integrity. Time and time again, I have been moved by their courage and inspired by the loving intention with which they approached reconciliation. Hearing their stories has galvanized me to look deeply within. In the past year, I have explored my automatic reactions when faced with conflict, questioned my need to be right, and asked myself why it is so hard for me to apologize. I have become less defensive, more able to listen, more willing to acknowledge my part in a relationship gone awry. I have grown to appreciate more deeply than ever how precious close relationships are. I want to preserve them and repair them, and whenever possible, avoid throwing them away.

I am grateful to the women and men who so generously shared their pain, their struggles, and their triumphs. I hope that their voices touch you as they have touched me, inspiring you to undertake reconciliation journeys of your own.

PART ONE

Preparing the Ground

CHAPTER 1

Growing Through the Pain: Estrangement, Time, and Maturity

To endeavor to forget anyone is a certain way of thinking of nothing else.
—JEAN DE LA BRUYÈRE, SEVENTEENTH-CENTURY FRENCH ESSAYIST

Two years ago, I made a self-serving decision that cost me two of my closest friends. At the time it seemed like a small thing to me—I pushed to get my son into a summer camp where the registration was already closed. But I did so at a cost to my friends, who wanted their child to attend as well. They felt betrayed by my insensitivity to their needs and appalled by my willingness to bend the rules. When they confronted me about it, I responded defensively, denying any wrongdoing and minimizing their concerns. By the time I got around to apologizing several months later, it was too late. The relationship between us and between our children, which had nourished and sustained both families for years, was over.

This estrangement, though not the most significant I have experienced, reminded me of the gamut of feelings that accompany such losses. I was amazed at the intensity, persistence, and mutability of my reactions. When it became clear that this was no passing argument, but rather the permanent loss of people I held dear, my emotions fluctuated wildly. I felt guilt and remorse on the

11

one hand, and indignation on the other. I was outraged at my inability to change the course of events, furious at my friends' unwillingness to forgive, and ashamed of my own shortsightedness and insensitivity. I wished I could turn back the clock and do things differently. I spent hours fantasizing both reconciliation and revenge.

More than anything, I was distressed at what the estrangement was doing to my children. My two-year-old walked around the house, asking repeatedly, "Why can't Ollie come over?" My seven-year-old's sole comment on the situation was, "It feels like a jagged hole with teeth."

For months, I couldn't shake my obsession with this estrangement; at times I was so filled with anger, longing, sadness, and grief, I could think of little else. I talked about it incessantly, initially wanting sympathy and validation; later, I sought help facing my own inadequacies.

By the following spring, when it was time to sign my son up for camp again, I was still sad, but the intensity of my feelings had faded. I had accepted my friends' decision to end our friendship. I had moved on with my life, and so had they. Wistfully, I watched their lives from afar, genuinely wishing them well.

Now when we meet, queuing up to fetch our kids at school, we make small talk. Under the circumstances, it is the best we can do. Yet a sense of loss lingers. Our failure to reconcile has marked us. There is one less safe harbor in our world.

The Pain of Estrangement

Obsession, discomfort, and rage are the hallmarks of estrangement, and sorrow is its center. Toby, a fifty-year-old man who was estranged from two of his closest friends, recalls:

> Last week was my birthday. I was surrounded by friends and family, yet throughout the evening, I felt an ache for my friends who were not there. For the past ten years, we've celebrated each other's birthdays, and their absence was a constant reminder of what I had lost. It was hard to take in the love of the people who were there, because I was so acutely aware of those who were missing.

The sense that "things are not as they should be" usually accompanies estrangement. So does loneliness. When Diane DeVito was cast out of her family, she had to cope with tremendous feelings of isolation.

> Being estranged from my family has really shrunk my life. I had a big extended family, and now I only have my husband. That's put a real strain on our marriage.
>
> My husband and I just bought our first house, and there were things wrong with it. We had no one to consult with, nobody to show the papers to. Our circle is very small, and that makes the world feel unsafe. If anything terrible ever happened to me, there's no one besides my husband who would help me. No source of money would come in. There's nothing, and that makes me feel very disconnected. The fact that I can't have children means I don't feel attached at either end of life. I have no ancestors, and I'm not going to have any children to carry on who I am in the world. When I die, that's it, and it's a very lonely feeling.

The impact of an estrangement is often directly proportional to the closeness of the relationship that has been lost. Molly Fisk, a poet who was previously close to her mother, found their estrangement excruciating. "Being out of touch with my mother felt like I'd had all my arms and legs cut off. It felt like I was not quite killed. I didn't know how to live without her. "

Estelle, a sixty-five-year-old woman who was estranged from her son, felt devastated as well.

> I thought I was a great mother. It was inconceivable to me that one of my sons would consider me such a terrible person that he wouldn't want anything to do with me. The fact that Danny felt that way came as a tremendous shock. For a long time, I felt sorry for myself. I missed sharing the good things that happened in his life. Danny also had some very bad things happen to him, and I never heard about them until years later. So he didn't have me, and I didn't have him. We lost years that way.

The Roots of Estrangement

Relationships become estranged for a multitude of reasons. People get sick of being mistreated, so they intentionally end relationships that were never healthy to begin with. Other times, rifts in relationships spring not from an unhealthy history but from a single act of betrayal—a wife cheats on her husband, a son empties his ailing father's bank account, a mother abandons her two young sons. Estrangements can be precipitated by lesser violations as well: a promise not kept, a confidence betrayed, a disappointment that lingers.

Philosophical, political, and religious differences sometimes stress relationships to the breaking point. When families are inflexible, offending members may be cast out for breaking the family's moral code. Jack, who grew up in a tight-knit Dutch community, learned this during an argument with his father:

> We were standing in the kitchen, and I said, "But I don't believe in God. All that stuff you're telling me about the Bible and how I should be living my life, I don't believe any of it." My father and I were both astonished I said that. From that point on, our arguments escalated, and we started seeing less of each other.

Estrangements often start because we lack the communication skills to prevent them: we don't know how to apologize, listen, or cool off and talk again tomorrow. Instead, a harsh word gets set in stone. Small slights are whipped up into unforgivable injuries. Jealousy festers. Misunderstandings are never discussed or resolved. An ultimatum, made in anger, comes due.

Other times, patterns of estrangement are passed down through the generations. When connections aren't strong to begin with, it's easy for families to drift apart. One man remarked, "My family has always been very easy to leave. You could move two doors down the street, and you'd be invisible to them."

One Disappointment at a Time

Some estrangements build like beads on a thread, one disappointment at a time. That is how the relationship between my mother and I came unglued—slowly, inexorably, over the course of many troubled years.

I am fourteen years old. I return from three weeks at summer camp to a letter from my father telling me that he is never coming home again. He has left for California to become a hippie, leaving my mother to pick up the pieces. She is stuck with a nineteen-year-old son experimenting with acid, a petulant teenage daughter, a business my father didn't bother to close out, and a house full of all the stuff he wanted to be "free" of. She has to face the failure of her marriage while figuring out how to pay the bills, keep up an old house, and parent two wayward teens. Her husband has abandoned her; it is the end of life as she wanted and expected it to be. Despite all evidence to the contrary, I blame my mother for my father's sudden disappearance. My disdain for her weaknesses grows larger with each passing day.

I am fifteen years old. I have cut school and am on a commuter train speeding north to Bayonne, New Jersey. I am going to receive the Knowledge of Guru Maharaj Ji, a young Indian boy who claims to lead sincere seekers directly to an inner experience of God. My older brother already lives in Maharaj Ji's ashram. Now I, too, want to experience the Divine.

When the train stops, I pull a crumpled piece of paper out of my pocket and hitchhike to the address scrawled on the front, joining two dozen other supplicants who have come in search of spiritual Knowledge.

A severe-looking man with a shaved head and saffron robes sits on a cushion at the front of the basement room. Mahatma Fakiranand's job is to sort out the sincere seekers from those who are not yet ready. After two-thirds of the group have been weeded out, he has the rest of us lie facedown on the orange shag carpeting, one at a time, prostrate before an oversize picture of the young Indian boy. He asks, "Would you cut your head off for Guru Maharaj Ji?"

"Yes," I assure him, "I would."

After the Knowledge session, someone gives me a ride to the train station; I don't reach my front door until 10 P.M. My mother is waiting at the kitchen table, her face flushed from crying. She looks at me in anguish, her words slow, agonized, and thick. "First your father, then your brother, and now you."

I am sixteen years old. After a miserable year living alone with my mother, trying to practice Knowledge and navigate through my junior year at Long Branch High School, I am graduating early. I have been offered a full scholarship to Wellesley College. I turn it down and decide to move into the ashram instead. My mother is crushed.

I am twenty-three years old; it's been two years since I left Maharaj Ji's ashram. I'm living in Santa Cruz, California, and have just flown to Miami Beach for my grandfather's ninetieth birthday party. In the middle of the celebration, my mother and I go for a walk on the deserted railroad tracks near my uncle's house.

I have asked my mother to take this walk with me because I have something to tell her. As I hop from tie to tie, I work up the courage to speak. "Mom," I squeak, my voice tight with held-back feelings. "I have something to tell you. I'm a lesbian."

My mother's face falls. A rush of emotion clouds her features. In an anguished voice, she says, "You've confirmed my worst fear about you."

I am twenty-eight years old. My mother has gotten over the shock at having a lesbian daughter, but our relationship is still precarious, a house of cards that might topple at any moment. Although we have both made valiant efforts to overcome our conflicts, I insist on holding her at arm's length; I need the three thousand miles between us.

I am calling to tell her why I have been particularly distant lately. I need to tell her that her father, the wonderful immigrant "Papa" we all loved and cherished, sexually abused me when I was a child. It is an extremely difficult call for me to make.

When I finally get out the words, "I think your father sexually abused me," they hang in the air, piercing and irrevocable. My mother gasps, and the light goes out of her world. All the struggles we've ever had fade into insignificance; we both know this is the big one—the one that will derail us for good.

In Order to Reconcile, the Wound Can't Be Too Fresh

It is no coincidence that people often experience lengthy estrangements before coming to terms with relationships that have troubled them for years. When disputes are new, feelings of anger, betrayal, and hurt are potent and pervasive. Time usually has to pass before most people are able—or willing—to reconsider a relationship that was so painful it had to end. As psychologist Hans Jorg Stahlschmidt once said, "Aging is the best therapist."

Andy needed time before he could consider reconnecting with his mother, Gwen. Gwen had been a fun-loving sixteen-year-old when she gave birth to him. The basics of providing for a child were more than she could manage. For the first few years of Andy's life, Gwen tried to do her best, but it was far from adequate. Finally, when Andy was three, Gwen ran away with her new boyfriend, who "wasn't into kids," abandoning her son to relatives who neglected him.

Years later, when Gwen got her life in order, she tried to reestablish a relationship with Andy, but he wanted nothing to do with her. Intellectually, he knew that his mother had been "a child having a child," but that knowledge alone was not enough to assuage his bitterness. "My mother devastated my capacity to trust another human being; I could only reconcile with her when I'd lived long enough to realize that the damage she did to me wasn't irreversible. It wasn't until I experienced my first mature, reciprocal love that I could begin to consider getting back in touch with her."

Even when the violations are not this deep, most people still require time and space to resolve relationships in which they have felt wronged. Bill, who had a falling-out with his best friend over a girl they both wanted to date, reflects on why it took ten years to work things out with Larry: "The whole thing seems so stupid now. I guess we both just needed to grow up."

Growing Bitter, Growing Sweet

Time, distance, and life experience can blur the edges of anger and blame, lessen the need to remember who was right and who was wrong, and open up new perspectives on old relationships. Yet time alone does not guarantee maturity or the ability to let go. We all know older people who have actively carried grudges for half a century or more. As psychologist Hans Jorg Stahlschmidt said, "Some people grow bitter, and some grow sweet."

We are all subject to turbulent, unpredictable forces in life, yet how we respond to those forces depends on a myriad of factors: our individual character, inner resources, luck, community of support, desire to grow, and our willingness to feel and ultimately transform pain. As General George Patton once said, "Success is how high you bounce when you hit bottom."

Ruth is a vibrant, energetic seventy-year-old. Twenty-five years ago, her husband took off to pursue a career in theater, leaving her with no source of income and four children to raise. For years she felt ashamed and betrayed, as if she had done something to drive her husband away. But she had children to care for and rent to pay, so she knuckled down and made the best of a bad situation. She got a job as a secretary and at night returned to school. Six years later, she earned a degree in special education and began to teach autistic children. She loved the work, and the kids loved her.

Now retired, Ruth plays mah-jongg, hikes with the Sierra Club, and raises money for political campaigns. Half the year, she tours the country in her thirty-foot mobile home, visiting national parks, spending time with her children and grandchildren, and dropping in on old friends. Whenever she is in Milwaukee, she always stops in to see her ex-husband, Charles.

> For a long time, I felt that Charles acted in his own self-interest to such a degree that he was terribly destructive to my children and me. I spent years fuming. Now I can see that he was a good man, but his own demons were so compelling that he believed he had to abandon us. I forgive him for that.
>
> Charles's choice forced me to be out on my own, and the way it turned out, being out on my own was wonderful for me. It made me realize how much strength I had and forced me to move in directions I otherwise would never have taken.
>
> I think it's self-defeating to live with past hurts. It makes you sick, embitters your personality, and prevents you from finding pleasure in the present. I had many good years with Charles. He was my first love, and he's the father of my children. Now he's old, and he's not going to live that long. What's the point of staying mad at him? I want to let go and forgive.

Life Shapes Us

Maturity is part of everyone's reconciliation story. Whether the ultimate result is a renewed relationship or simply a sense of resolution inside, "being worked on by life" prepares us to move on. Life shapes us and surprises us; it can humble us and wear our sharp edges away.

Sometimes it is a growing sense of fulfillment that enables us to feel receptive. Other times, tragedy opens our hearts.

My father died in August 2000. We lovingly erected an altar full of old photographs in his memory and kept a seven-day candle burning there. Six weeks after his death, I was awakened by our dog, Tyson, at four in the morning and immediately realized that our house was on fire. Our dining room, where the altar had been, was ablaze. I woke up Karyn, wrapped the kids in blankets, and we escaped with our lives.

Three days after the fire, I was standing in front of the house with my friend Bob, telling him how devastated and broken I felt inside. Lovingly, he responded with a story: "A man went to see his spiritual teacher after having been through a number of tragedies, and his teacher gave him the following mantra to recite: 'Heart breaks . . . open. Heart breaks . . . open. Heart breaks . . . open.' "

When tragedy occurs, and life as we know it is temporarily suspended, a door opens in our lives. We are given the opportunity to rethink our priorities, deepen our compassion, and open our arms to the people who love us. When the tragedy happens to someone we love—or used to love—we are also faced with a choice—whether to respond with indifference or compassion, disdain or love. Rachel Thomas faced such a crossroads with her sister Vivian.

Rachel Thomas: Flying to My Sister's Side

After so many years, your mind tells you that too much time has passed, that it's too late to be close again. But I opened my heart in a minute. Vivian needed me, and in an instant, I was there.
—RACHEL THOMAS

Rachel Thomas is a schoolteacher and the mother of a grown son. She grew up in rural Oregon in a poor family. Rachel and her sisters spent their summers picking beans in the fields to earn money for school supplies, clothes, and lunches. Competition between the six Thomas kids was fierce. "There was so much conflict, we never banded together. It's a miracle I have any relationships with my siblings at all."

Rachel was the first person in her family to go to college. She became a teacher and a hippie. She wore long dresses and braids, cared deeply about the environment, and took her students on camping trips. Rachel's family scorned her unconventional lifestyle. "My whole family thought I was weird; they saw me as an embarrassment. My mother was sure the Communists in California had taken over my mind. I wasn't really a rebel, but they saw me as pushing the envelope all of the time.

"One time I was visiting my sister Vivian right after she gave birth to my niece, Madeline. Her husband, Michael, met me in front of the house and said, 'You better behave yourself, or you can leave right now.' He saw me as a threat and told me that he didn't want me to influence Vivian. I felt hurt and shocked, and stayed angry for years."

After this, Rachel had little contact with her sister. Two years later, Rachel gave birth to a son, Daniel. When he was four months old Rachel got a call that her mother was dying. "I took Daniel with me to see her one last time. My mother died shortly after we arrived. I stayed several more days, until the funeral.

"While I was there, I was taken aback because I had this beautiful baby that everyone else in my life adored, and my sisters had no interest in Daniel whatsoever. In fact, Vivian was mortified that her in-laws might meet me because I was an unwed mother.

"I didn't understand the animosity Vivian had toward me. Right after the funeral, she came up to me and said she had realized that she wasn't like me in any way and that she didn't want to be my sister anymore. I was stunned."

We Have to Fly to Reno Tonight

For seven years, Rachel and Vivian had nothing to do with each other. A pair of family reunions softened things between them, though the sisters would never have been considered close. "Then one night, when Daniel was seventeen and I was directing *West Side Story* at the high school, Daniel walked into my rehearsal, came on stage, and said, 'Mom, your sister Vivian is dying, and we have to fly to Reno tonight.'

"Vivian had caught the flu from one of her first-grade students. She'd gone through a couple of antibiotic treatments but had never really recovered. One night, she said to Michael, 'I can't breathe. You need to take me to the hospital.' They admitted her, and within moments, her body started shutting down, one organ at a time; she was dying of acute adult respiratory disease. The doctors in Intensive Care forced her body into a coma so she wouldn't exert any energy. They said later that if she'd even blinked an eyelash, she would have died.

"By the time Daniel and I arrived, Vivian had been on life support for twenty-four hours, and everyone expected her to die. The moment I walked into her hospital room, my heart just flew open. I wanted my sister to live.

"For five days we held a vigil in the ICU. During that time, I connected deeply with my niece, who was a senior in college. Madeline didn't really know me, but I was more open to emotions than the others and she took advantage of that. I also felt very close to Michael. He was cracking open. He needed to express his feelings, his fears, and his love for Vivian, and he saw me as a safe person to do that with."

By the end of Rachel's visit, it looked like Vivian was going to live. She had passed through a critical window, even though she was still unconscious. "I went home to finish out the semester. There were a lot of phone calls back and forth. No one knew how fully Vivian would recover.

"I flew back to Reno during my spring break. After forty-five days, Vivian had just come out of the coma. She was extremely weak. Her muscles had atrophied; she had to learn to walk again. I remember taking her for wheelchair rides outside. I massaged her a lot.

"I saw Vivian's illness as an opportunity, and I decided to take it. I could have held back and let our history stand in the way. I could have said that she and I didn't have a strong enough bond for me to be one of her main caregivers, but I decided to take the risk to be available.

"During this time, Madeline and I kept growing closer. We spent days together getting the house ready for Vivian to come home, and I got to know her. She was so ready for me to be her aunt.

"When I came back that summer, Vivian had just gotten home from the hospital. She was still extremely weak. She could hardly make it up the stairs. She and Michael both welcomed me. I helped in any way I could.

"It felt good to have an open heart around them, to no longer care about being right or wrong. I didn't need to make sense of everything that had gone on before. All that mattered was that Vivian was my sister and that we had each other now. I never realized how important she was to me until I almost lost her."

I Couldn't Believe It

Over the course of the next few months, Vivian made a complete recovery, surpassing all of her doctors' expectations. She went back to teaching first grade, and gradually, her life returned to normal.

The following fall, Rachel got a call at work telling her that Madeline had been killed in a car accident. "I stood in the middle of the principal's office, doubled up, crying. After all those years of being denied a relationship with her, I had just gotten to know Madeline, and now she was gone. I couldn't believe it. I flew out to Reno immediately.

"Vivian let me in in a deep way around Madeline's death; she still does. I think a lot of the things that she and Michael feared about me are the things that they value most about me now—my spirituality, my comfort with emotions, my willingness to talk about what's really happening. I talked about Madeline's death, about their loss. I brought up things other people were afraid to say. During that first year, I called them every week."

A year after Madeline's death, Vivian still had not taken her clothes out of the garbage bags that came from the burned-out car. "They had gasoline on them and smelled like smoke, and she couldn't face them alone, so I said, 'I'll come out.' We went through each bag, sorted through all of Madeline's clothes, and decided what to do with them. The fact that she trusted me to do that with her really touched me.

"Madeline's death bonded Vivian and me forever. It's bittersweet knowing that we feel even more connected in part because she died."

Death as a Teacher

Death echoes through many reconciliation stories. When people die or we go through life-threatening crises, it can make us realize that we may never get another chance to make peace with the people who have mattered in our lives. Mindy, a labor and delivery nurse, was about to have a hysterectomy, and there was a chance that cancer was involved. A week before her surgery, Mindy made a list of all the people with whom she had unresolved business; it included her sister, two friends, an ex-lover, and a former boss. Systematically, she contacted them all. "The surgery put me in touch with the fact that my life could end tomorrow—or today. We only have this short opportunity to love people, and I no longer wanted to waste my time holding on to grudges and resentments."

Even when a relationship has not been stretched all the way to the breaking point, a crisis can be a catalyst toward improved relations. Jeannie and her mother were both obstinate about their beliefs. Whether they were discussing a book, a news event, or something that had happened in the family, they each believed that they were right and that the other person was wrong. Every time they got together, they ended up in a major fight.

Two years ago, when Jeannie's mother was diagnosed with lung cancer, Jeannie stepped in to care for her.

As I bathed my mother and changed her Depends, it felt like the circle was completing itself. My mother had changed my diapers and bathed me as an infant, and now, at the end of her life, I was doing the same for her. As I witnessed her vulnerability, I was able to let go of all of the grievances I'd held against her.

Our reconciliation was essentially tied to the knowledge that time was running out. She was going to die, and after that, there would be no more chances. Knowing that allowed the love that had been swimming below the surface of our relationship for years to rise.

Jeannie was fortunate. She had the opportunity to take care of her mother, a mother who wanted her care, and the willingness to do what was required. Yet even when direct efforts at reconciliation remain impossible, one person's death sometimes opens the door to healing with someone else.

My friend Nona Olivia grew up wild and rebellious in southeast Texas. When we met, I was nineteen and she was a spirited twenty-four-year-old single mother, completely estranged from her family. We met in a spiritual community devoted to becoming enlightened—which we eventually left to explore the bigger world. For five years Nona and I did everything together: we worked together, lived together, drank together, got stoned together, and traveled together. Being older and more sophisticated, Nona taught me to be bold and outrageous in the world. But then we had a huge fight and stopped speaking. Neither of us thought we would ever be friends again.

Over the next four years, Nona's mother died of a pulmonary embolism, her father died of emphysema, one of her closest friends died from AIDS-related complex, and another from breast cancer. Their deaths affected her profoundly. Years later, Nona recalled:

Up until that point, I'd always had the attitude "Don't mess with me!" I was very tough, well-defended, mean, and impatient. I was kind of like a dog who'd been beaten. If anybody reached out to pet me, I'd snap at them. I went through relationships like people go through jelly beans—I just chewed people up.

I was so grief stricken at all the loss. I felt vulnerable and fragile. Maya and Dan had both died in their thirties. My mom and dad were dead—and ambivalent relationships are the hardest ones to lose. I saw that life is completely unpredictable and that love is all we've got. People being right or wrong didn't seem to matter anymore. The people I loved suddenly became very precious to me.

After all of that dying, the problems that had driven Laura and me apart were just a blip on the screen compared to the love I felt for her. It became clear to me that having fights that drove people away from me was an indulgence I could no longer afford. So I contacted Laura, and we started rebuilding our friendship. That was fifteen years ago, and now we're closer than we've ever been.

The Lessons Children Bring

At one end of the life cycle, death shapes and changes our lives. At the other, birth transforms us. When we become parents, we are changed irrevocably, and the impact of that change reverberates through every aspect of our lives. Relationships—resolved and unresolved—are re-examined, childhoods relived. In a visceral way, we have the opportunity to come to terms with the parenting we received or failed to receive, delineating the ways we want to emulate our parents and ways we want to differ. From our new vantage point, we can more accurately assess our assumptions about the people who raised us, because for the first time we truly understand the territory that comes with the job.

Becoming a parent also moves us up the generational ladder. Our primary role is no longer that of a son or daughter, but rather as a caregiver of the next generation. When we first hold our babies in awe and wonder, and begin to grasp the immense responsibility of nurturing a vulnerable human being, we understand in a whole new way the challenges our parents faced in caring for us. Whether they handled their responsibilities well or failed miserably, they too once held a tiny infant in their arms and probably vowed to do the best they could.

Most parents want to do well by their children. Even when circumstances, lack of experience, limited resources, or immaturity get in the way, parents usually imagine the best for their child. Phyllis, who was estranged from her parents for years, realized this soon after her daughter, Caitlin, was born. "When I was young and angry, I felt like my parents intended to hurt me. But once I became a parent, I saw just how many mistakes you can make in the name of being a good parent. Even when I do my best with Caitlin, I sometimes make gross errors. That gives me a lot more compassion for the mistakes my parents made with me."

Children often provide us with the impetus to reach out to estranged family members. People say, "I wanted an uncle for my children," or "I want to know my grandchildren." We are often willing to make changes for the sake of our children that we would not make for ourselves.

Marcus is a sculptor who works as an artist in the schools. He grew up in an athletic family that belittled his artistic talents. As a young man, he fled his rural home and moved to St. Paul, Minnesota, where he found new friends and creative inspiration. For the next fifteen years, he established himself as an artist and rarely spoke to his parents or his three brothers. Despite the recognition he was garnering as a sculptor, he still felt like a failure in their eyes.

At forty, Marcus married and had a daughter. Becoming Angie's father opened up his world: "I spent years defending against the need to be close to people, but when Angie was born, the walls began to melt. I wanted Angie to have a sense of connection with blood family that I never had."

Maturity Allows Us to Embrace Paradox

Paradox is woven through the human experience. As the mother of young children, I experience it every day. Each morning, I walk into my children's rooms and stand for a moment, filled with awe. As I watch the rise and fall of their fragile, narrow chests, I am filled with a love beyond any I ever imagined. An hour later when we are tussling over coats, boots, and lunches, and are increasingly late for school, I feel trapped and angry, my rage ready to blow. Before I ever get to work and sit down to officially "begin my day," I have experienced the full gamut of feelings that a person in love can have. I have never hated or loved so passionately before. It is only in the most intimate of relationships that we discover the best and worst we have to give.

When Molly Fisk began considering the possibility of reconciliation with her family, she made a list of all the things she had gotten from them that were good and all the things she had gotten that were bad. When she was done, there was a substantial list on both sides. The fact that those two realities could coexist was a revelation to her. "Holding both of those things in my mind simultaneously taught me that people aren't all bad or all good. In my opinion, nobody's a real monster. People may do monstrous things, but they can still have good qualities. Understanding that has been very important in my life."

Molly's exercise reveals the complexity of human beings. The father who taught you to ride a bike could never hold down a job or keep a roof over your head. The brother who told wonderful stories tied you up with belts when your parents left you alone. Your mother, who lovingly sewed you shoes from the softest cowhide, screamed "I hate you" one dark and rainy afternoon. The friend who made you laugh until you cried spread rumors in the eighth-grade cafeteria that you were having sex with the boy down the street. The enemy you were taught to hate and fear plays the violin so sweetly it breaks your heart.

As one man explained, "It's hard to speak of the violence and the tenderness in my family because there was so much of both."

Paradox is part and parcel of deeply knowing another human being, and it is at the heart of reconciliation. When we grow large enough to embrace our own faults and to honor the flawed humanity of another human being, we open the door to connection, integration, and love.

At sixty-seven, Carol had been estranged from her oldest son for twenty-two years over his refusal to come to his father's funeral. Finally, she decided to lay her burden down. "There are certain unresolvable issues between my son and me, and I've gotten to the point where I'm comfortable letting them be. People evolve; people change. To hold him responsible for something that happened so many years ago is counterproductive when he's grown and changed into someone else."

Maturity allows us to soften our stance, to relinquish absolute requirements, to accept another person's failings, while at the same time acknowledging our own. Mature people learn to embrace relationships that are imperfect. As one man told me, "I love my daughter, but I don't love everything about her."

In his book *How to Forgive When You Can't Forget*, Charles Klein describes an exercise used by Rabbi Pesach Krauss, who worked as a chaplain at Memorial Sloan-Kettering Hospital in New York. In his work with cancer patients, Krauss held up a piece of paper with a single dot in the center and asked his patients to describe what they saw. Many described only the dot, and when they did, he reminded them to notice all the white space on the page. "The dot," he would tell them, "is the pain and suffering you are experiencing because of your cancer. And the white space is all that is good and precious in your life. By shifting your perspective, you can see how small and insignificant that dot is compared to the goodness of life."*

To Everything, There Is a Season

Gaining this sense of perspective takes time. No matter how much we want to let go of resentment and find compassion, we cannot force ourselves to grow. We can set the intention, lay the groundwork, and take the initial steps to heal, but we cannot will ourselves into a different state of consciousness.

Everything on earth has its season. In order to mature, we need the grounding life offers, the nourishment of people we love, and the wisdom only time and distance can provide. By cultivating the qualities that help us grow sweet, rather than bitter, we can grow receptive to deep healing within ourselves and with the important people in our lives.

---

*Charles Klein, *How to Forgive When You Can't Forget* (New York: Berkley Books, 1995), p. 43.

CHAPTER 2

Building a Self:
The Importance of Autonomy

One of the best things about my life now is having the time and space to finish relationships I ended twenty years ago

—NONA OLIVIA

In order to achieve reconciliation, we need to have a self to reconcile with. We need to know who we are, what we value, and what we believe in. We need to know where we stop and where the other person begins, to be able to say, "This is me. These are the ways I am the same as you, and these are the ways I am different." It is not until we are whole enough to approach the other person, not because we need to but because we choose to, that real reconciliation can begin.

When my friend Nona and I were estranged, it was largely due to an unhealthy dependency at the core of our relationship. Neither of us had the self-awareness, communication skills, or individuality necessary to sustain a healthy friendship. Recently, when we were discussing our years of estrangement, Nona said:

> In retrospect, I can see that our break from each other had nothing to do with what we thought it was about at the time. You and

I *wanted* to be close, but we had no idea how to do that. We were both far too needy.

When we met, we bonded in a way that was boundaryless. It was as if we were these arteries that weren't getting enough blood, and then we connected and started feeding into each other in a symbiotic way. It wasn't until we had tie-off surgery and were cauterized that we could become separate individuals and reconnect.

The Importance of Boundaries

When we are entwined with another person in a way that limits our freedom, independence, or personal integrity, it is extremely difficult to have a healthy relationship with that person. Before reconciliation can occur, we need to be able to establish boundaries that protect us from undesirable interactions or harm.

Until we can say "no" in a relationship, our "yes's" are meaningless. Telling our mother to stop criticizing our children, our daughter to stop returning our car with an empty gas tank, or our buddy Bob that we won't spend time with him if he keeps canceling our plans when something better comes along are important steps toward self-respect. Part of autonomy is loving ourselves enough to know how we want to be treated.

Ideally, this discussion of ground rules should be mutual—with both sides making requests and both sides willing to listen. A father asks his daughter to arrange regular times for him to visit his grandchildren; the daughter agrees but asks him to stop telling off-color stories in front of them. One friend asks another to honor her confidentiality; the friend agrees but asks that past transgressions, now acknowledged, be laid to rest. A shifting of boundaries has to take place in order for a new relationship to begin.

This kind of give-and-take, which should be part of any intimate relationship, is especially important in relationships where boundaries have been unclear, power has been skewed, or trust has been broken. Ground rules give people a way to rebuild trust and feel safe again. Although they do not need to be permanent, and often recede in importance as trust builds in the relationship, ground rules give us a starting place—a way to feel protected as we reengage.

There is no guarantee, however, that the person on the other side of the estrangement will be receptive to our requests—or ready to negotiate on his or her own. But even a grudging acceptance can make at least some degree of progress possible.

Anna French was estranged from her mother for almost twenty years. In the last decade, since she became a mother herself, Anna has worked hard to rebuild their connection. Their reconciliation has only been possible because Anna established a few key ground rules.

When I began healing around my father's abuse, I wrote my mother several letters addressing the subject. Instead of being willing to meet me halfway, she was enraged. My mother was on her third husband by then, and she had turned my father's memory into a shrine. In retrospect, she believed they'd had this perfect marriage.

That was my first ground rule. Whenever my mother would start immortalizing my father's memory, I would stop her: "We can't talk about how perfect your marriage was because my experience with him was different. The subject is off limits."

My second ground rule had to do with this family story that was always told about me. My father died when I was twelve. I was devastated and got heavily into alcohol, sex, and drugs. Later, it became a family joke. My mother would say, "You were such a difficult teenager! I hope your daughter is as horrible as you were."

When I realized why I had been wild, the kind of pain I had been in, and how absolutely unsupportive my mother had been, I set a second boundary: "You are no longer free to tell those stories about me."

The third one was about my weight. I'd gained a lot of weight as a teenager; I stuffed my pain with food. And I told her she could no longer discuss my weight.

My mother responded with a kind of eye-rolling, grudging consent, but I didn't care if she rolled her eyes or not. My priority was keeping myself safe—and it worked. We don't talk about those things anymore.

In cases such as Anna's, where one person has been deeply hurt by another, ground rules for renegotiating contact are essential. Unfortunately, the deeper the violation and the more dysfunctional the family constellation, the less likely it is that such boundaries will be respected.

Yet even in circumstances where direct limit-setting might be fruitless or even dangerous, we can still quietly establish ground rules on our own. By identifying situations that hook us into old patterns of relating, we can gradually develop new ways to respond. Screening calls, shortening visits, visiting on neutral turf, or bringing a friend along are all strategies that have been used successfully.

Ginger grew up in a poor family with an unstable mother. She lacked decent clothes for school and was frequently hit and belittled. Once she was old enough to escape, Ginger stopped seeing her family.

> Those years of estrangement were the best thing that ever happened to me. I explored myself. I traveled. I learned enough skills to gradually start having contact with my family again. Before that, I was so enmeshed in family dynamics that I couldn't figure out how to be with them and take care of myself at the same time.

Through her exposure to healthier people and ideas, Ginger developed new tools for dealing with her family's criticism, small-mindedness, and despair.

> When I started seeing my family again, I made two promises to myself. First, I was going to take care of myself. Second, I was no longer going to deny my past. If they didn't want to talk about it, that was fine, but I was no longer going to edit out my childhood to protect them.
>
> I have this mantra I use when I go to visit my parents. It's an old Kenny Rogers song: "You've got to know when to hold 'em, know when to fold 'em, know when to walk away, and know when to run." If I'm not in touch with all of those things, I don't

go home to visit. But when I am and I'm feeling strong, my visits home are fairly successful. And if at any time I feel the need to walk away or run, I honor that. The two times I didn't were big mistakes.

Even if we never discuss our new ground rules with the other person, the fact that we have created them shifts the paradigm of the whole relationship. As we make new choices and behave and respond accordingly, change starts to occur. Shawnee Undell, who has studied four generations of women in her family, observes:

> Change gets passed down through the generations, but it also reverberates in the other direction. When change happens in me, there's a dynamic shift that happens with the older people. Even if we're not in regular contact or don't discuss what has happened, ripples start to occur. When I make a big shift in myself, something is freed up for them, and patterns people have been locked in for years sometimes give way.

When Injuries Are Unforgivable

When miscommunication, insensitivity, or conflicting needs damage relationships, clarifying boundaries can open the door to reconciliation by ensuring that similar injuries won't be repeated. But when deeper wounds cause estrangements, the requirements of healing are far more complex, long-term, and demanding. When someone violates our trust, betrays our deepest values, attacks our individuality, or in the worst case—uses physical, sexual, or psychological violence to control us—a terrible imbalance occurs in the relationship, leaving us reeling, full of self-doubt, and sometimes unable to function. The shock alone can be devastating.

Marjorie was nine months pregnant when she found out that her best friend was having an affair with her husband. "In an instant, the bottom dropped out of my world. I dropped the teacup I was holding, and it shattered all over the floor. Then I heard this rasping, desperate sound, the wail of a dying animal. It wasn't until later that I realized the sound was coming from me."

When such an injury occurs, reestablishing our sense of equilibrium becomes a Herculean task. In her book *Forgiving the Unforgivable: Overcoming the Bitter Legacy of Intimate Wounds*, Beverly Flanigan calls this process "balancing the scales."

Flanigan says there is an intricate system of balance that operates in relationships—in which each person brings resources to the relationship and each person benefits from resources the relationship has to offer. One partner in a marriage provides humor and optimism; the other brings skills and discipline to the mundane tasks of daily life. One friend gives the other a listening ear; the other provides a welcoming extended family. Although one person may give more or take more at a particular time, there is an overall balance that feels fair to both people involved. Everyone experiences adequate love, trust, and freedom of choice, the three elements Flanigan believes to be essential to healthy relationships.

When one person commits an "unforgivable injury," this sense of equilibrium is destroyed. A parent fails to protect a child from harm, a wife admits her long-term affair, an adult child belittles and neglects an aging parent. In all of these instances, one person commits an act of intimate betrayal that throws the relationship off balance. The scales are tipped heavily toward the person who violated the relationship's moral rules, while the other person is left gasping for air. Balancing the scales is a process by which the damaged person reclaims the power, choice, and resources he or she lost in the wake of the betrayal.

Donna Jenson grew up in a family devastated by violence, and she believes the length of time it took her to heal was directly proportional to the magnitude of the trauma she suffered.

> When my father raped me, a mountain fell on top of me. I was eight years old, and it was painful on every level you can imagine. It splintered my wholeness. Healing from what my father did has been incredibly difficult. Pulling myself back to wholeness has meant pushing the mountain off me.
>
> What my father did took ten minutes, and it's taken me more than twenty-five years to regroup. There's almost physics in this to me: the weight of the trauma is equal to the weight you have

to lift in the healing, and that healing takes time. There's no way around it. There are no shortcuts. I had to lift that weight myself.

There is no substitute for the work that is necessary to heal from loss and violation. As Rumi, the Sufi poet, says, "The cure for pain is in the pain." Attempting to reconcile before we've done the work of healing discounts the fact that grief and anger are as essential to the reconciliation process as compassion and love.

Dana Roper: Returning the Gift He Gave Me

When I was twenty-two, I had my first astrology reading. I never said a word to the astrologer about my family. He looked at my chart and said, "There's this extraordinary presence in your life. It's either your mother or your father, and it's unbelievably powerful. It was either the best thing that ever happened to you or the most destructive thing." Then he asked, "Do you know which way it went?" And I said, "Oh yes."

—DANA ROPER

For more than fifty years, Dana Roper has struggled to come to terms with her father—a critical, domineering man who ruled her life and invaded her psyche. "I grew up in Canada with my parents and my older sister. My father was an alcoholic. When he drank, he'd get sadistic. His sadism took the form of humiliation and verbal cruelty. Whatever I loved, he found a way to demean.

"Yet despite his cruelty, my father gave me some wonderful things. My love of bodies comes from him. My father taught me to play football, baseball, and tennis, to drive a car at seven, and to shoot a gun. He taught me massage. His touch always felt comforting and loving; there were never any sexual overtones. It was the only thing I had with him that felt safe.

"I learned to love touching, and I became really good at it.

That's given me pleasure all my life. However, the kicker with him was that he'd make me massage him on demand. I would always comply, but this rage would well up in me."

In her twenties, Dana began what would be more than fifteen years of therapy, trying to overcome her father's devastating influence on her life. During these years, their relationship consisted of occasional phone calls and very short visits. "My father could be charming and enjoyable for a short period. I made sure that I never saw him for more than a few hours at a time."

When Dana was forty, she reached a major turning point in her relationship with her father. "He called and said something incredibly humiliating to me, and I said, 'You've been humiliating me my whole life, and I just want you to stop!' He laughed and said, 'All right.' And he never humiliated me again. I remember thinking, 'That's all it took?' I was furious. I was relieved.

"Once after that, he called to tell me he was coming to town. I hadn't seen him in five years. We went out to dinner, and he was lovely and charming. He put his arms around me and said, 'I just want you to know I'm proud of you and I love you.' It was a lovely moment, but I still didn't trust him."

Realizing What Might Have Been

True reconciliation requires a deep acknowledgment of the injury we have suffered. In Dana's case, it was not until she was forty-three that she finally recognized the source of her deepest grief about her father. "I had done tons of therapy, but I finally went to a great therapist. For twenty years, I'd been talking about how mean my father was. What this therapist said was, 'It's deeper than that. What's the real wound about?'

"I started talking about how I hated going to my father's penthouse but loved his art collection. I then realized that my father recognized good art: he knew feeling; he knew sensuality; he knew when something had heart and soul. You could tell because he had beautiful things in his place and he cared about them. His art wasn't ostentatious. He surrounded himself with beauty because it mattered to him.

"When I visited him, I used to wake up early when nobody was up, because that's when I would feel safe. Then I'd walk around touching his things and looking at them. His art moved me.

"My father was also a brilliant businessman. He read widely and had broad interests, as I do. He had a great spirit, but it was perverted by alcohol and child abuse. I'd always known that my grandfather had beaten my father, but what I started to realize was that if my father had gotten help, his intelligence and charisma could have had the most wonderful impact on my life.

"I grew up to become a poet, an artist, and a philosopher. All of that came from him. If he hadn't been so hurt, we could have had extraordinary conversations. Instead he ended up with a daughter who hated and avoided him. We both could have had so much more, and that was tragic.

"I remember sobbing in grief in my therapist's office as I started to deal with this. I wasn't evolved enough then to feel compassion for him; I was still too busy fighting off his humiliation. But I did have compassion for myself for the first time, which was a great triumph."

I Came Here to Do Something

Just before her fiftieth birthday, Dana got a call from her sister saying that their father was dying. At that point in his life, Dana's father was a broken man: he had gone from being a millionaire to a pauper, prostate cancer had spread throughout his body, and he had lost his home and family. Dana's sister, who had always borne the brunt of his rage, had taken him into her home to care for him.

Dana flew to Arizona to see her father and to support her sister. When she arrived, her father was asleep. "I went in to see him, and what I saw was a very old man curled up in a fetal position on the bed. When he woke up, I watched my sister interact with him, and their interactions horrified me. She practically threw his food at him. If he reached for her hand, she'd pull her hand away. I asked her why she didn't touch him, and she said, 'I loathe his touch, and I'll never touch him.'

"I was shocked because touch was the one area in which I felt safe with him. Then I saw her give him a beer. I said, 'Why are you giving him alcohol?' And she said, 'He's a ninety-year-old alcoholic. Do you think I'm going to stop him now?'

"I wanted to flee. I thought, 'This is why I hate my family. They're so sick.' But then I said to myself, 'I came from a cruel, vicious family, and I am committed to healing this kind of cruelty. I came here to do something. What can I possibly do for this man?'

"Then it came to me. 'Of course! I can touch him.' So I went into his room and said, 'Would you like me to rub your head? I can help with the pain.'

"He said, 'I'd really love that.'

"I sat down on the bed. I held his head in my hands and said to myself, 'I'm okay now, and this man is really suffering. Give him back the most important gift he gave you. Give him the gift of touch.'

"I asked him where the worst pain was, and I started to massage his head. I could feel the pain leave his body. I got very meditative, and he went into trance for a while.

"I was holding him like a little baby, his head in my hands, and suddenly I felt this huge shift—I was now the adult, and he was now the child. In that moment, I knew he couldn't torment me anymore. I had set myself free, and now I could give to him. It was the first time in my whole life that I ever wanted to.

"At one point, he woke up and looked at me, and damn him, he tried to get me one more time. He said, 'Well, you can't get away from having to rub your old father's head, can you?' It had that sadistic little jab in it, and I felt my chest and my insides just tighten. I wanted to smash my fist into his face. At that moment,

I could have gotten lost in rage and gone back to being a child. But then I laughed, and thought, 'He can't stand to receive. This is an abused man who's never been receptive in his life, and I just spent half an hour pouring love into him, and he got scared. I know this, because I do it in my own life; I get scared when the good stuff comes.' Inside myself, everything became clear: 'That's all this has ever been about—his fear.' I felt tremendous compassion for him, and in that glorious moment, I knew the war was over.

"I looked at my father and said, 'Shhhhhh.' I put my hand on his forehead and stroked over his eyes, and said, 'Just relax.' I put him right back into trance, and I went right back into loving. I wanted to ease his pain.

"I massaged him for another half hour, until he was asleep. Then I stood by his side and held his hand and just looked at him. Then he woke up and looked me in the eye, and I felt him simply receive. In that moment, he looked at me with absolutely no hostility or meanness. His look was clean, deep, and honest, and full of love. He let me in, human being to human being. I smiled at him, and he said, 'Thank you. I love you.' Then he went back to sleep.

"That's when I left. I knew I had done what I had come to do. I'd said good-bye to him in the most healing way possible."

When It's Time to Move On

When we balance the scales in a relationship, as Dana was able to do, we rebuild our sense of self and reclaim the moral integrity that was taken away from us. Although it seems to take forever, one of the paradoxes of healing is that focusing on our pain is what enables us to move through it.

Beyond a certain point, however, identifying with past injuries can be limiting. While it is often empowering to identify as "a battered wife," "an abandoned husband," or "the mother of a drug addict," in order to claim our legacy and heal from it, aligning ourselves with our injuries only benefits us for so long. Ultimately, a label that initially brought strength, solidarity, and understanding can become a prison from which we must free ourselves.

Elizabeth Menkin, whose sister was killed by a drunk driver, recalls her decision to give up her identity as a victim.

> Anybody who's been wronged goes through a period where they feel righteously angry. As appropriate as it feels at the time, it gets old. Yet there's an attraction to staying angry and victimized because you can say, "Poor me! It's all *her* fault. None of this is under my control." To put on your shoes and lace them up and walk out of the swamp of victimhood is a powerful thing to do.

Yet no one can tell us when it is time to move on. Ben, who spent much of his adult life struggling to come to terms with a cruel, unpredictable brother, recalls:

> I finally got to the point where I realized "I cannot change the past, so mulling it over and over isn't going to do any good. I need to move on so I can enjoy the rest of my life." But that's not something anyone else could have decided for me. I had to come to that realization on the inside. It's not a head thing; it's a whole body thing. I had to earn the right to say it.

People come to this crossroad when their focus naturally shifts toward their present life or when they recognize the price of holding on to a painful past. As one man put it, "I realized I couldn't hate and love simultaneously, and I wanted to love again."

As we gain mastery over our emotional wounds, we gain a sense of freedom that enables us to move on. It is from that place of autonomy that we can reconsider relationships with people we were sure we'd left behind.

Kathleen Ryan:
When Memories Are Disputed

Being connected is more important than being right.
—KATHLEEN RYAN, INCEST SURVIVOR

Kathleen Ryan grew up believing she had wonderful parents and a wonderful life. Then, when she was twenty-six, it all started to slip away. "I'd always had trouble in relationships, but then my problems started spilling over into work. Even my boss pointed it out to me. I was in sales, and I'd always been very successful. I was alarmed by what was happening to me, so I got into therapy.

"Six months later, on a business trip, I was accosted by a drunk businessman. It was horrible, and when I talked about it in therapy, I began to recall sexual abuse from my childhood. Eventually, I remembered it was my father."

As Kathleen got deeper into dealing with the incest, she began to withdraw from her family. "It felt really hard to be around them. Everything was always so 'perfect' in my family, yet beneath the surface, this other reality existed. I wanted to yell at them, 'Can't you see what this family is really like?' "

Kathleen chose not to tell her family about the incest, but they noticed changes in her behavior. Three years into her therapy, Kathleen and her mother had a huge confrontation. "My mother said she'd heard rumors that I was saying I'd been abused, and she asked me about it. I confirmed what she'd heard and said it was my father. She yelled, 'How could you say that? He's a good man!'"

Soon afterward, Kathleen broke off contact with her parents. "I was in a real crisis. To protect my fragile emotional state, I asked my parents not to call me."

Contact with her family was minimal until she got a call from a reporter with the biggest newspaper in her state. The reporter wanted to know if she would agree to be interviewed for an article in which her parents were telling "their side of the story."

Kathleen declined. A few weeks later, she read the published story. "The article was a nightmare. Basically my parents portrayed me as an idiot who'd been brainwashed by my evil therapist.

"I felt humiliated. The fact that they weren't willing to talk it out with me, but instead went public, was, for me, the final emotional cutoff between us. For four years, I didn't have any contact with my parents, and during that time, they joined the False Memory Syndrome Foundation (FMSF) and became the contact people for their state. Someone sent me a video of them addressing a group on false memory syndrome. It was painful, and it infuriated me.

"At one point, I got a very angry letter from my mother. It was a diatribe asking me how I could be so susceptible to my therapist. Receiving that letter was particularly painful because I'd always been close to my mother. I still missed her terribly."

During the four years she didn't speak to her family, Kathleen felt split inside. "My personal life was taking off. I was very happy with my husband and extremely successful in my career. I stopped therapy because I didn't need it anymore. But it was hard being cut off from my family, especially during the holidays. I imagined being shut out, on the outside forever."

Then, remarkably, things began to change.

I Wanted to Hear My Mother's Voice

Kathleen and her husband decided they wanted to start a family, and Kathleen got pregnant. Although she was thrilled, impending motherhood brought up a lot of issues for her, so Kathleen went back into therapy. "I started talking about my mother. Becoming a mother and not being in touch with her just felt wrong. Yet there were obstacles that kept me from reaching out. I was scared, I didn't know how my parents would react, and I wasn't entirely sure what I wanted from them. The last barrier, which was really big for me, was that I'd come of age in a survivor culture that said, 'If they don't admit to what happened, you can't have a relationship with them.' For a long time, I believed that, but then something changed for me.

"Part of it was my pregnancy, and part of it was maturity. Younger people can afford to be passionate and have ideals that they refuse to compromise on. But I was getting older. I was tired of being ostracized and estranged. I realized that winning wasn't as important as being connected. So I gave up wanting to win.

"I recognized that there were other things to talk about with my family besides whether or not I was abused. Things didn't have to be all or nothing; there could be something in between that would be comfortable for them *and* comfortable for me."

Deciding to Call My Parents

When she was nine months pregnant, Kathleen finally decided to call her parents. "I was shaking as I dialed the number. I didn't know what to expect. Would they hang up on me? Would they yell at me? I was so terrified I couldn't sit still.

"My dad answered the phone. I wasn't too happy about that. I said, 'Hi, it's Kathleen. Is Mom there?'

"My dad said, 'No she's not. Won't you just talk to me?' He was begging me to stay on the phone.

"I checked it out with myself, and I realized I felt okay talking to him. I said, 'Look. I want to tell you right up front that I'm not interested in talking about the abuse. Maybe later, but not now. I just called because I missed you guys and wanted to be in touch.' Setting that boundary was really important for me. Frankly, I think my dad was relieved; he didn't want to talk about the incest either.

"My dad's voice was shaking. He told me how much they had missed me and worried about me. We talked about the family. I told him I was pregnant. He told me he'd had a quadruple bypass. We both said how hard it had been not to talk for all those years. Both of us cried.

"This whole time, my husband was sitting right there next

to me, ready to take the phone away if things got too hard. He didn't leave until he knew I was okay.

"Eventually my mom got home, and then all three of us were on the phone. My parents kept saying they'd prayed for this and that it was a miracle. I was able to tell them I'd missed them and that I loved them. For me, that had always been the most difficult part of being a survivor—hating my parents and loving them at the same time. When I finally got up the courage to speak to them, I realized I could talk to them *and* stay true to myself, that they could never take that away from me."

I Was Able to See My Parents as People

Kathleen called her parents after her son was born, and talked with them every few weeks in the months that followed. "During every conversation, my dad would say, "When are we going to see you?" I heard that for more than a year. Basically I ignored it; I just didn't feel ready.

"Then I heard that my grandmother was dying. I wanted to say good-bye to her, but I knew if I went to see her, I'd be seeing my parents.

"I drove down and spent the morning with my grandmother. Afterward, I had lunch with my parents. I was really nervous, and so were they. We spent most of the time on small talk. Then right before I was about to leave, we started talking about the estrangement. The conversation was very tearful. I brought up the article, and my mother apologized. She said, 'I knew that article was going to hurt you. We learned our lesson about the media. A lot of things we said were out of context; they printed a lot of things we thought were off the record.' Hearing her apology was huge for me because I never expected any acknowledgment from my parents at all.

"Then my mother broke down crying, saying I must think she was a really bad mother. She just fell apart. And the thing that stood out for me was that my father just stood there. He didn't try to comfort her or reassure her. He did nothing.

"Witnessing the pain in my parents' relationship had a deep impact on me. It explained a lot of things about them. Seeing their lack of intimacy enabled me to see them not as parents but as people—as partners in a couple whose relationship was broken."

The Elephant in the Room

Several years into their reconciliation, Kathleen finally decided she was ready to talk to her parents about the abuse—or rather, that she was ready to talk about *not* talking about it. "I brought it up, and we both acknowledged that there's no room for movement on either side. Eventually, we agreed to disagree."

With incest no longer on the table between them, Kathleen and her parents have shifted away from an adversarial stance. For her parents, that's included a lessening of their focus on "false memories." "For years, my mother spouted all this FMSF propaganda. Now, she doesn't do that as much. Interestingly enough, I think what they went through is similar to what survivors go through. You know how when you first realize the incest, you're obsessed with reading stuff and being involved, and then your need to do that gradually fades? I think for my parents, with the false memory stuff, it's been basically the same. They were really active, but their need to be involved in it has faded. They've moved on to other things in their lives."

Ironically, despite her mother's ardent belief in false memories, Kathleen believes that somewhere inside, her mother is rooting for her. "Many women of my mother's generation couldn't be strong, but they taught their daughters to be strong. My mother did that for me, and I know that a part of her is cheering me every step of the way—because I stood up to my dad, something she could never do. In spite of everything, I've always known that."

Establishing Terms of Engagement

Seattle psychotherapist David Calof mediates between survivors of abuse and their families. In circumstances where the perpetrator takes responsibility for what he or she has done, and offers to make reparations, the potential for deep healing between the two parties is enormous. But where there is a disputed history, the family mediation session takes on a very different form. Then the goal is not to reach consensus on a shared perception of truth, but rather to come up with what Calof calls "terms of engagement." Terms of engagement are rules by which the two parties agree to abide so that they can interact peacefully in limited circumstances. Terms of engagement might include agreements to not discuss certain volatile topics, requests that certain kinds of jokes or stories not be told, boundaries about touch, discussions about where, when, and how visits should take place, or conditions under which grandparents and grandchildren get to see each other. When history is disputed, Calof says the best that can be hoped for is "a peaceful coexistence and not a great closeness." But for many families, this kind of negotiated settlement is better than total estrangement or hostility.

Mediation in such circumstances needs to be handled with tremendous skill and sensitivity, and a rigorous screening process must be done to ensure that the mediation will benefit both parties. It is crucial that the mediator be unbiased and that both parties enter the mediation with realistic expectations. Calof tells each side that everyone will probably leave the mediation thinking that some of their needs were met and that many of them were not, and that that will be an indication that the mediation was fair.

For mediation to be successful, both parties must agree that the purpose of the meeting is to come up with rules of engagement, rather than to decide who is telling the truth. As much as possible, both parties need to come to the table with equal power and resources. If meditation is attempted before these conditions are met, it can backfire. But when these conditions are met, it is possible for deeply estranged families, even those with a disputed history, to work their way back into a limited reengagement.

The Difference Between Reconciliation and Capitulation

In circumstances where there is a dispute about what has taken place, particularly when one party has historically had more power than the other, there is a fine line between reconciliation and capitulation. Capitulation is the antithesis of autonomy; it's backing down from what we know to be true because holding on to that truth is too painful or because the consequences are too costly.

The choice to have a relationship with someone who does not acknowledge our version of history can look a lot like capitulation. But there is a huge qualitative difference between someone who recants because the pain of separation is too great, and someone who has done sufficient healing to negotiate a relationship with a person who sees the past through different eyes. In one instance, the self is sublimated and personal needs are ignored or sacrificed. In the other, we hold steady to our own truth and choose to relate anyway.

When we capitulate in a relationship, we experience shame, self-doubt, and self-hatred. Anger festers, and we may find ourselves responding to the other person with coldness, jabs, sarcasm, aloofness, or with subtle or overt cruelty.

Reconciliation, on the other hand, is expansive. Reentering a relationship from a place of strength and wholeness enables us to feel more generous inside. As we relax in our own truth, we learn to stay present in the moment, responding with good humor, flexibility, and a gentle heart.

Donna Jenson, who is attempting to reconcile with her mother, can feel the difference between "capitulation" and "reconciliation" in her body.

> When I talk to my mother from that caved-in place, all this anger bubbles around and my stomach gets knotted up. I'm sweaty. My breathing is shallow. My mind starts racing, saying nasty things about my mother and nasty things about myself. But when I accept my mother for who she is, when I see her as someone who's gone as far as she can go, I open up to having a connection with her at the level that's realistic. When I do that, I

feel centered. My stomach stays relaxed. I can actually hear our voices talking to each other, instead of a chorus of judgmental, critical voices in my head.

Then I'm being who I want to be. I'm not reacting or being a "damaged daughter." When I hang up the phone, I'm simply able to go on to the next thing I'm doing in life. I don't have to waste time stomping around my office, not being able to find my glasses.

Reconciliation becomes possible as we rebuild ourselves into people who are no longer capable of being hurt in the same way. Molly Fisk, the poet who reconciled with her mother, says:

> From the outside, our relationship looks the same. But on the inside, I know that my mother can no longer hurt me the way she could before. I can imagine showing her a new poem and having her not like it or having her say something cutting to me, and although it might sting, it wouldn't surprise me the way it used to every single time. I am not available to be devastated by her anymore.
>
> I already had the worst thing happen that could happen. For seven years, I lost her. Now that I have her again, I'm as close to her as I was before, but I'm not vulnerable to her in the way I once was. I've grown up, and I don't *need* her anymore. I love having her in my life, but if she were gone, I know I would survive.

It is this kind of autonomy that enables us to change the dynamics of an estranged relationship. As we establish ourselves as separate individuals, we increase our capacity for self-care and gain the clarity required to reassess unresolved relationships.

CHAPTER 3

Finding Clarity: The Task of Discernment

Approach each new problem not with a view of finding what you hope will be there, but to get the truth, the realities that must be grappled with. You may not like what you find. In that case you are entitled to try to change it. But do not deceive yourself as to what you find to be the facts of the situation.

—BERNARD BARUCH, ECONOMIC ADVISER TO U.S. PRESIDENTS

When we are embroiled in a dispute or are suffering through an estrangement, emotions often run high: jealousy, rage, bitterness, sadness, and grief all vie for attention. Even when we grow to "accept things as they are," we usually don't have to scratch too far below the surface to discover feelings of anger, loss, and hopelessness. Our perception of the estrangement—what caused it, who was at fault, and why it has continued—is usually strongly biased toward our point of view. Any objectivity we might have were we to look at someone else's circumstances is muddied by our own sense of injustice and need to be right. It is very difficult to step back from the middle of an estranged relationship and see it clearly. Yet that is exactly what we must do. Until we develop a broader perspective and greater clarity, it is difficult to determine which way to proceed.

A discerning eye cuts through emotion, habit, expectations, and desire, and enables us to keenly perceive a situation as it is. We lay bare our strengths, weaknesses, needs, and motivations—as well as those of the other person. We seek to understand the mistakes we made—and that the other person made. We strive to see the chain of circumstances that led to the break in the relationship so we can understand the options and risks we face in trying to restore it. Discernment enables us to recognize possibilities, learn what the other person means to us, and discover whether our deepest goal is to mend the relationship or let it go.

WHAT'S HAPPENING NOW?

To find clarity in the midst of an estrangement, it is helpful to do an internal assessment of where things stand right now. Choose a particular relationship you are struggling with and write down several statements that characterize it: "I haven't talked to my sister in three years. I'm scared to call her and think she may be feeling too proud to call me. The last time I saw her, at my brother's wedding, I felt incredibly awkward and anxious." Or if the relationship is with your daughter: "Every time I talk to my daughter, I feel like I'm walking on eggshells. She's clearly angry, yet she won't tell me why."

Next, make a list of all the complaints you have about the other person. Begin with the big things: the welts your father left on your thighs when he beat you, the years it took you to overcome your sister's indifference, your grandfather's cruelty, your ex-husband's shocking betrayal. If your complaints are smaller, don't let that stop you. Whatever has bothered you, write it down: the fact that your friend shows up late when you go to the movies, the way your brother-in-law always chews with his mouth open, the mean, stupid trick your brother played on you the summer you were nine.

Once you have exhausted all the resentments you carry, take a stab at your own regrets—the things you wish you had said or done differently with that person. "I'm sorry I never took my little brother to the county fair." "I'm sorry I confronted my father with so much rage; I wish I'd waited." "I wish I'd gone to Mario's funeral." "I wish I'd spent more time in my friendship with Lonnie listening and less talking about my own problems."

Taking stock in this way can help you see the old baggage you may still be carrying in regard to the other person, and sometimes it levels the playing field. Marty, who was estranged from his sister, recalls:

All the stuff Janet did to me has always been crystal clear in my mind. I had no trouble whipping out a list of all the ways she had wronged me. When it was time for me to sit down with a blank sheet of paper with the word "Regrets" at the top, I was sure I'd never come up with a thing. But fifteen minutes later, I had nearly filled the page. I remembered all the times I had withheld my affection, turned up my nose at her attempts to reconcile, and talked badly about her to the rest of the family. As I wrote, it became clear to me that our estrangement was a lot more complex than I thought.

After you have written out your resentments and regrets, make another list that spells out the ways the estrangement is benefiting you. This may seem like a crazy thing to do, but even a situation that hurts you may have rewards, such as sympathy or safety.

Honestly looking at the ways you may have benefited from an estrangement can help you recognize conscious and unconscious attempts you may have made to maintain the status quo. You can also use this information to evaluate whether you want to (or are prepared to) attempt reconciliation at this time.

Now make a list of the ways in which this estrangement is hurting you. Ask yourself: "What price am I paying by not having this person in my life? What is this estrangement costing me?"

Answers to these questions frequently revolve around several themes: "My hatred and bitterness are consuming me." "I feel disconnected from part of my history." "My children don't know their cousins." "I can't love fully when I'm carrying around this much hate." Or, "I'm still letting what happened in this relationship define me."

Finally, as the last part of this assessment, evaluate the conflicts that led up to the estrangement in light of a piece of wisdom my father shared with me: "Evaluate your troubles by how far into the future they will affect you." Ask yourself: "How long will the issue that led up to this estrangement affect me? Is it affecting me now? Will it affect me at the end of a week? In a month? In six months? In a year? In two years? In five years?"

Looking at the length of time something will affect you can give you a realistic sense of the injury you have suffered. Although there are some things worth getting upset about—and perhaps even terminating a relationship over—many issues that seem critical in the moment lose their significance when you project their impact over time.

This exercise can be particularly revealing. One man said, "The interesting thing for me was seeing that the estrangement itself was having a more long-lasting effect on my life than the precipitating incident ever would have had on its own. It made me think twice about whether cutting off Robin had been such a good idea."

You can also use these last questions as a yardstick. When someone says something that upsets you and you feel yourself start to react, ask yourself, "How far into the future will this affect me?" If your answer is relatively short term, it may be worth taking a breath and letting the incident go. And if the impact is going to be severe and long-lasting, you can assess your response in light of that information.

These six tools—characterizing the relationship, recording

complaints and regrets, inventorying benefits and costs, and evaluating the long-term impact of an injury—can provide an initial appraisal of an estranged relationship and give you a better sense of how you might want to proceed.

What's My Role in This Estrangement?

Reconciliation is only possible when we come to terms with the depth of the injury we have sustained. Yet looking at what was done *to* us is not the whole story. It is essential that we look beyond the ways we were wronged and consider our part in the estrangement.

When a relationship is damaged to the breaking point, it is natural to blame the other person. While there are situations in which one person is entirely responsible—like when one spouse beats another—most of the time, both parties contribute to the dynamics that end a relationship.

While our role may not be apparent at first, with reflection and distance, we can usually recognize how our actions, lack of awareness, miscommunication, or insensitivity played a part in the relationship's demise. As we dig beneath our defensive reactions and initial perceptions, new truths and perspectives often emerge.

Ned, whose wife walked out on him, recalls:

> For a long time after Natalie left me, I felt like a victim. But when I thought about it more, I realized that she'd been telling me for years how self-centered I was. When I look back at our marriage, I realize I never once put Natalie's career or needs ahead of my own. I always expected her concerns to take a back seat, figuring we'd get around to what she wanted—later. But years went by, and later never came. Finally, she had enough of my selfishness and left.

Sometimes this dawning awareness of our part in a relationship's failures comes slowly. Other times, the picture becomes clear all at once. Stacey and her best friend, Fran, stopped speaking after a fight about how to divvy up the bill in a restaurant. The two friends had gone out for Moroccan food. Stacey had ordered the special: barbecued lamb over couscous. Fran had a bowl of lentil soup and some flatbread. Over dinner, they each had a glass of wine and enjoyed the belly dancers. They caught up on each other's lives, at one point laughing so hard over Fran's antics at work that they cried. It was what they loved most about each other—how easy it was to laugh uproariously when they were together.

After dinner, Stacey ordered dessert, and Fran declined. Both enjoyed the mint tea traditionally served at the end of the meal. A tall, turbaned waiter stood at his full height and poured steaming sweet tea into tall glasses on the table—from three feet above. They watched, delighted, at his casual and practiced aim. It was the perfect end to a wonderful meal.

When the bill arrived, Stacey assumed they would split it evenly. Fran pulled out a pencil and started to calculate what each of them had spent. The two women fought about it. Finally, so as not to create a scene, Fran paid half but left the restaurant fuming.

Afterward, Fran refused Stacey's calls. Stacey stomped around, feeling hurt, perplexed, and angry.

> At first, I couldn't believe how ridiculous Fran was being. Why was she making such a big deal about how we split the bill? I couldn't believe she'd be willing to throw away our whole friendship over such a petty thing. But as time went by and her silence grew, I began to wonder if maybe something else was going on. By the time I ran into our mutual friend Petrina, I guess I was ready to listen. Petrina reminded me that I come from a family that's well-off and that money has never been an issue for me. Then she reminded me of Fran's situation: she's a single mom who's gone back to college, and money is really tight for her. When I heard Petrina say that, the whole picture suddenly became clear. I thought about all the times Fran wanted to eat at home when I insisted on eating out, all the times she lobbied for an inexpensive place when I pushed for something fancier. I thought about how embarrassing that must have been for Fran and how hard it might have been for her to bring it up.

The more I looked at my own behavior, the more I was faced with my own insensitivity.

It is humbling to accept the fact that our own stubbornness, selfishness, or lack of awareness has contributed to the loss of a relationship we once held dear. But it is only from this place of honesty that reconciliation can begin.

What's the Bigger Picture?

When we are embroiled in a conflict with another person, we typically see it from our own narrow perspective, thinking in terms of the dynamics in *our* family, *our* friendship, or *our* marriage, rather than considering the larger societal forces that may have contributed to the way the relationship played itself out.

Exploring the context in which a particular estrangement took place can broaden our perspective. Donna Jenson, whose mother failed to protect her from an abusive father, recalls:

> I needed to recognize the larger, more universal context of our relationship—not just *this* mother hurting *this* daughter. I had to see that this problem wasn't just about my mother and me. It was about two females living in a sexist world, being working-class, living in a culture that doesn't have a lot of resources for families burdened by alcoholism, violence, and poverty. I looked around and saw there was a bigger world in which our family festered and grew. Seeing that bigger context increased my understanding and deepened my compassion for my mother.

Bridging the Generation Gap

In *Another Country: Navigating the Emotional Terrain of Our Elders*, Mary Pipher explores the psychological chasm that exists between today's baby boomers and their aging parents. Baby boomers, Pipher says, are a generation that values self-reflection, discusses personal matters freely, and sees the benefit of "working through their pain."

Many of their parents, who grew up during the depression and lived through two world wars, do not share this worldview. They survived hard times with humor, by taking care of each other, and making the best of things. They learned not to "dwell on things" and believed it was best to "keep problems within the family." They learned to laugh in the face of tragedy. When confronted with hardship, they kept their feelings and disappointments to themselves.

The older generation, Pipher says, often views their children's efforts to express their feelings and dig through the past not as mental health but as betrayal.

> Older parents are angry at their grown children's complaints. Parents label their children whiners. To them it looks like their children have so much more than they had as kids and yet they don't appreciate it. On the other hand, children are skeptical of their parents' protests that their families were happy. Adult children sometimes confront their parents about abuse when the parents felt they were only providing good discipline.
>
> There are many fractured families as a result of such collisions. Adult children want to acknowledge and forgive, but not pretend that bad things never happened. Older people view their children as hothouse flowers who distort history and only remember the bad. We say we want to know the truth. Our parents ask, "Now, why do you want to bring that up?"*

This cultural clash is at the root of many of the conflicts baby boomers experience with their elders. Understanding the difference between these two perspectives can produce more peace between the generations.

One way to do this, Pipher explains, is to recognize the difference between "deep structures" and "surface structures." Deep structures are the underlying motives a person brings to an interaction: "I love you." "I only want the best for you." "I want our family to stay con-

---

*Mary Pipher, *Another Country: Navigating the Emotional Terrain of Our Elders* (New York: Riverhead Books, 1999), p. 105. Excerpted with permission of the author.

nected." "I want my grandchildren to grow up with good values." More often than not, family members across the generations agree about deep structure, but the way they express this deep structure— the words and actions they use—is determined by the time and place in which they were raised and their life experience. It is at this level— the surface structure—that so many conflicts and estrangements arise.

When I read Pipher's words, I immediately thought of my father and my brother. Abe, who died at eighty-one, was raised in an era when authority reigned supreme. The medical advances in his lifetime wrought miracles and saved lives. From his viewpoint, doctors were always right, and anything that couldn't be proved scientifically was hogwash.

At forty-six, my brother, Darren, is an acupuncturist deeply committed to alternative medicine. When Abe had his first heart attack, in 1988, Darren urged him to get acupuncture, take herbs, and try alternative modes of healing. Abe consistently repudiated Darren's advice. In his mind, the cardiologist was the supreme medical authority. He wondered what gave his son the right to think he knew more than a doctor. For years, my father's dismissal of Darren's ideas hurt Darren. Darren, after all, was just trying to be helpful. He loved Abe, wanted him to be more comfortable, and most important, wanted him to stay alive.

Between my father and my brother, the deep structure was the same. They both cared about Abe's health and wanted him to get the best care possible, but the surface structures of their lives prevented them from ever reaching the same conclusions.

We can alleviate estrangements based on surface structures by digging down below the disagreements to find the common ground. As Pipher tells us:

Many of the tensions between generations are not personal. The difficulties are nobody's fault. We can't change our histories, but we can educate ourselves about them. . . . We need translators and interpreters rather than declarations of war.

People are most alike in their feelings and least alike in their thinking. The conflicts among surface statements often disappear if deep structures are understood. When people are evaluated in terms of their motives, they are easier to respect and forgive.*

Van, the father of three sons, experienced this tension with his parents, who were extremely critical of the way Van and his wife were raising their boys. Things had gotten so bad that Van avoided his parents for months. His parents, who felt increasingly uncomfortable around their grandchildren, weren't making any overtures either.

Finally, Van invited his parents out to dinner. Midway through the meal, he addressed the tension between them. "I asked my parents to stop criticizing my parenting. I said it was really getting in the way of me wanting to be around them, and that if they had to judge me, I didn't want them to do it in front of me."

Van's parents were taken aback but agreed to try. Then they asked Van to stop criticizing them for the mistakes they had made in raising him. They also said they might have to leave when Van's kids were running wild because they couldn't handle the noise.

Van felt good about his parents' requests and said he would do his best to honor them. Since then, both sides are moving toward genuine acceptance.

> Sometimes when Bailey is having a tantrum or Quinn is bouncing off the walls, my parents say good-bye, that they'll see us next week. But they say it matter-of-factly. It no longer has that sting of judgment. Our arrangement is a relief to all of us; I don't have to rein in my kids, and my parents don't feel stuck having to watch our family circus.
>
> Since we talked, I've realized that my parents raised me in another time and place when ideas about parenting were different. They were basically loving, good people who wanted the best for me, so I've backed off on telling them how I wish they'd let me cry. They, in turn, are keeping their opinions to themselves, and we're all enjoying each other a whole lot more.

---

*Pipher, *Another Country*, p. 72.

Van and his parents were able to work through their differences by focusing on the deep structure instead of the surface disagreements. Because both parties brought openness, good communication skills, and a similar desire for reconciliation to the table, the outcome was ideal. Unfortunately, such synchronicity does not always exist.

What Is the Other Person Capable Of?

While other people can always surprise us—and while it is important to leave the door open to unexpected surprises—it is useful to look objectively at the other person's capabilities when we consider reconciliation. Nadine struggled to do this with her mother.

It took me years to accept that my mother could not give me what I wanted. The main thing I wanted, just once, was to be more important to her than her husband. I wanted to come first, and I never had. Whenever there was a choice to be made, her husbands always came first and my sister and I lost out. As kids, we always bore the brunt of her screwed-up marriages. She never picked a mature, healthy partner.

The man my mother is married to now is very immature. He's sexist, racist, and Neanderthal. Whenever my sister or I confronted him about some horrible sexist joke he was telling, he'd get very insulted. At one point he said to my mother, "They're not allowed in my house," and my mother said, "Okay."

I said to her, "What do you mean, 'Okay'? Why can't you say to him, 'I'm going to take my kids into consideration before you'?" And she said, "Honey, I can't do that for you." As much as I didn't want to hear her say that, having her say it really helped me.

I had to accept that my mother is always going to be in dysfunctional marriages. Then I had to ask myself, "Is my mother more important to me than having to deal with her screwed-up husband?" and I decided she was. So my sister and I learned to zip up our mouths around certain things that offend him even though that has not been an easy task.

Accepting the limitations of the people in our lives does not make our path easy; it just clarifies the terrain. Once we get clear about the things we cannot change, we can stop yearning for a fantasy and decide what, for us, is enough. Colleen Carroll did this with her father, an emotionally shut-down man.

> All my life, I tried to get my father to acknowledge Mom's cruelty toward me and my sister. I thought if I could just find the right words, I'd be able to get my dad to wake up to reality. Finally, after forty years of trying to change my dad, I've come to understand that changing people doesn't work.
>
> I've had to accept that my father is a grown man in the latter stages of his life. His daughter killed herself, he lost his wife, he had prostate cancer, and if none of those major events made a dent in his denial, no magic words of mine were going to make a difference. I finally accepted that my father is where he is, and who he is, and that it was no longer my responsibility to change him. The freedom from that impossible task has been liberating.

Despite her father's limitations, Colleen chose to make peace with a circumscribed relationship. She wanted to provide a grandparent for her son and stay in touch with her last surviving relative. Someone else in her situation might have decided to stand up for the truth, to not settle, and to create a surrogate family of people who could more readily support her. And those would have been equally valid choices.

The Changes Were Going to Have to Happen Inside of Me

Assessing the other person's strengths and weaknesses, as Colleen did, is pivotal in determining the kind of reconciliation that is possible. I learned this for myself in November of 1999 during a long car ride with my mother.

My mother, Temme, and I are driving north to San Francisco. We've just passed the outskirts of Santa Cruz, and the two-lane coastal highway opens up before us. I like road trips—the feeling of freedom and the sense of heading off on an adventure. For me, the car is a good place to talk; there's a unique feeling of privacy created in the front seat.

My mother has flown to California for an extended winter visit. She's been here two weeks so far. Although we've spent quite a bit of time together, the kids have always been with us; we have never been alone. I have something I want to talk to her about, and I know this may be one of our few opportunities. So despite my nervousness, I plunge ahead. "You know, Mom, I'd really like to be closer to you, but sometimes when we're together and you start telling stories that go on and on, I feel further away from you. I feel more like an audience and less like we're in a conversation."

I hear a sharp inhalation beside me, then the sound of angry tears. These are familiar sounds; I know them well. Since my mother is a very emotional woman, I've never had to question how she feels. Now she is very upset.

"Oh no," I think to myself, "I never should have said that."

Temme lights into me, her words sharp and angry: "I was really looking forward to today because we haven't had a chance to talk, but you were just waiting to pounce on me, weren't you? I knew you didn't really want me to come on this trip today, and now you've sabotaged the whole day by starting it off with so much negativity."

I feel my neck tighten and my body tense. An old sinking feeling starts at the base of my spine and moves straight toward my head, threatening to engulf me. I am dissolving quickly, and soon I will be nothing more than a puddle on the floor mat, sloshing remorsefully under the clutch.

I stop listening. I tune her out, a survival skill I mastered years ago. As numbness spreads through me, I keep my eyes fixed on the road, wishing I could feel something, anything. But there is no room for my feelings; Temme's are taking up every inch of space. I feel my mind snap shut and my heart harden. Pretty soon, there will be nothing left of me at all.

We're driving up Highway 1, the spectacular road that ribbons all the way from Mexico to Canada. I've had so many wonderful trips up this road—the elephant seals, the hang gliders, the surfers, the whitecaps—they're all streaking by as I sit locked in misery. I look out the window, wishing I could fly.

Then with conscious intent, I force my attention back into the car. I'm an adult, and I'm the one who instigated this mess; I'm the one who needs to clean it up.

Temme is still talking. I come in on the tail end of a speech I know by heart. "Why did you attack me like that? How could you be so insensitive?" As my mother's hurt spews out, I grow colder and more rational.

Like clockwork, our old patterns play themselves out. My mother pauses, then I know it's my turn. It's the old parry and thrust I know so well: she attacks, and I defend; I attack, and she defends. I respond automatically to my cue. "I wasn't trying to attack you," I say, my voice lofty and superior. "I was just trying to tell you something I thought might bring us closer together." I cringe as I hear myself defend my insensitivity. How arrogant and self-righteous I can be! All my mother needs is a compassionate word, a kind gesture, for me to reach over and take her hand, but something in me is frozen. I can't move.

She counters, "Well, it sure didn't feel that way to me." Lamely, I try to hold my ground. "No, really, Mom. I want to be close to you. That's why I told you it was great when you wanted to spend the winter here. It took a lot of courage for you to come here, and I admire you for it."

She responds, "I admit, you've been very generous. The maps you got for me, the kids' artwork in my room. You've invited me for dinner. You sent me all those newspapers with ideas of things to do. But underneath your niceness, there's always this formality, this coldness, this meanness just waiting to strike."

"Mom, all I said is that when you tell a lot of stories, I find myself tuning out. I don't feel connected to you, and I want to feel more connected. That's why I said it. You have to admit it, Mom," I say, my voice softer now, "you do go on and on."

It's quiet on her side. The tears, I realize, are back. She's staring out the passenger window, lost in a private sea of pain. Finally, she turns to me, her voice thick. "Do you have any idea," she says to me, each word deliberate, "what it's like to live alone? You have no idea! There is a hole in my life where family should be. Telling stories about places I've been and things I've done helps fill that loneliness. Why deny me that?"

My heart drops. I can't believe she's saying this about herself. Despite our history of estrangement, I've always admired my mother. "Mom," I say, "there are lots of great things about you. Look at what you've accomplished. Your husband walked out on you and you went to night school and got your master's degree. You pulled your life together financially. You've built a terrific network of friends. You have your theater and your health. You've traveled all over the world. There are a lot of good things in your life. Besides," I continue, "you don't have to be interesting for us. We like you just the way you are. You don't have to embellish yourself with stories."

My words don't penetrate. Her face is still anguished, her body pulled away. "You don't understand," she tells me, her voice wracked with pain. "You don't know what it's like to be so far from my children and grandchildren. Everyone else has their family with them for holidays and birthdays, and I never have mine. You moved three thousand miles away—and I know you did it to get away from me."

I say nothing. What she's accusing me of is true, and we both know it. She goes on: "I don't blame you for that. What's done is done, but now you live here. You've made a life here—and I see that it's a good life. I accept that you're never going to move back to New Jersey. But I don't think you understand my situation at all. You're young. You're in the prime of your life. I'm past mine. My life is getting smaller, and I'm alone. In my social circle, people are dying, and a number of them are younger than me. I'm at the acceptable age for death, and I've started to face my mortality. What's wrong with telling a few stories if they help me feel better?"

Wow. This wasn't what I intended. I didn't want to hurt her like this. I thought I was doing the right thing, but obviously I wasn't.

More than anything, I want to close up this wound and move back into the present, back into this glorious, sunny winter day. Then somehow, miraculously, we do. Neither of us wants to lose any of the ground we've so tenaciously carved out; we've fought for every inch, and we're not going to let old history defeat us now. I push past my coldness and take hold of her hand. She pulls herself back from the precipice, and we ease back into now. The terrible moment passes as we reach the Pigeon Point Lighthouse and continue north on 1 toward Half Moon Bay.

The rest of the drive—across 92, with the rolling hills famous for pumpkin patches and Christmas tree farms; and on to 280, a straight shot north to the city—we manage small talk: the kids, the garden, the fence Karyn and I are planning to build, the storytelling conference Temme recently attended.

But what I remember most about that drive north is that I finally understood that my mother was not my enemy, but rather a complex, imperfect aging woman too vulnerable to experience that conversation as anything other than an attack. Driving up to San Francisco, on that sunny winter morning, I

realized with absolute clarity that any changes I needed to make in our rela-
tionship were going to have to happen inside of me.

Years ago, the questions for me might have been "Do I want this relation-
ship? Is it worth it to me?" But those questions had long since been answered. I
was committed to her, and she was committed to me. Now we were trying to
figure out how to be two adult women together, and I realized that I cared
enough about her to never want to repeat this scene again. The question I faced
now was "How can I find in myself the love, compassion, and acceptance for my
mother that she so deeply deserves?"

What Kind of Person Do I Want to Be?

In an estranged relationship, one of the few things we have power over
is how we respond to the other person. It is up to us to establish our
own standards of conduct, rather than accepting our family's definitions, our friends' definitions, or society's definitions of the kind of person we ought to be. In estranged relationships, particularly those in
which there has been a serious betrayal, old norms and rules of behavior no longer apply. We don't have to be the same kind of sister we used
to be before the rift with our brother took place. We don't have to obey
our family's rules about how sons *should* interact with their fathers if it
has been six years since ours has spoken to us. We don't have to treat
our friend the same way we treat other friends who have not betrayed
our trust. Instead, we get to look at each relationship and decide what
makes sense given our unique circumstances. Yet violating age-old
standards is unsettling—and can leave us feeling uncertain. Donna Jenson has given this matter a great deal of thought.

> For twenty-five years, I've struggled with what it means to be a
> good daughter. For a long time, I only saw two options—being a
> good daughter or a horrible daughter. In my mind, not visiting
> my mother meant I was a bad daughter. Not forgiving her made
> me a bad daughter as well, because my mother was as much a
> victim as I was.
>
> After years of working on this, I've readjusted my thinking.
> Now I feel okay about the way I'm relating to my mother, given

our history together. I call her every week to make sure she's okay. I ask, "How are you doing, Mom? How's the diabetes?" Although our conversations aren't deep, they're not phony either. It's human kindness at the depth that makes sense for this relationship.

Donna's choice to reconcile with her mother, despite a lack of truth between them, is one many people make as their parents age, grow ill, and move toward death. Sharon Tobin faced this crossroad when she learned that her mother was terminally ill.

Sharon Tobin: Choosing Compassion for a Dying Parent

My mother had been awful, but I didn't want to be awful. I didn't want to abandon her and do all the same things to her that she had done to me.

—SHARON TOBIN

"My mother should never have been a mother. She was only sixteen when she married my dad. She gave birth to me the next year. Then my father went off to war. She was left with a severely asthmatic child. My mother could not cope with caring for a sick child, so she abandoned me to a series of abusive foster homes.

"When I was thirty-two, I'd done enough recovery to decide that I wanted to talk to my mother about what had happened to me as a child. Her response was negative, and she changed the subject. When I pressed her, she finally said, 'I've never been able to help myself. I certainly couldn't have helped you.'

"For the next ten years, I pulled way back from her. During those years, I went to therapy and explored who I was as a person. Part of what I learned about myself was that I didn't want my mother to die with me regretting how far I'd pulled away from her. So I started driving down to have dinner with her once a month, but there was no sharing of anything real between us.

"Sometimes when I left her, I'd drive two blocks and have to park the car to deal with my rage about some snide remark she had made. It was very clear to me that my fury had little to do with what was happening in the present. It all had to do with the past. I knew our relationship wasn't satisfying to either of us, yet there was no place for it to go."

What Kind of Daughter Do I Want to Be?

Six years after Sharon starting seeing her mother again, her mother was diagnosed with cancer of the mouth and told she had three to six months to live. Sharon recalls, "For twenty years, I'd been working with dying people. When I realized my mother was terminally ill, I knew that I didn't want to regret what I had or hadn't done while she was dying.

"I started to focus on the kind of adult person I wanted to be, rather than on the kind of mother she had been. My mother had been awful, but I didn't want to be awful. I didn't want to abandon her and do all the same things to her that she had done to me. I wanted to live that last period of time with her in such a way that I could respect myself and hold my head up. So I decided to go through her dying process with her. In all honesty, that decision was more for my sake than for hers.

"At first, my mother wanted me to live with her and be her full-time caretaker, but I knew there was no way we could spend more than four hours together without her becoming extremely agitated. I also knew that staying in her house would make me bitter and resentful. But I wanted to make sure she had care and got to die the way she wanted to, so we began to make arrangements.

"I coordinated all of her care, and every Wednesday I spent the afternoon and evening with her. During one of these weekly visits, I decided to make one more attempt to confront her about the way she had abandoned me. She made a joke about it.

"At that moment, something shifted in me. The child part of

me absolutely recognized, 'This is never going to be a meaningful mother-daughter relationship. She is not going to be a mother to you. She never has been.' It was the most freeing thing that's ever happened to me.

"The adult part of me looked at her and felt this incredible sadness. My mother had been one of these bright, beautiful teenage girls who looked around at the world and decided to give up. My mother had never chosen to live; she had just chosen to exist. I realized that most of the bad things that happened to me were due to the fact that she didn't stand up and fight for herself or for me. It was wrong, but it was totally consistent with who she was. Realizing that enabled me to see that the abuse I suffered had absolutely nothing to do with my soul. It belonged to her, not to me. And it was that change in perspective that allowed me to take care of her and then let her go.

"When my mother died, I felt so finished. I was relieved that that part of my life was over. A weight dropped off me, and I felt peaceful. Since then, there have been no remnants of anger or upset. The only thing I've felt is sadness at who my mother might have been."

DOES THIS RELATIONSHIP WARRANT RECONCILIATION?

In clarifying how you want to respond to an estrangement, it is important to honestly assess your hopes, expectations, and reasons for seeking reconciliation. If you are seeking an apology that will never come, hoping for a personality change that would require a miracle, or trying to find a way out of facing irretrievable losses, your attempts at reconciliation will most likely lead to disappointment and further estrangement. Until you can approach an estranged relationship realistically, your hopes will probably be dashed again and again.

In considering whether a particular relationship warrants

reconciliation, it is critical to be honest about what you are feeling and what you want from the other person. The following questions can help clarify your thinking:

- What is the importance of this relationship in my life?
- Do I share enough history or common ground with this person to accept the difficult aspects of the relationship?
- Have I worked through my own pain and anger sufficiently to approach this relationship in a new way?
- Is there potential for this relationship to evolve into something new?
- Would the relationship be worth it to me even if it didn't change?
- Can I be in this relationship and still feel good about myself?
- Do I have the time, energy, and resources necessary to rebuild this relationship?

A Personal Decision

The decision whether or not to attempt reconciliation is highly personal. We may recognize that our grievances are dwarfed by the significance of the relationship and choose to do everything we can to rebuild it. Conversely, we may conclude that the relationship is no longer as important to us as it once was and decide that it is easier or more beneficial to let it slip away.

Decisions about whether or not to seek reconciliation can also vary *within* a relationship. Sara and Tom Brown, a couple who split up, spent years deciding whether or not to get back together again. Their story is a good example of the kind of discernment that is necessary when assessing the viability of a relationship over time.

Sara and Tom Brown:
Facing a Broken Marriage

When Tom suddenly wasn't there, I was thrown into a situation where I was making all of the decisions. I discovered that I didn't need a husband; I didn't need anyone to take care of me. I discovered that I was an intelligent, independent person who could take care of herself. I grew spiritually during those years, and I wouldn't give up any of that.

—SARA BROWN

Sara and Tom Brown were married for twenty-one years when a hidden enemy derailed their marriage. The events leading up to their separation came as a total surprise to Sara, who was left alone with two teenagers to raise. "I knew something was drastically wrong with our marriage, but I didn't know what it was. There was no communication between Tom and me; we were yelling at each other a lot. Tom didn't participate in the family, and he was treating the kids unfairly; it often felt like it was us against him.

"Things came to a head when Tom and I went away for a long weekend to Palm Beach, Florida. While we were there, Tom had seizures and had to be rushed to the hospital; he stopped breathing and almost died. The doctor came to me and said, 'Your husband has advanced alcoholism and liver disease.' That's how I found out that Tom had a drinking problem.

"In retrospect, I realize he'd been having tremors for a while. I'd asked him to go to see the doctor, but he insisted, 'Nothing's wrong with me.' I'd smelled this really strange smell on him, but I had no idea what it was. I later found out it was acetone, something the body gives off as a by-product of alcohol.

"I've often asked myself how I missed the signs. Alcoholism just wasn't in my awareness. We generally didn't keep alcohol in the house. We would go out to dinner and have a glass of wine or two. That was all.

"Tom had always had an amazing capacity to hold his liquor;

he was famous for it in college. I realize now he must have been drinking very heavily those last few years, but he never got sick and he was incredibly good at covering it up. No one in our social circle and no one in his family had any idea. And since I never saw liquor around, I didn't attribute our growing problems to alcohol."

I Just Had to Let Go of Him

"Tom was hospitalized for two weeks. Then we flew home, and he went right into an alcohol treatment program. I immediately got into therapy with a woman who specialized in alcoholism, and I started going to Al-Anon. I learned about the disease and how pervasive it is. I found other spouses of alcoholics, and that kept me going.

"Six months after we got home, I realized Tom was drinking again. He was hiding it, but I found some bottles. At that point, he was still denying that he had a problem. I got angry and gave him an ultimatum: 'You can either stay here and get help, or you can leave.' Tom chose to move out.

"If Tom was going to drink himself to death, and it seemed as though he was, I wasn't going to go down with him. I was determined to do everything I could to survive and help my kids, and I couldn't do it with him here. If he got help as a result of being out of the house, that was good, but what I really cared about was my own mental stability and the children. Reconciliation was the last thing on my mind. I knew as long as he kept drinking, there would be nothing between us."

Trying to Survive

Sara had little contact with Tom once he moved out. "There were periods when I didn't even know where he was living. From time to time, we talked on the phone about the kids, but generally he was far too interested in the bottle. There were times I had to tell my son he couldn't go with his father because Tom was drunk.

"That first year, I didn't think about Tom a lot. I had a daughter who was considering college and a son entering adolescence. Mostly, I just focused on trying to get through each day.

"By choice, I had only worked part-time since my kids were born, and it was hard getting a full-time job. When I finally did, I hated it, and I wasn't making enough for us to live on.

"Tom was good about sending money for the kids; he was very generous. At one point, I went to a divorce lawyer but found out that Tom was sending me more money than any judge would give me, so I left things the way they were. I did whatever was necessary to keep the family functioning.

"During this time, Tom was in and out of four different rehabs. He got fired from his job. He had seizures again and almost died. When I heard about it, I thought, 'What will it take for him to hit bottom? He's lost his family. He's lost his job. He's lost his friends. What's left?' I fully expected him to drink himself to death."

He Seemed to Be Able to Listen

Two years after his initial hospitalization, Tom quit drinking, but Sara didn't hear about it for a while. "I wasn't in enough contact with Tom to realize that he was staying sober. During that year, I was focused on helping my daughter apply to college, and my mother fell seriously ill. I didn't hate Tom, but I didn't have time for him. During the first year of his sobriety, he was pretty much on his own with AA and his therapist.

"But he did tell me when he was having his first anniversary of sobriety, and I went to that AA meeting. After that, we started talking on the phone. He'd call to talk about the kids, and I'd start talking about my mother's illness. He seemed to be able to listen, something he'd never been able to do before. I started to feel like I had an ally. It was helpful that he knew her and cared about her; I didn't have to explain everything. Those phone calls met a mutual need. I needed to talk, and Tom wanted to participate more in family life.

"That spring, I was feeling particularly needy. My mother died in May, and my daughter was going off to college. I felt as though I was losing the two most important women in my life, and Tom was a safe person I could talk to about it. I wasn't thinking of him as a husband at that point; he was just an old friend I could talk to on the phone.

"That summer, Tom got our son a job working in a friend's business. Tom lived an hour away, and he would drive over to pick Sean up in the morning. Then they'd drive another forty-five minutes to the job site. At the end of the day, Tom drove Sean home and then drove back another hour to where he lived. He was spending almost four hours a day commuting, largely because he wanted to be with Sean. That impressed me. It showed me that he had gotten beyond the point where AA and getting through the day was his whole life. Still, he was only with us in bits and pieces. He was not back fully into our lives in any way, shape, or form."

It Was Strange Going on a Date with My Husband

That fall, Sara got tickets to hear some music, and she spontaneously asked Tom if he wanted to go with her. "It was strange going on a date with my husband. I'd lived with this man for more than twenty years, yet I felt a lot of anxiety. I even bought a new dress and some lingerie. I hadn't gone out on a date in years.

"We went to the concert and had dinner. We had a very good time, and there was definitely a physical attraction between us. We talked a lot and then came back to our house. I remember standing with Tom in our front hall, talking; I hadn't actually invited him all the way in. We were just standing in the hall, not knowing where things were going to go next. Then he kissed me.

"Up until that point, there'd been no physical contact between us at all, but I think at that moment, we were both aware of a strong physical need. I'd gone three years without a man in my life, and it was nice to be close to one again. I didn't expect it to happen so quickly, but we had a really good time. The evening was comfortable.

"Things went forward from there. We kept dating. Pretty quickly, it turned into him coming here, largely because he wanted to be with Sean. We would cook dinner and listen to music, watch a movie, and just lie beside each other on the couch. We did ordinary things.

"We laughed a lot that winter. We're both reserved people, and I remember laughing more than we had our whole marriage.

"I noticed that Tom was open to trying things that he would never have tried before. He was more caring and interested in what was happening with me and the children than he had ever been. He wasn't turning back into the man I had been married to."

Can Someone Really Change This Much?

As Tom and Sara tentatively found their way back to each other, they went for a lot of counseling, both individually and together. It was during one of their first joint sessions that Sara dared to voice her deepest hopes. "I said to the therapist, 'Can someone really change this much? Can he be turning into somebody I'm liking much better than the man I remember?'

"She said, 'Yes, people can change. They can be very different if they work at it and they want to be.'

"After that session, we went to a marriage counselor with the specific intention of figuring out where our relationship was headed. I could feel that I was starting to trust Tom; we were beginning to share more intimately. I wanted to explore, 'Where can it go from here?' 'Do I want it to go any further?' 'Can the trust between us be reestablished given the damage that's been done?' And, 'Can we learn to do things we were never able to do before?' I knew I wasn't willing to settle for what we'd had; I wanted more in a relationship now.

"In therapy, we realized we had a lot to learn about being in a healthy relationship. We spent a lot of time learning to communicate, express our feelings, and not clam up when things got tough. Tom was willing to do all of those things; the man I knew twenty years ago never could have.

"Four years after Tom's first hospitalization, we went away for the weekend. We had a really nice time together; we stopped at a beach, and I said to him, 'I think we ought to try again.' I told him I loved him and that I wanted him to move back in.

"I hadn't planned it. In fact, I surprised myself. I couldn't really verbalize why I was ready. It was a gut feeling, and I went with it.

"He moved in two weeks later, and that was seven years ago. We just celebrated our thirty-first anniversary together."

Believing That People Can Change

One of the paradoxes of reconciliation is that we must accept another person's limitations while simultaneously staying open to the possibility that he or she might change. Although we might have a pretty good idea how a particular person is *likely* to react, sometimes even the most recalcitrant person can change.

Dana Roper spent twenty years coming to terms with a cruel, homophobic father. Just when she finally accepted the fact that he would never change, all of a sudden he did.

I came out to my father when I was twenty-four. He was fine with it for about an hour. Then he gave me a lecture about what a shame it was because I would have made such a good breeder.

A year later, I wrote to tell him I was fighting an antigay

initiative. He wrote back and said, "People like you would have all been killed in the pogroms if it weren't for the fact that you can't reproduce." Then in the next paragraph he said, "But I love you."

I thought, "This is the kind of crap I've grown up with my whole life." That was the point at which I really broke off with him.

Twenty years later, when I was forty-five and he was eighty-five, we were having one of our rare phone conversations and my father asked, "How are things with you and your lover?"

I said, "I can't believe you're asking me about my lover after twenty years of refusing to talk to me about being a lesbian!"

He said to me, "If you live long enough, you can get over anything."

And the thing was, he meant it. I could hear the warmth in his voice. So I said, "We're doing really well, and I'm in love."

He said, "I'm happy for you," and I believed him. Then I said to myself, "I'll be damned. It took him twenty years to go from being the fascist who said I should be killed to 'I'm happy for you,' but he got there."

As one woman put it, "I like to be realistic, but I always stay open for a miracle."

Different Circumstances, Different Choices

In the world of emotions and relationships, there is no one "right way" to respond; no blanket approach that works across the board. In some cases, what is called for is a fierce determination to do whatever we can to make things right again. In others, the best solution is to walk away.

One man, who lived with an unpredictable, alcoholic roommate, recalls: "Week after week, I kept trying to work with this dynamic and talk about it. Finally, after months of struggling to do the right thing, it dawned on me that the right thing was to move. So I gave my notice and left, and that was the appropriate resolution."

In relationships where more is at stake, it is harder to move on. Out of loyalty, desperation, or need, people sometimes try repeatedly to reconcile relationships in which they are consistently treated badly. In these cases, walking away from a conflict can be especially empowering.

Sylvia, who is sixty-four, fretted for a long time over her relationship with a friend.

> My friend Betty was very negative. Every time I saw her, she was full of bad feelings. She'd complain that her son had done this, her son had done that. She hated her mother. I got tired of hearing about all her problems. She was a beautiful woman who had a lot going for her: she had a good job, she was intelligent, she owned her own house, and she had two sons who loved her. But every time I saw her, I felt like I had to be her counselor. By the time we ended the friendship, I couldn't stand it anymore.
>
> When Betty's mother died, I wanted to go the funeral, but Betty told me not to come. Being excluded really hurt me, and I never called her again. She called a couple of times, and I never returned her calls. It's bothered me a bit, but basically I think I did the right thing. I listened to her for years, and I just didn't want to do it anymore. I have my own health problems and troubles in my life, and I need friendships where things are more equal.

Other times, people decide that the benefits of a particular relationship are worth the compromises they would have to make to keep it. Albert, an eighty-year-old man, recalls:

> Olga and I had been friends for twenty-seven years. She's thirty years younger than I am, but we'd been close for a long time. For years, Olga had a key to my place so she'd always have a place to stay when she came to town. Over the last ten years, she's probably slept here fifty or sixty times.
>
> Once she was visiting, and we decided to go to a movie. On the way over, she kept criticizing my driving. When we got there, we had quite a few blocks to walk. I walk quite slowly these days, and before I even locked up my door, she raced off

ahead of me. I called out for her to wait, but she didn't. When she reached the corner, she turned back and shouted, "Which way do I go?" I told her, and she continued on without me. That really upset me.

After the movie, Olga had to use the bathroom, and there was a mix-up about where we were supposed to meet afterward. I waited for her in the lobby; she waited by the bathroom. When she finally found me, we were both very angry. After that fiasco, there was a complete break between us. For weeks, my partner, Regina, urged me to call Olga, but I wanted nothing to do with her.

Six months passed. Finally, Regina told Olga, "Albert's not going to have anything to do with you until you apologize."

So Olga wrote Albert a letter and used those words: "I apologize."

Albert called and formally accepted Olga's apology and their relationship resumed, but Albert didn't feel the same about her and thought he never would. "I didn't trust Olga anymore. I felt she might turn on me at any moment."

But after Olga visited a couple of times, Albert found himself enjoying the old relationship: "Olga and I have such a long history. I knew her children the whole time they were growing up. Now they're in college, and I realized I'd miss not hearing about them. I still feel a little wary around Olga, and I don't think that I'd go out alone with her again, but in general, I feel more kindly toward her now."

In this instance, it was the potential loss of history that motivated Albert to accept a flawed friendship. Many people consider reconciliation for just that reason. Others, like Dana Roper, seek reconciliation because it is essential to *their* well-being.

My efforts to work things out with my father have always been for me, not for him. Hating my father leaves me with tight places in my chest and makes me a smaller person than I want to be. That's the thing that always motivates me to go deeper.

HOW CLOSE DO I WANT TO BE?

Every relationship fluctuates in terms of closeness and intimacy. Even with the people we are closest to, there is a rhythm of being connected and being separate, bonding and pulling back into ourselves. There are times to unburden the heart, to hold each other close and be there in need, times for boisterous laughter, anger, conciliatory words, or pillow talk. When life is busy, we sometimes pass like ships in the night, knowing that later we will dock together again. This ebb and flow of closeness—this breathing in and breathing out—is part of any healthy relationship.

With each person, we determine our level of closeness and the ways we like to share our time. We rack up long-distance phone bills with our cousin, play bridge with our son-in-law, and let the new baby crawl all over our lap. It is natural for each relationship to seek its own level and its relative degree of importance in our lives. Yet the amount of proximity and contact we want—or that is available—can vary by day, by season, or by year.

Estranged relationships are no different. They, too, find their own level, and they, too, evolve over time. When we reenter into a relationship after an estrangement, we need to consider the kind of contact we think will serve the relationship—and us— best. The following questions can help you think about the kind of connection that you hope to create:

- Am I trying to repair a relationship that was once intimate and loving? If at all possible, do I want to return to the level of closeness we once had?
- Under what conditions would I consider a partial or compromised relationship?
- Do I want to set up "terms of engagement" (see p. 46) so we can successfully negotiate a limited rapprochement?
- Am I trying to clean up unfinished business so I can let the relationship go?

- Am I looking for reckoning and truth-telling? Or do I want to pick up the relationship in the present and let sleeping dogs lie?
- Would it be wise to reengage around some safe, neutral activities and see how things evolve? Or do I need to address the roots of the conflict right from the start?

Answering these questions can help you glean an overall sense of direction. If you believe deep reconciliation is possible and that is what you want, you will probably approach things differently than you would if you were only seeking a circumscribed reengagement. In many instances, however, you will not know what you want—or what is possible—until you begin interacting with the other person. In that case, the question to ask might be "Am I ready to find out?"

Am I Prepared to Deal with the Outcome?

When we decide to make a gesture of reconciliation, timing can be crucial. We call our brother, and he says he just picked up the phone book in search of our number. We send our niece a wedding gift, and a note crosses in the mail saying, "Isn't it time we get together?"

There are moments of serendipity. There is luck. There are times when grace meets opportunity. Other times, the fates are against us: a letter returns unopened, a number is unlisted, an e-mail bounces back. We finally locate our stepfather's address, only to learn that he recently died. When it comes to human relationships, there are never guarantees. The question, then, is not "Is this the perfect time?" but rather "Am I prepared to deal with the outcome, whatever it might be?"

Elizabeth Menkin faced this quandary when she was offered the opportunity to meet with the woman directly responsible for her sister's death.

Elizabeth Menkin: She Owes Us a Life

There's an old Yiddish phrase, "When you go out for revenge, you have to dig two graves."

—ELIZABETH MENKIN

On April 27, 1993, twenty-five-year-old Susanna Cooper was out drinking peppermint schnapps at a friend's home. She left the house, drove to a roadside tavern to use the bathroom, and tried and failed to get a ride home. Still drunk, she got back in her car and drove two more miles down the road, veered across the center line, and smashed head-on into a car driven by forty-seven-year-old Elaine Serrell Myers. Myers was killed instantly. Cooper sustained severe injuries that put her in a coma and almost killed her. When doctors checked her blood alcohol level in the emergency room, it was .20, twice the legal limit for Washington State. It was later discovered that Susanna Cooper had been arrested for drunk driving four years before.

Elaine's sister, Elizabeth Menkin, is a hospice doctor for the Kaiser Santa Teresa Medical Center. Like most people who lose a family member to a drunk driver, she was consumed with anger and obsessed with vengeance. She and her brother-in-law spent hours swapping revenge fantasies over the phone.

As a hospice doctor, Elizabeth understood the importance of grieving. As part of her own grieving process she traveled to the crash site to see it for herself. On that trip, she and her nine-year-old daughter, Aileen, visited the wrecking yard where Susanna's minivan had been towed after the crash. Aileen looked in the backseat and saw toys. She turned to her mother and said something that would profoundly influence the path the Serrell-Myers family would take in their grief: "Hey, Mom. She's got kids." Susanna Cooper, it turned out, was the single mother of two young children.

Elaine and Elizabeth's father, Peter Serrell, was deeply affected by this news. He began asking himself, "What kind of lives are her children going to have if she doesn't turn her life around? How many generations does this tragedy have to destroy?"

Peter remembered a presentation he had heard by Marty Price, founder and director of the Victim-Offender Reconciliation Program Information and Resource Center of Camas, Washington, about a promising new trend in corrections called restorative justice. In restorative justice programs, perpetrators of crimes are brought face-to-face with their victims, with the assistance of a trained mediator. Perpetrators are confronted with the human consequences of their crimes, and victims have the opportunity to speak their minds and express their feelings to the person who hurt them—a process that contributes to the healing of the victim. Offenders take responsibility for their actions by creating a restitution agreement with the victim that attempts to right the wrong as much as possible. This agreement does not preclude or replace a court sentence, and the restitution can be monetary or symbolic. Anything that creates a sense of justice between the victim and the offender can be included in the restitution agreement.

Peter Serrell felt that restorative justice might do more to dissuade Susanna Cooper from drinking and driving, and possibly taking another life, than simply going to jail. He called Marty Price.*

---

*In an article titled "The Mediation of Drunk Driving Deaths and Other Severely Violent Crimes," Marty Price explains that most victim-offender mediation programs work primarily with juvenile offenders who have been charged with property offenses and other nonviolent offenses. He writes: "The mediation of severely violent crimes is not commonplace. However, in a growing number of victim-offender programs, victims and survivors of violent crimes, including murders and sexual assaults, are finding that confronting their offender in a safe and controlled setting, with the assistance of a mediator, helps to return their stolen sense of safety and control in their lives. Increasingly, mediation is helping to repair the lives of surviving family members and offenders devastated by drunk-driving fatalities."

Realizing I Still Had Some Control

Initially, Elizabeth was too busy struggling with her own rage and grief to be interested in mediation. She didn't know how she wanted to respond to her sister's death, but watching how others had reacted to drunk-driving tragedies gave Elizabeth a clear sense of what she wanted to avoid. "My brother-in-law and I went on a TV talk show with other victims. Among the guests was a woman whose daughter had been killed two years earlier by a drunk driver. This woman's whole identity revolved around being incensed by this criminal and what he did to her daughter, and her rage was consuming her. My brother-in-law and I shared a limo back to the hotel with her, and we got out of the car saying, "My God! I don't want to go that route.""

Choosing Compassion

What leads one person to choose vengeance and another compassion is hard to define. For some, a deep sense of spirituality creates the bridge to inner healing. For Elizabeth, a combination of circumstances enabled her to choose a more compassionate path. "One of the seeds was my father making it clear that he was going to pursue the mediation. He didn't ask for our blessing or need us to cooperate. He just wanted to let us know that he was going to do this, and he hoped it didn't bother or offend us. If we were interested, he would keep us informed, but we were under no obligation to join him if it wasn't to our taste.

"It was kind of like hors d'oeuvres that are being passed around at a party. No one is going to be insulted if you leave them on the tray. And after the fourth or fifth time the waitresses walk by in their little starched uniforms offering you these tidbits, you think, 'I'm tired of being hungry. They're kind of funny looking, and I'm not sure they're going to taste good, but maybe I'll try one.'

"My initial response to the mediation was 'Yuck! Why would

I want to do that? I'd have to be in the same room with her, and I'd want to crawl across the table and strangle her. Why should I go to the effort of having to control those impulses?' That's how I felt at first. And my father just patiently gave me updates."

In mid-November, Susanna decided to plead guilty and spare the Serrell-Myers family a trial. That was another turning point for Elizabeth. "Once it was clear there wasn't going to be a trial, we were asked to write victim-impact statements for the judge to use. Mine went through several drafts. The first said I thought Susanna should have her eyes poked out. I knew from the Washington statutes that she wasn't going to get more than twenty-six months in jail, so it was clear to me that the criminal justice system wasn't going to keep her from driving drunk again—and I figured she couldn't drive if she was blind. At the time, I was searching for an answer to the question 'How can I get a guarantee that this won't happen again?'

"Then I had to rewrite the thing so the judge would take it seriously. I found myself thinking back to the Jewish High Holy Days a few months earlier. Yom Kippur is the time when Jews are supposed to focus on forgiveness. At the time, it felt like a cruel joke. Elaine had been dead for five months. How could I ever forgive someone for taking my sister away from me?

"But then I remembered a blackboard I had seen in the religious school with the definition of 'teshuvah' on the board. 'Teshuvah' is a Hebrew word that comes from the root 'to turn around.' And on the board were the five R's of teshuvah: recognition, remorse, repentance, restitution, and reform. They're the stages you have to go through in order to be forgiven for an offense.

"At first I hooked into that list as a way of staying pumped up: 'Look at this list. She hasn't done any of this. Why should I forgive her?' But a little voice inside of me said, 'No she hasn't done those things, but have you given her the chance?'

"I reached a point where I started to ask myself, 'What choices do I still have in my life? I can't change what happened in the past, but I still have choices about the future.' For me, realizing that I did have some control was a toehold I could use to climb out of my pit of grief."

Preparing for the Mediation

Before victims and perpetrators are brought together in a mediation session, particularly in the case of a violent crime, meticulous preparation and screening are done. A specially trained mediator often spends months meeting separately with the victims and the offender to make sure that the victims are clear about their motives and expectations and that the offender is truly sorry and ready to hear what the victims have to say. Victims and offenders are not brought together until and unless offenders admit their guilt, exhibit remorse, and express a desire to make amends for the hurts they have inflicted. Participation is voluntary for all the parties involved.

Elizabeth describes the importance of those preparatory meetings: "A lot of people think that the punch line of the mediation is the meeting with the offender, but that was just the coda to the symphony. The first movement, the second movement, the theme, and variations were the meetings with the mediator. In our early meetings, Marty would ask us, 'What's in this for you? Why would you want to do this? Do you want to do this?'

"People often assume what we did was altruistic, but really, we did it for selfish reasons. You might think that not wanting Susanna to kill someone else was altruistic, but it wasn't. If I ever found out that she had killed somebody else, I knew I would be so enraged that I would have to kill her, and that would ruin my life. That was a real fear for me."

Marty Price recalls his memories of those early meetings. "Family members shared their pain, discussed the loss of Elaine, and brainstormed requests they might make of Susanna that could meaningfully address their loss. No one was interested in monetary compensation. Rather, they wanted Susanna to be rehabilitated and to use her experience to help keep drunk drivers off the road. Their main concern was breaking the cycle of tragedy."

During the same period he was meeting with the Serrell-Myers family, Marty was talking with Susanna Cooper. He wanted to make sure she was prepared to hear what the Serrells had to say and also that she wouldn't arrive at the mediation with so little insight into what she had done that Elaine's relatives would end up feeling hurt or revictimized.

In Marty's first meeting with Susanna, she denied having a drinking problem. He told her, "I don't think the Serrell family would find that credible." He gave her the homework of going for an alcohol-abuse evaluation, which helped her realize that her level of drinking seemed normal to her only because so many around her abused alcohol.

Marty also helped Susanna face the impact of what she had done. When he first met her, her sorrow and remorse revolved around what she had done to herself. Although she was devastated that she had killed someone, her grief was self-centered. She was sad about her injuries, distressed at how she'd hurt her family, upset that she had to abandon her children while she was in the hospital, a nursing home, and, later, jail. She wasn't nearly as concerned about the larger circle of pain she had created. So Marty asked Elaine's relatives if he could pass along their victim-impact statements for Susanna to read.

Their statements broke through Susanna's shortsightedness and self-pity. By the time the mediation took place, she had acknowledged that she was an alcoholic, demonstrated genuine remorse, and sincerely wanted to make amends to the Serrell-Myers family.

Elaine's family members also went through a transformation during the preparation period. Elaine's husband, David Myers, who initially had fantasies of slicing up Susanna Cooper with a beer bottle, later took the position of advocating for the woman who had killed his wife. Realizing that Susanna would be facing such a large number of Elaine's relatives, David said, "It's an uneven playing field. Susanna ought to have someone at the meeting who loves her to be by her side and hold her hand. She needs a support person."

I Don't Have to Lift a Finger

Elizabeth clearly remembers the five-hour session with Susanna. "She entered looking as though she expected to be torn apart by a pack of dogs. Her small build, ponytail, and side-brushed blond bangs made her look twenty-five, but her face showed a strain and fatigue uncharacteristic of that age. My physician eyes noticed that she was gaunt and walked with a limp, there were scars on her legs and a vertical scar showing over her blouse on the center of her chest. I had heard that after the wreck she had been airlifted to the nearest university medical center for treatment of a cardiac rupture, multiple fractures, and multiple internal injuries. I wondered about the invisible scars, how she felt about having survived.*

The standard format for victim-offender mediations is that the victims speak first. But since Susanna had already read all of the victim-impact statements, Marty had her talk first. "Susanna tried to speak, but for the first five minutes, she could only cry," Elizabeth recalls. "Finally, she managed to say, 'I want to tell you how sorry I am, but I know that's not good enough.'

"Part of me was saying, 'You're right! That's not good enough!' But I also felt tremendously relieved: 'Oh good! I don't have to beat her up because she's already miserable. I don't have to lift a finger.' She was like the dog on the floor with her neck bared. She didn't defend herself or make excuses. The way Susanna put it was that she was so depressed that she didn't see how she could go on living if she didn't try to say she was sorry."

---

*This one-paragraph description of Susanna Cooper comes from "Life After Death," a first-person article written by Elizabeth Menkin published in *West Magazine*, part of the *San Jose Mercury News*, on September 4, 1994. Copyright © 2001 *San Jose Mercury News*. All rights reserved. Reproduced with permission.

Each family member then had a chance to talk about the impact of the crash and to ask Susanna questions. In the article she later wrote for *West Magazine*, Elizabeth recalls: "The main question on my mind was: 'How could you do such a thing?' Instead, I asked her what she could recall about the decisions she made that day—the decision to drink as much as she had, and to drive herself home.

"The answer was disappointing and blunt: 'I don't remember nothing.' Her injuries had been so severe she had no recollection of the week preceding the wreck. All she knew about what she had done she had learned from others.

"Aileen asked, 'What did you do when you found out you had killed someone?' Susanna answered simply, 'I cried,' her eyes filling with tears again. She went on to describe herself as a softhearted person who carries spiders out of the house rather than killing them.

"My father explained that he had initiated the mediation with the hope it would help him feel he could do something positive, not just suffer the pain of losing his daughter. My mother tearfully expressed her resentment. Not only had she lost a daughter, but the violent tragedy had so changed her husband she felt she had lost him, too. Elaine's husband had much to say. He had lost his partner in love and in work, and Elaine had been robbed of her future at a time of wonderful personal, professional, and spiritual growth.

"Susanna listened intently to each speaker without averting her gaze and without fidgeting. She wiped her tears frequently."*

Elizabeth was really impressed with Susanna's courage. "The deck was stacked against her in terms of verbal prowess, yet she was able to be there and take the lumps."

The final part of the mediation involved coming up with a restitution agreement. Susanna agreed to attend AA meetings and to participate in victim-impact panels while in prison. She promised to find ways to fight drunk driving in her community,

---

*Menkin, "Life After Death," p. 4.

pledged to further her education, complete her GED, attend parenting classes, write weekly to her children, attend church, and give 10 percent of her income to charity. She also agreed to write a quarterly letter to Peter Serrell reporting on her progress.

In the years since they made this agreement, Susanna has followed these stipulations with varying degrees of success. She served her time in prison and completed a work-release program. During this time, the Serrell-Myers family supported her efforts to create a better life for herself and her children. When Susanna attended community college to study accounting, they paid for her tuition and books. Ulitmately, Susanna had to drop out because she couldn't manage the hour-long commute without a driver's license. Since then, she has worked at several jobs. She struggles to honor her commitment to stay in touch with the Serrell-Myers family. They continue to hope that she will learn to make better choices for herself and are still grateful that she participated in the mediation.

She Owes Us a Life

The relationship between Susanna Cooper and the Serrell-Myers family is unique. Because of Susanna's tragic mistake, they will be tied together for the rest of their lives, but the nature of their connection is often misunderstood. Elizabeth recalls: "A TV interviewer once asked me, 'Oh, so you've become friends?' And I said, 'No it's not exactly that.'

"The thing that says it best is the film *To Live*. It's a movie that chronicles the life of a Chinese family over three decades. In one part of the story, the little boy in the family is on his way to school, but he's been up late and is tired, so he lies down next to a wall and falls asleep. Meanwhile, a man in the town is out driving drunk, and he bashes into the other side of the brick wall, which falls over and kills the boy. Later in the movie, the character that killed the boy has fallen on some bad times, and he's coming around to see the mother and father of the little boy he killed.

It's clear that he's depressed and is thinking about suicide. So he's making his rounds to say good-bye and give his things away. And the boy's mother says to him, 'You owe us a life. You do not have our permission to throw yours away.'

"That's the relationship. I care about what Susanna does with herself because she owes us a life and she doesn't have my permission to throw hers away."

From Discernment to Action

Reconciliation requires tremendous inner clarity and strength. This is true whether we are reconciling with a parent, a child, a friend, or someone whose reckless behavior has rocked our world forever. Whenever we are faced with someone from whom we are estranged—whether by hate, fear, sadness, or negligence—we are faced with the task of ascertaining the kind of relationship we want to pursue. Once the answer to that question is clear, we can move beyond personal healing and self-reflection to the more active phase of reconciliation: reaching out to the other person to see what relationship, if any, it is possible to reclaim.

PART TWO

Marshaling Your Strength

CHAPTER 4

Taking the First Steps: Gathering Courage

Why not go out on a limb? Isn't that where the fruit is?
—FRANK SCULLY, AUTHOR OF <u>BEHIND THE FLYING SAUCERS</u>

When we make the decision to extend ourselves to someone from whom we've been estranged, we enter unknown territory. No one can guarantee a positive outcome when we reach out through a hurt, angry silence. Risk and reconciliation go hand in hand. As aviator Amelia Earhart once remarked, "Courage is the price life exacts for granting peace."

Relationships that have ended because of misunderstanding, hurt, or anger can only be repaired when one person in the relationship—or both—take responsibility to set things right. Doing so requires tremendous courage. Every time we face a family member, a friend, or an enemy, and say, "Can I have you back in my life?" we lay bare our deepest desires and admit our human needs—all to someone who has hurt us or whom we have hurt in the past.

Yet facing fear is part of what makes us truly alive. As diarist Anaïs Nin once wrote, "Life shrinks or expands according to one's courage."

This chapter is filled with stories of people who found the courage to initiate reconciliation. All of them were scared but took the risk anyway. Whether their efforts bore fruit or were thwarted, they gave it their best shot and laid their hearts on the line, demonstrating that they were people willing to fight for a relationship.

Gary Geiger: Facing the Man Who Shot Me

If you'd been in the back of that courtroom in 1982 and had said to me, "In another decade, you and that man who shot you are going to be making speeches together," I would have said, "What, are you crazy? I want to take a gun to him!" Wayne and I have come a long way since that sad day in August of 1981. It's sure changed both of our lives to reconcile like we did.

—GARY GEIGER, ROBBERY VICTIM

At the age of thirty, Gary Geiger was the victim of a terrible robbery. It was the summer of 1981, and in the months leading up to the attack, Gary was an athlete in peak physical form. He competed in track and field, winning local competitions and making a name for himself as a runner. "At the time of the robbery, I wanted to be a coach and was looking for a shoe sponsorship. Meanwhile, I got a job as a night auditor in a motel in Albany, New York, working from eleven to seven in the morning. The motel was not in the best of locations, and there was no security."

One hot summer night, five young men came into the lobby at a quarter to three in the morning. They surrounded Gary. "At first, they were polite. Then I saw that one of them had a gun. He said, 'This is a stickup! Give me the money!' I must have hesitated for a moment, because one of them yanked my glasses off. Another guy hit me on the side of the head. They told me to get down on the floor, which I did. They asked where I kept the money. I told them it was in the drawer and I gave them the key, and they took the money. Then they ridiculed me, kicked me, and pushed me into the back room.

"When we got back there, they saw our safe—which was locked. One of the young men put the revolver to my temple and said, "I'm gonna blow your head off if you don't open that safe." At that point, I was cut and dazed, and I believed he was going to shoot me. I mustered up all the courage and sincerity I could and said, 'Look, I'm the night auditor. They don't give me the combination to the safe. I *can't* open it.'

"The leader of the group said, 'Knock him out,' and the young man hit me in the back of the head with the gun. I pretended to be unconscious, but I could hear the sound of their sneakers echoing through the lobby. I thought, 'I'm alive! They got what they wanted. They're out of here!'

"I jumped up. As soon as I got to my feet, I heard this loud cannonlike sound and felt a burning sensation in my abdominal area. I knew I'd been shot. The guy that shot me ran out the door. I felt my way to the front desk area and called the manager. Within three or four minutes, the paramedics arrived."

Gary was rushed to the hospital and barely survived. The bullet had penetrated his right lung and broken three of his ribs, but when it reached his stomach muscle, it stopped dead in a place where it couldn't be removed. The doctor later told him, "If you hadn't been in the incredible physical shape you're in, we wouldn't be talking right now. If your stomach muscles hadn't been strong enough to stop that bullet, it would have bounced around all of your vital organs and you would have bled to death before the paramedics got there. You are one lucky man."

I Was in My Own Prison

But in the weeks and months to follow, Gary didn't feel like a lucky man. Like many crime victims, he suffered from post-traumatic stress disorder, and life as he knew it came to an end. "That night changed everything. After the attack, I felt angry, guilty, and afraid. I was very depressed. I worried about whether I was going to be the same person I was before; I wondered if I'd be able to compete again. The day that I was shot, I could run one hundred meters in less than eleven seconds. When I went to my sister's house to convalesce, I couldn't even *walk* one hundred meters.

"Then I went back to the motel, working during the day. They kept giving me fewer hours. Finally, they sent me a letter saying my services were no longer required. I went to the manager and said, 'What gives? I almost gave my life for this place, and now you're firing me?' He said the incident had generated a lot of negative publicity, and it was bad for business. So he fired me.

"Now I was without a job, I was forced to move out of my apartment, and I had to sell my car to meet expenses. To show you how much I lost, I woke up one morning at the YMCA with seventeen cents in my pocket. It wasn't until a year after I got shot that I found a job and started working again."

Gary was also haunted psychologically: "I was plagued by nightmares and by unanswered questions. I wanted to know who these young men were and why they seemed so angry with me. I wanted to know what I had done wrong. Did they know me? Were they trying to kill me? And once the young men were apprehended, I worried that they or their friends might retaliate because I put them in jail."

I Walked Out of That Courtroom a Very Angry Man

In the year following the robbery, Gary went through two trials. The first was for the leader of the group, the second for the man who shot him. Both were awful for Gary. "During the first trial, the leader of the group had his friends sit in the back of the courtroom to intimidate me. And the second trial—that was as bad as being shot. I was on the stand for two hours, and I got into a shouting match with the defense attorney. She accused me of drinking that night, which was totally untrue. She accused me of being a racist because I was white and the assailants were black. She said I couldn't have made the identification because my glasses had been pulled off. Being on that witness stand was one of the worst experiences of my life."

Ultimately, the man who shot Gary, twenty-one-year-old Wayne Blanchard, was convicted and sentenced to twelve to twenty-five years in prison. But knowing that Blanchard was behind bars did not bring Gary any peace. "I should have been ecstatic, but I was angry. It wasn't just being shot and seeing him again in that courtroom. It was being instructed that I could not tell that jury what I was going through as a result of this crime. I wasn't allowed to talk about my nightmares, about walking the floor every night, about having shakes from head to toe. I couldn't talk about my fears that the friends of the defendants would come after me. I couldn't talk about losing my job and not being able to compete again. I wasn't allowed to say any of that. I was only allowed to testify about what I saw and experienced that night. As the victim of the crime, I did not have a voice. I was a mere witness—a piece of evidence—as far as the state of New York was concerned.

"But this had happened to *me*. It was personal. I wanted to know why Wayne had shot me. I wanted to ask him right then and there, 'Why did you pull that trigger when I complied in every way? Why did things get so violent?' I wanted to tell him, as well as the jury, what I was going through. But I never got the chance. Consequently, when I walked out of that courtroom, I was a very angry man."

For the next ten years, rage ruled Gary's life. "I invented road rage. I took my anger out on the people who were closest to me: my family, friends, and coworkers. I overreacted all the time. I was in and out of relationships. My whole life was a mess."

I Knew Immediately That This Is What I Wanted to Do

In 1991, Gary started seeing a psychologist and learned that he had been suffering from post-traumatic stress disorder. Then a year later, Gary saw a TV show that changed his life. "They showed this teacher from New York City who was blind in one eye. He was sitting at a table in a prison with a mediator, and directly across from him was the young man who had hit him with a baseball bat and taken out his eye. The narrator said this was a new program called victim-offender mediation. The prison was right here in New York. I remember thinking, 'This is incredible! This is what I want to do!'"

Gary tracked down Dr. Tom Christian, the mediator, and went to see him. "He asked why I wanted to go through such a process. I said I needed the answers to my questions and that not having them was getting in the way of moving on in my life. He asked if I was out for revenge, and I said, 'Not anymore.' Then we did some role-playing. Dr. Christian told me I was a good candidate for the program and that the next step would be for him to ask Wayne if he wanted to participate."

Two months later, Gary got his wish. Wayne Blanchard, now thirty-two, agreed to the mediation.

I'm Truly Sorry for What Happened That Night

On July 20, 1992, Gary and Dr. Christian drove to Ellenville Prison, a maximum-security prison in upstate New York. "I'd never been inside a prison before. They brought us in and put us in an antiquated auditorium. It was more than eighty degrees, and there was no air-conditioning. Wayne's counselor kept telling me how skeptical he was about this whole thing. I was the first victim who had ever set foot in that facility, and he couldn't see any good coming out of it. I wished he'd be quiet and leave me alone.

"Finally, it was time to start. There was a knock on the door, and out came the man who shot me. I noticed right away that Wayne didn't look the same as I remembered him. He was sweating profusely, and so was I.

"Tom told us to treat each other like human beings and to look at each other when we spoke. I gave a little introduction about why I was there, and Wayne talked about why he accepted the invitation to participate. Then we went ahead. The whole thing lasted an hour, but it felt like fifteen minutes.

"I had a little pile of three-by-five cards on which I'd outlined everything I wanted to cover. I told Wayne, 'There are questions that have been haunting me for eleven years, and only you can provide me with the answers.'

"I asked him if he was the person who shot me. He said he was. I asked him why he shot me. He said he was the lookout and that when I jumped up, he thought I was going for an alarm. He fired what he thought was a warning shot, and then took off. I asked if he had tried to kill me, and he said no, that if he'd wanted to kill me, he would have fired more than once.

"I was satisfied with Wayne's answers. He responded honestly and was very open. He told me things about the crime I hadn't known. Then I described the aftermath of the crime, something I think every offender should hear from his victim. I needed to tell him that it wasn't over that day or the day he was sentenced either. For me, that was just the beginning. I said, 'Wayne, I know you've lost a lot, but let me tell you what I've lost.' Then I told him everything—the nightmares, the shaking, the anger, the fear—and I really felt like I was getting through to him. Here was this big, tough man who had been in jail for half of his life, and I could tell I was breaking down his armor.

"Up until then, everything had gone according to my outline. Then something happened that I never planned, that I never thought possible. Wayne looked right at me, eyeball to eyeball, man to man, and gave me this little speech. He said, 'I'd like to say something to Mr. Geiger. I'm truly sorry for what happened in that motel that night. I'm not only sorry for the pain that you feel, but for what your family had to go through and for the problems it's created in your life today.

" 'I have a lot of pain in me as well from all of this. My life has been jail, jail, jail. I really haven't had a chance to live my life out in society because of the stupid things that I did. If I had it all to do over again, it would have never happened. As far as the bullet being inside of you, there's nothing I can do about that. I can only say I'm sorry, and I really am. And as I told Mr. Christian, that's the main reason I accepted to have this confrontation with you—if there was something I could say or do that could help you pull through this and put it behind you, I would be glad to do it. Again, I'm truly sorry for what happened that night.'

"What an apology! The way it was delivered—wow! Here's this individual who's been incarcerated for half of his life. He's not supposed to show emotion, and this guy has a tear in his eye. And there's nothing in it for him. He wasn't promised anything for doing this—not early parole, not a letter in his file, nothing. He was doing this for me—and for himself.

"Wayne's apology was the reparation I'd been waiting for, and when I heard it, the burden I'd been carrying lifted right off my shoulders. After years of building Wayne up as a monster, he was now a human being to me, and I was a human being to him; I wasn't just a faceless victim. Right there, in that moment, I forgave him, and I told him so.

"Then it was time to end the mediation, and it was an awkward moment. This man shot me. What was I going to say? 'Thanks for coming? Have another happy five years in prison?'

"I thought, 'What the hell. It went well. I got my answers. It's time to end this thing.' So I said to him, 'The first time you and I met, you had your hand extended to me in anger. Now,' and I stood, Wayne stood, and Tom stood, 'I want to extend my hand to you as a sign of healing for both of us.' Wayne just grabbed hold of my hand and held on to it.

"That's how it ended. When we were finished, Wayne's counselor was the first to reach me. He said, 'You know, I've worked with Wayne for a couple of years now, and no one has been able to get through to this guy. But let me tell you something. You got through to him!' We made a believer out of him."

Before Wayne was taken back to his cell, Tom arranged for Gary and Wayne to have a few private moments together. "I thanked Wayne for accepting the mediation. He said, 'I really meant what I said. I'm truly sorry for what I did. And when I get out, if you'd like to get ahold of me, I'd sure like to talk to you again.' 'Yeah, I would like that, too.' Then we gave each other an awkward embrace, and that was it."

Confronting Wayne face-to-face profoundly changed Gary. As far as he is concerned, there was life before the mediation and life after. "I walked out of that room a different man. I still had problems, but nothing like before. Once I confronted my past, I no longer had to relive it. The nightmares and fears were gone. I stopped blowing up at people. My coworkers and my family would be the first to tell you how much I've changed."

I'd Have to Say He's Still a Work in Progress

You might expect that Gary and Wayne's relationship would have ended the day of the mediation, but six months after their meeting, Gary visited Wayne in prison and the two men began to correspond. In July of 1994, when Wayne was paroled, he and Gary continued their relationship on the outside. Gary recalls: "I could have let it go. After the mediation, I could have said, 'This is great for me,' and forgotten all about Wayne Blanchard. But I saw something in that mediation. I saw a man who took advantage of the programs that had been offered to him. Wayne had furthered his education. He had some excellent goals. And I thought, 'If I could be like a big brother to him, maybe I can guide him toward the right path, and he can start making some good choices.' I didn't want Wayne Blanchard to get out of jail and victimize anyone else.

"No one had ever taken an interest in Wayne before. He'd lost his father when he was young. Wayne has fifteen brothers and sisters, and he got lost in the shuffle. I think I was the first person who ever reached out to him.

"Once he got released, we'd get together for coffee. I'd have him over for dinner, and we'd kick things around with each other. I took him by the hand and helped him fill out job applications. I taught him how to dress for an interview. I taught him what to say. Wayne's an excellent house painter, and I got him work with a couple of friends of mine.

"I haven't hovered over Wayne, but I've found ways to guide him. And he's got himself going pretty good. He has a wonderful girlfriend. They plan on getting married down the road. But it's an arduous transition making it back into society, and sometimes Wayne slips back into the streets. He doesn't commit violent offenses anymore—those days are over—but I'd have to say he's still a work in progress.

"When I don't hear from Wayne, I know things aren't going 100 percent great. But now I'm starting to hear from him again, so I know he's righted himself. When he calls and wants to talk, I see him. But if Wayne ever got in trouble, I've made it clear in no uncertain terms that my involvement with him is over."

If We Can Reconcile . . .

Gary and Wayne now give motivational talks together at colleges, churches, and high schools. "When Wayne tells our audiences that I saved his life, he brings tears to my eyes. Wayne says if I hadn't taken an interest in him when he came out, he probably would have screwed up and ended up back in state prison—and he's very sincere when he says that.

"Wayne's developed into quite a speaker, and I think the two of us really make a good team. People's first question to us is always, 'How can it possibly be that you two are here together?'

"Our message to the kids is 'If *we* can reconcile, think how you can handle the conflicts in your life.' That message has gotten through to many of them. We're a powerful example of reconciliation, and it makes quite an impression on the kids."

That Day Is Just a Memory Now

It has been more than twenty years since Gary was shot, and the trauma that once dominated his life has receded into the background. "That day is just a memory now. As Wayne so aptly put it in our mediation, 'There's nothing I can do about taking the bullet out. I wish I could.' We both have to go on, and that's the crux of it. That's what the mediation did—it allowed me to move on. It allowed Wayne to move on, too.

"The mediation empowered me. I'm back to my sprinting again. At one point this summer, I was ranked tenth in the world in my age group. I'm thrilled that I'm able to run. On the Internet, I coach young people all over the country. I give them tips on running, and, sometimes, on life. And it's all an offshoot of that mediation."

The Courage to Face Uncertainty

When we find the courage to face someone who has hurt us—or whom we have hurt—there is no telling what the outcome will be. Each reconciliation is unique. Being open to the evolving rhythm of a reconciliation requires flexibility and the willingness to enter uncharted territory. As one woman put it, "The essence of any healing work is surprise."

Receptivity requires taking risks with people—opening the door to see if they've changed, assessing whether our growth might affect them, determining whether a new dynamic might be created. It entails setting aside fixed ideas, rigid expectations, and a legion of defenses; it means approaching the other person with an open heart and a spirit of curiosity.

Even when reconciliations are not as far-reaching or significant as we might hope, they can still be beneficial. Wendy Richter learned this firsthand when she reached out to her parents after an estrangement of thirty years.

Wendy Richter: Sometimes It's Enough for Things to Be Just a Little Bit Better

If I hadn't known they were my parents, I never would have recognized them. If we'd passed each other on the street, I wouldn't have had a clue.

—WENDY RICHTER

Wendy Richter grew up in an extremely abusive home. She ran away at seventeen and never looked back. She survived a rough adolescence on the streets and grew up with the help of some caring people who took the place of the family she left behind.

With their help, she turned her life around and focused her energy on helping other kids who had nowhere to go. "When I was twenty-nine, I founded the National Child Rights Alliance, whose goal is to provide sanctuary for kids who need to get away from their families. Promoting the NCRA and our Children's Bill of Rights was at the center of my life for a long time."*

Years passed, and Wendy wanted nothing to do with her family. "In my case, getting away for thirty years was necessary. It freed me up to find people who related to the world and to each other in a very different way. I created my own voluntary family with people I have no blood ties with. They remain, to this day, my real family."

But in the last two years, forces in Wendy's life coalesced to open the door to her family of origin. "Nine years ago, my husband and I adopted two children, both of whom had been in foster care. One day, when my daughter was six, she said to me in

---

*The National Child Rights Alliance was founded in 1986 by seven youths and adults who had been abused and neglected as children. Their mission was to stop child abuse and to increase the level of social justice available to young people. NCRA played a key role in numerous court cases involving children's rights and drafted a bill of rights for young people, which defined young people's rights to liberty, safety, survival, education, free speech, nondiscrimination, free choice, and to an attorney.

this singsong voice, 'First I was with my birth mom. Then she gave me away to my foster parents. Then she gave me away to you, but you haven't given me away yet.'

"I felt like someone had put a stake through my heart. We had done everything to protect this child from the idea that she could ever be removed from us. We had assured her that she had love and permanency with us, that our family was forever. The fact that she still expected to be given away really upset me.

"Our son, who is very emotional, has also indicated that he was afraid he would lose us. He kept asking me about my relationship with my parents. From my point of view, leaving my family was the safest and healthiest thing I could have done, but all of a sudden it struck me: my son hears this as 'Someone can do something that upsets Mom so much that she'll cut them off forever.'

"That really disturbed me, but it still wasn't enough to make me want to see my parents. But then I heard about the Truth and Reconciliation hearings in South Africa. I thought, 'You can't pick people who have been through more horrific oppression than the blacks in South Africa. No one knows what suffering means more than they do. And if they're willing to go through Truth and Reconciliation hearings, maybe it's time for me to face my parents.' "

Two years earlier, Wendy's sister, Claire, had seen her on TV and contacted her. It was the first time the sisters had spoken in twenty-eight years. Wendy agreed to see Claire only if she promised not to tell their parents. "My sister was sensitive to my feelings, but from time to time, she'd ask if I wanted to see our parents. One day, after I'd been mulling all of this over, I finally said, 'Okay.'

"Two months ago, my sister and I went to a get-together my parents were having. It was a pleasant reunion. Everybody was very nice to each other. I felt like a polite person meeting other polite people. I know that sounds like it was dreadfully tense and phony and superficial, but it was simply the best any of us could do under the circumstances.

"I can't say that seeing my parents has led to any wonderful reunification. I've seen them just that once, and I probably won't see them again, except on very rare occasions. That might be different if there was truth in our reconciliation. Unfortunately, there isn't, and I don't expect there to be. My father is mildly demented now, and my mother isn't capable of facing the truth for her own reasons.

"My reconciliation story doesn't have neat edges and a nice tidy bow to make it look wonderful, but things don't always have to be wonderful. Sometimes it's enough for things to be just a little bit better. One step forward is still one step forward. In my case, seeing my parents brought me one step closer to understanding and one step farther from warfare. I'm grateful for that and also for what that means to my kids. It gave them the message that in the hardest of times, people can still communicate across very difficult lines. There doesn't always have to be a war."

Fear Doesn't Have to Stop You

When we reach out to someone from whom we've been estranged, it is natural to feel afraid. Not knowing whether we face acceptance, rejection, or indifference can freeze us in our tracks. It is natural to worry that old injuries will be restimulated and that the vulnerability we reveal will be used against us. But just because we feel fear, it doesn't have to stop us.

Many people have the erroneous idea that they have to master their fears *before* they act. Were that the case, none of us would ever attempt anything new. In order to achieve our goals in life, we need to move forward despite our fears. As John Wayne, the actor, once said, "Courage is being scared to death, but saddling up anyway."

Certainly, not all fears can or should be overridden. Fear warns us of danger; it can let us know when holding our position or retreating is the best course of action. However, *some* degree of fear will accompany all the major risks we take in life.

What Am I Afraid Of?

When we're feeling scared, it can be helpful to ask, "What is the *worst* thing that could happen?" In identifying our worst fears, we sometimes realize that we are not ready to move forward. Other times, we recognize that we are willing to take the risk—or that the "worst thing that can happen" is not as bad as we imagined.

When my friend Nona considered reaching out to me after our estrangement, she came to the conclusion that she really didn't have much to lose. She later told me, "I'd already lost our friendship, so taking the risk to reach out wasn't that hard. What were you going to say? 'I hate you,' again? 'Remember how I hated you before? Well, I still hate you!' "

On the other hand, we may feel terrified, as if our whole world is teetering on a precipice. Malcolm felt this way when he decided to talk to his sister about his decision to give the bulk of his money to charity, rather than to his nieces, as he had originally planned.

When I walked into my sister's room, my heart was beating like crazy. Everything that mattered to me was at stake. I loved my sister and her family, and I was scared I might never be close to them again. Fortunately, my sister was able to hear what I had to say. She understood my reasoning and was able to honor my decision.

FIRST STEPS

When you're deciding how to respond to a gesture of reconciliation or are considering making one of your own, ask yourself the following questions:

- What result do I want from this interaction?
- What are the risks involved in confronting this particular situation at this time?
- If this goes badly, what is the worst thing that can happen?

- Do I have the inner resources to handle a disappointment if things don't turn out the way I want them to?
- Is this really the best time to do this?
- If I wait, might feelings or circumstances change?

Taking the First Step

When we are the ones initiating a reconciliation, we need to assess the best way to reach out. Should we write a letter? Send an e-mail? Pick up the phone? Invite the other person over for dinner? Search for them on the Internet? Arrive on their doorstep with a single red rose? The possibilities are endless.

To end our estrangement, my friend Nona sent me a photo of herself bathing a curly-haired toddler in the sink. "I had a son," said the brief note scrawled on the back. "His name is Jasper."

I couldn't believe that Nona had had a son and I hadn't known about it. I had missed her whole pregnancy, labor, and birth; I hadn't gotten to cook her my famous bone soup when she was postpartum, fold her son's tiny clothes, or smell his sweet, precious head. Now her son was a toddler, standing up and splashing in the sink—and I still didn't know him. It just felt so wrong to me; the reasons I had been angry with her seemed petty by comparison. So I called Nona to congratulate her on her son's successful entry into the world, and soon after, our estrangement slipped away.

Many times, an oblique approach is best. My friend Mary had a falling-out with her sister. Rather than confront her sister directly, Mary started showing up on weekends to hang out with her nieces and nephews. Her sister's kids adore Mary, and she adores them. Slowly, between wrestling matches, basketball, and Monopoly, the icy climate between the sisters began to thaw.

Misha and her sister Sonya are both teachers. Literature helped them end their estrangement. "We both love to read, and we like the same kind of books. So instead of being silent at family gatherings, we started to sit together and compare notes on what we'd been reading. It gave us a safe way to reconnect."

Mickey Jeppesen had to take a different route when he mustered the courage to reach out to his father. Since he had never known the man, his first step had to be trying to track him down.

I have an unusual last name, and I typed it into the People Search on Yahoo. Three names came up. I ended up introducing myself to aunts and uncles I never knew I had. Through one of them, I found my dad. He was traveling around, working carnivals.

I called, and his wife answered. I said, "I'm his son," and she said, "Wait a minute. Which one are you?" I told her, and she said he'd always thought I was a girl.

Later that day, my father called back and we talked. I was twenty-one years old, and it was the first time I'd ever heard my dad's voice. I wanted to cry, but I was too proud; I wanted to be a man. Finally, I did cry. I told him, "I need a father. If you knew half the stuff I've been through, you'd be mad at yourself for not trying to find me."

And he said, "I did try to find you, son, but your mom kept on running from place to place. I wanted to know you."

Then my dad told me I had four brothers and four sisters. The oldest is thirty-eight years old, and the youngest is seventeen. So I started calling them up and saying, "You're my brother," "You're my sister." I've met a couple of them already, and when I can afford it, I'll meet the rest.

My dad and I met for the first time this past year. When I first saw him, it was weird—he looked like a littler version of me. I gave him a hug, and then I couldn't stay away from him. We talked about my life and what I've been through, what I've seen, and what I believe in now. I told him all the times I tried to find him, how hard it was for me to live without him. Then he told me about his life. I found out that my dad had a rough life, too. Nothing I said shocked my dad because he was just like me when he was a kid. He got beat like I did. He stole from stores like I did. I was just a younger generation of him.

Now my dad and I talk once a week. Getting to know him has been awesome. He's the father I never had.

Slow but Steady Wins the Race

Although some reconciliations happen all at once, with years of bitterness instantly giving way, it is much more common for reconciliation to take a slower course. Expecting too much or revealing too much can impede the gradual path that most successful reconciliations are built on. As one woman put it, "You don't heal a relationship all in one visit. It takes quite a few."

By taking a small step, testing our footing, and taking the time to check the reaction of the other person, we build the confidence to take a second small step—if and when it is appropriate. Although tiny steps may not seem like much, they add up to a lot when laid out in a long, steady row. Small changes—not just big dramatic ones—transform relationships. As Shawnee Undell once said, "When you change the trajectory of something just slightly, it completely changes the ultimate destination."

Taking Risks Gradually

When most people are scared, they hold back. However, to compensate for their fears, others leap out with bravado, stretching far beyond what is comfortable—ending up so far out on a limb that they have to backtrack later on. Taking risks gradually, so we can bring our whole self along, enables us to sustain the advances we are making.

Molly Fisk, the poet who reconciled with her mother, deliberately rebuilt their relationship slowly.

> In the process of writing poetry, I started to realize how much of my ability to look at the world was formed by my mother. My mother is a painter, and she taught me to look underneath leaves to see how the colors there were different from those on the top of the leaf. She taught me to study the refraction of light. My powers of observation were very much trained by her. I use those abilities all the time in my work, and I enjoy them immensely. I started to feel grateful to her for that.
>
> That's when I began thinking, "Maybe I ought to reconnect with my mother." I thought about it for a year. I always thought

about it in the car, where I do not have a phone. Only after I'd driven thirty or forty miles in the car, would I suddenly think, "You know, I should probably get in touch with my mother." I made sure I never had that idea when I was anywhere near a phone or a piece of paper.

Then last September, I put together a book of poems, and I decided to send my mother a copy. I included a note thanking her for teaching me how to look at the world. Then I said, "If you'd like to come up here and have lunch, I'd like to see you."

My mother sent a letter back saying she'd love to. Twice she made plans to come, and both times, something came up. One time she had the flu, and the other time she hurt her back. Even though I preferred to see her here, I finally decided to visit her.

We met at a restaurant, and it was fun. My mother looked older. She looked little. She gave me a great big hug, and I gave her one back. Then we sat across from each other and talked and talked.

Molly and her mother rebuilt their relationship slowly, largely because Molly needed to take care of herself along the way. "It was a while before I invited my mother into my home. We only met in public at first."

Molly also made a real effort to stay in touch with her feelings. "Every time I was about to make an arrangement to see my mother, I'd stop and ask myself: 'Is this something I really want to do? Is this something I think is important? Is my body telling me anything? Am I suddenly eating a lot of chocolate cake?' And, 'What will it cost me?' "

This kind of attentiveness can be helpful in the early stages of a reconciliation, particularly when we are beginning to see someone around whom we've felt off-center in the past. But such vigilance doesn't have to be permanent—unless we're dealing with a hostile or negative person, in which case watching our back remains perfectly appropriate.

In most instances, when both people in a relationship *want* to reconcile, the rapport grows naturally. As trust accrues, both people gradually reduce the level of caution they bring to the relationship. Eventually, it becomes possible for them to relax and be themselves without monitoring the relationship's every up and down.

That's how things worked out for Daniel, a fifty-year-old environmental science teacher who had a falling-out with a colleague. For a number of years, he and Abby had been friends, but then they had a huge fight.

It was over something stupid, but at the time, I was livid. Abby said some really cruel things about me, like, "Anyone who ends up in a relationship with you would have to be in really bad shape." She accused me of having all sorts of prejudices. She said horrible, nasty things.

I was deeply hurt by the intense level of cruelty she directed at me. I couldn't believe that someone I thought of as a friend could turn on me like that.

Afterward, I kept a wide berth around Abby. We never mentioned the incident, but I never trusted her again. Meanwhile, we had to work and live together for three months every summer. We managed to maintain a working relationship, but I always felt like I was sneaking around a big dead elephant in the room.

This past summer, after four years of holding on to all this resentment and distrust, I got up the courage to approach Abby. I was definitely nervous, but I asked her to take a walk with me. We walked down the dirt road to the ocean. I said, "You know that big fight we had a few years ago? I want to air it out and let it go."

Abby was immediately receptive, and to my surprise she apologized for being mean. She told me about some of the stresses she had been going through at the time.

After we talked, I felt a huge weight drop from me. I told her I loved her, and she said the same to me. Sitting down on some rocks by the ocean, we hugged each other and cried. We left the rocks arm in arm, feeling really close.

Looking back, it was the single best thing I did all summer because I got a completely new relationship with Abby. She supported me in ways she never had before, prompting me to get benefits and a raise. In lots of different situations, she's shown that she cares about me. Now I feel really glad to be around her, and it all came out of my commitment to bring this up and let it go.

Daniel was fortunate. Abby was receptive to his overtures and eager to reconcile. But even if she had been hostile toward him, that would not have diminished his courage.

If Abby hadn't been able to step up to the plate or respond in kind, I would have felt bad, but it wouldn't have lessened the value of what I had done. In the course of that conversation, I made a sincere effort to end a painful estrangement, owned up to my mistakes, and showed compassion for someone who had hurt me. Those things would have been valuable for me no matter how Abby responded.

The Courage to Face Yourself

When we reach out to someone from whom we've been estranged, as Daniel did, we essentially say to the other person, "I'm willing to learn about your perceptions, feelings, needs, and ideas. I want to know what you've experienced in your relationship with me." We agree to a two-way dialogue in which both people express feelings and bring up issues to resolve. This kind of active engagement is very different from only *thinking* about the relationship, where we hold all the cards and retain all of the control. As Kay Kessler discovered, it takes great courage to walk into a situation in which you are not the only one with a grievance.

Kay Kessler: Growing a New Relationship

Having a chance to make peace with both of my parents before they die creates a sense of wholeness that I don't even know how to name.

—KAY KESSLER

Fresh out of college and working on Wall Street, twenty-one-year-old Kay Kessler felt dissatisfied but didn't know what to do with her life. So she moved to Ann Arbor and married her college boyfriend. Her parents paid for a lavish wedding, and Kay landed a job as a fiscal officer for an insurance company. Two months later, Kay fell head over heels in love with Valerie, a woman she met at work. Thus began a dozen years of estrangement from her parents. "My mother and father were very traditional people. They were liberal enough to see movies and plays with gay characters, but they weren't prepared to deal with it in their own family. After I told my parents, my mom stopped eating. Both my parents symbolically sat *shiva** for me and said I was dead, but my dad couldn't follow through with that. He sneaked in occasional calls to see if I was okay."

Four years later, Kay and Valerie packed up their Honda 750 motorcycles, drove across the country, and moved to Santa Barbara. They'd been there less than a week when Kay had an almost fatal motorcycle accident. "I cracked my head and was unconscious for ten days. It was a very serious injury, and my parents never came to see me. When I think back on that now, I'm amazed that they were able to cut themselves off from me to that extent."

Seeds of Change

Kay and Valerie eventually split up, and Kay continued to have relationships with women. She worked as a top executive in a real estate company and traveled in her free time. Then, at twenty-eight, she had a reunion that directly affected her relationship with her parents. "I reconnected with my cousin Leslie and found out that she was a lesbian, too. Leslie moved to Santa Barbara, and my aunt and uncle flew out to visit her. Shortly afterward, my parents showed up.

Shiva is the formal mourning period that Jews observe in their homes in the first seven days after someone's death.

"I was cautious on that first visit. I had a professional career so it was easy to talk about that, but I steered clear of any talk about my personal life. My parents loved Santa Barbara—they liked the warm climate and the laid-back lifestyle. That helped them see that I was making at least some choices they could approve of.

"My parents came back a few more times. They were getting ready to retire and began to consider moving here. That was pretty amazing, considering how poor our relationship was at that point.

"I was in my midthirties by then, and I'd been going through a lot of changes myself. I'd been out as a lesbian for thirteen years, and I was considering dating men again. However, when my parents made the decision to move here, they knew nothing about that."

We've Really Changed

Kay vividly recalls her parents' announcement that they wanted to move to Santa Barbara. "We were out eating lunch, and my parents said, 'We want to move here and start looking for a house. Is that okay with you?'

"I burst out crying and said: 'No! I don't want you living here! You've been so mean and cruel to me. You've been judgmental of everything I do! Now I'm dating a man. What if I decide I don't want to be with him and that I want to be a lesbian again? If you're going to continue to be mean, I don't want you here!'

"When I stopped talking, my parents just looked at me. Then they said, 'You've been mean, too.'

"I said, 'I have?' and then I just broke open. I had reached a point in my life where I was ready to look at my own behavior, and so I listened as they told me how painful our estrangement had been for them. They said I'd been critical about how they lived and judgmental about the things they cared about.

"As I listened to them, I could see that what they were saying *was* true. I *had* rejected much of their world. I *had* been critical.

They'd say something about me being a lonely old lesbian, and I'd say, 'Well, you're going to be lonely, too! You don't have any intimacy in your friendships. At least I'll have friendships my whole life.' I came back at them with judgments that were just as big as the ones they were throwing at me.

"It felt good to start recognizing my part in what had happened, but I still wasn't sure I wanted them living near me. So I said, 'But how do I know you're not going to judge me anymore?'

"My parents looked at me and said, 'We've really changed. We've grown to accept you for who you are.'

"I countered, 'Well, what if I change again? What if I decide I want to be with women again?'

"They said, 'Whatever you decide to be will be fine with us. We've finally come to accept that you're our daughter and your happiness is the most important thing to us.' "

That's How the Deeper Reconciliation Began

After that conversation, trust began to accrue on both sides, but Kay still felt cautious. "When I thought about them moving here, my biggest fear was that they were going to intrude on my life. So I initiated another conversation with them to clarify our expectations of each other. I didn't want them to have any expectations about how often I was going to see them. I said if they had judgments about how I was living my life, I didn't want to hear them. I said I didn't want them interfering in any of my decisions. I also said I didn't want to have to take care of them—that I didn't want to 'give them my life.' At the time, I had this erroneous idea that just because they were in their sixties, they'd need me to take care of them. They just laughed at that one. And now it's even funnier—because they barely have time to see me, and I'm the one who wants to see them more.

"My parents agreed to all of my conditions. Then they moved here. I continued living my life. Eventually, I met Ted, and we decided to get married and start a family, and I felt like my parents kept the proper distance and relationship to that."

You've Done That to Me My Whole Life

The next turning point in Kay's reconciliation with her parents came when she quit her job. "I'd been a CEO for ten years. When I quit, I felt lost and sad. My parents stopped calling me again. A month went by, then two months. I didn't hear from them. Finally, I called them and said, 'What's going on with you? I'm having a hard time, and you never call to ask how I am.'

"So they came over. I said, 'I don't know what's going on, but I'm having a really hard time, and you're my parents and you're the last people in the world to ask me how I am.'

"Then my mom burst out crying and said, 'I can't stand that you're hurting. I can't tolerate it, and I don't want to be around it.'

"I screamed, 'You've done that to me my whole life!' We had this huge fight, where my mom confessed her inability to deal with my sadness.

"I said, 'The impact of that on me is disastrous. You're telling me that when I have those feelings, I shouldn't call you. Those are conditions in our relationship that I can't tolerate.' We had a good cry together, and my mom said she'd make an effort to learn why it was so hard for her to handle those emotions.

"It was at that point that our deeper reconciliation began. My parents both started doing things so they could understand and be closer to me. That meant a lot to me because I'd assumed that my parents were always going to stay the same. To make 'growth' part of being in our family was such a gift. Our relationship now had an element of learning in it, which is exactly what I'd always wanted."

I Had to Learn to Say, "I'm Feeling Hurt Now"

As her trust grew, Kay began taking more substantial risks with her parents. One of the main ones was learning to speak up when she felt hurt. "For me, moving to this deeper level of closeness required that I recognize when I was feeling hurt or when my parents were doing something that upset me.

"My usual pattern when that happened was to withdraw. I'd say something mean or remove myself from the conversation and then hold a grudge against them. I'd assume that they were insensitive and incapable of understanding me. So the first thing I had to do was interrupt that habitual response.

"Then I had to get up the courage to say something, and I had to learn how to talk about what I was feeling in ways that weren't critical or hostile. For instance, if my father started to talk non-stop without inquiring about what I was thinking, I would say, 'You know, it's hard for me when you do that, Dad. If we're going to have a conversation where we learn about each other's thoughts, I need you to pause so you're not just talking *at* me.'

"I had to believe that my words could affect them, and as I experienced more instances in which that was true, I was encouraged to do it more. The trust built up, more and more."

As she felt safer with her parents, Kay also took the risk to share more intimate parts of her life. "I had been private for good reasons, but I began to say things that were in my heart or that I was troubled by. I remember telling my mom: 'Ted and I really need therapy. We've got twelve-month-old twins, neither of us is sleeping, we're both working hard, and we don't have time to talk about things. I'm scared issues are building up, and we really need someone to help us talk to each other.'

"I remember sitting there, crossing my fingers, thinking, 'Is she going to freak out and start worrying about me?' Part of me expected her to panic or to try to shut me up. But instead, she simply said, 'That sounds like such a great idea.' "

A Deep Blessing

This kind of acceptance continues to grow. Kay reports: "I was talking with my mother a couple of weeks ago. She said, 'Our friend Joe has cancer, and so-and-so's husband just died, and so-and-so is depressed, and I'm worried about this person's health.' She had five or six people who were sick, dying, or really distraught. Then at the end, she said, 'Other than that, everything's fine.'

"I started laughing because that's so much who my mom is. I've come to appreciate her positive outlook. It's hard to maintain a commitment to joy, and as I've gotten older, I've come to realize that my mom has something pretty special—to continually claim happiness as part of her life. I used to feel disgusted by her because I thought she was avoiding the realities of life, but now I know that she feels life and hurts inside *and* that she is eternally optimistic.

"My joke back to her was 'Ma, when you die, I'm going to write on your gravestone, "Other than the fact that she died, everything was fine."' That kind of humor flows freely between us now."

The Courage to Change

As Kay's story makes clear, an initial overture of reconciliation is just the beginning. Deepening a relationship requires that we take additional risks, sustain vulnerability, and alter ingrained patterns of behavior.

All of us have habitual ways of responding to conflict. By becoming aware of the strategies we regularly use when faced with conflict, we free ourselves up to try new approaches. Instead of making a retort that escalates the tension, we can use humor to defuse it. Instead of withdrawing, we can come forward with more vulnerability. Instead of counterattacking or defending ourselves, we can try finding the grain of truth in what the other person is saying. The more versatile we become in our emotional repertoire, the more flexible and successful our relationships will be.

Lisa, who reconciled with her stepfather after a ten-year separation, recalls how hard it was for her to change her usual responses.

> I needed courage going into every encounter with him. For me, the question was always "Will I be strong enough not to break down and cry? Will I be able to access my skills so I don't revert back to the way I responded as a teenager?" That always felt like the greatest risk for me—that I would stop acting like an adult and turn back into a whiny child.

After reconnecting with me, my friend Nona had to find the courage to stick things out in our relationship.

> I realized that people were irreplaceable. I had other friends besides Laura, but there was no one else like her. She was one-of-a-kind, a precious gift I had to work to keep in my life. I was in therapy at the time, and I remember how hard I had to struggle to learn how to maintain close relationships in spite of conflict. Before when I'd gotten mad at people, I'd just thrown them away.

Frank's challenge was to change the negative view he held of his older brother.

> I'd always judged Ernie harshly. I saw him as a dreamer who could never accomplish anything in the real world. When Ernie finally called me on it, I had to admit my arrogance—and from then on, I looked at Ernie through different eyes. I recognized that he had vision and that he often perceived solutions where I saw none. Ernie brought hope to people, and I realized that that was as valuable as any practical contribution I might make. At first, it was scary to see Ernie as a peer because I'd gotten a lot of mileage out of feeling superior, but when I climbed down from my pedestal and saw Ernie as other people do, I gained a wise, compassionate man as my brother.

The Myth of the Cowardly Lion

There's an erroneous idea about courage—either we have it, or we don't. But in the right circumstances, all of us have the capacity for courage. The step we take may be a small one, but it is a step nonetheless.

One of my favorite literary characters is the Cowardly Lion from *The Wizard of Oz*. The Lion believes he's a coward, yet despite his lack of faith in himself, he repeatedly meets challenges, faces enemies, and prevails. At the end of the story, when the Wizard gives the Lion a medal of valor, it is not to bestow courage upon him but rather to acknowledge the courage he already has.

We, too, are Cowardly Lions. Despite our belief that we don't have what it takes to reconcile, we do. Courage lies dormant inside of us until our own desire to act draws it forth. Once we decide to attempt reconciliation, the courage to do so will arise. Even though we might be uncertain, frightened, or shaking in our boots, we can hold our higher purpose in mind and act anyway.

Courage is the willingness to face each new challenge with determination, awareness, and an open heart—and all of us, no matter how scared we are, can do so.

CHAPTER 5

Persistence Over Time:
The Importance of Determination

Being defeated is often a temporary condition. Giving up is what makes it permanent.

—MARILYN VOS SAVANT

In the summer of 1994, seventy-three-year-old Alvin Straight set off on his 1966 John Deere lawnmower and drove 240 miles—from Laurens, Iowa, to Mt. Zion, Wisconsin—to visit his ailing brother, Lyle, who had suffered a serious stroke. The two men had not spoken in ten years, and Alvin decided it was high time they reconciled.

Alvin, who walked with two canes and was suffering from emphysema, couldn't see well enough to get a driver's license, didn't like buses, hated trains, refused to fly, and did not want anyone to drive him. He knew that this was one trip he had to make on his own—his way—so he hitched a makeshift trailer to the back of his power mower, covered it with a green tarp, and hung an orange hazard triangle on the back. He loaded the trailer with camping provisions—a blanket, a Styrofoam ice chest, a generous supply of cigars and braunschweiger, and fifteen gallons of gas—and set off across America's heartland.

David Lynch's 1999 film, *The Straight Story*, immortalizes Alvin's historic journey. In one scene, Alvin tells a pair of battling twins why he embarked on his unprecedented pilgrimage: "There's no one knows your life better than a brother that's near your age. He knows who you are and what you are better than anyone on earth. My brother and I said some unforgivable things the last time we met, but I'm trying to put that behind me. And this trip is a hard swallow of my pride. I just hope I'm not too late."

Traveling an average of five miles an hour, Alvin encounters a variety of people on his remarkable odyssey: aging war veterans, bicycle racers, farmers riding their tractors, and just plain folk. One of his first nights out on the road, Alvin befriends a young, pregnant girl who has run away from home. Alvin shares his fire, his hot dogs, and his blanket with the girl. After she tells him her story, he shares one of his own: "When my kids were little I played this game with them. I'd give each of them a stick and ask them to break it. Of course they did, easily. Then I told them to take all the sticks and tie them in a bundle and to try to break them then. Of course, they couldn't. 'That bundle,' I told them, 'that's family.'"

In the morning Alvin gets up and the girl is gone, but a bundle of sticks lies tied together on the ground.

Throughout his extraordinary journey, people are similarly touched by Alvin's quiet wisdom. Finally, six weeks into his trip—after eating roadkill, coping with mechanical failures, near-catastrophes, and summer rainstorms—Alvin pulls up in front of his brother's shack, gets off his lawnmower, and calls out his brother's name. Lyle shuffles to the door, learning heavily on a walker. The brothers sit on the porch in silence, and Lyle looks out at Alvin's rig. He asks, "Did you ride that thing all the way out here to see me?"

Alvin says, "I did, Lyle." Lyle's eyes fill with tears, the two brothers look up at the stars, and the movie credits roll.

More than anything else, in Alvin Straight, we see a man who is resolute and single-minded. It is this kind of tenacity that reconciliation requires.

Determination is about making a commitment; it's deciding what we're going to do with the cards that life has dealt us. Psychologist

Hans Jorg Stahlschmidt believes it is these choices that determine the quality of our lives: "When we allow ourselves to love, we are inevitably disappointed and hurt. In choosing to be intimate with another person, we put ourselves in a situation where our shortcomings invariably show. We are all human, and at times, we're going to fail each other."

Stahlschmidt believes the way we respond to these failures is a vital measure of our resilience and strength. "As a psychologist, one of the most important indicators of psychological health is how people are able to repair. It is the nature of relationships that we are going to get injured. The question is 'How are you going to respond to that injury?' Through an injury, deepening can happen. Without injury, the relationship will never deepen."

Many people report that their relationships are more precious and intimate after an estrangement than they were before, but they don't get that way without a lot of hard work. Determination is the commitment to persevere despite the impediments that arise.

Being Resolute in Your Goals

Beth Tanzman is a very determined sixty-seven-year-old woman. Despite a daunting set of obstacles, Beth tracked down her cousin Marvin after being out of touch with him for thirty years. Their reconciliation, which has been richly rewarding for both of them, has led to a reunification of a whole extended family. And it would never have happened if Beth Tanzman hadn't set her sights on finding the one man who had always made her childhood special.

Beth Tanzman: I Just Had to Find Him

The estrangement between Marvin and his mother was so profound that when she died, no one called to tell him. The way he found out his mother was dead was by going to the cemetery to visit his father's grave—he saw his mother's grave right there beside it.

—BETH TANZMAN

"I came from a family full of cold, buttoned-up people. I'm sure they loved me, but it was never expressed. There were never any hugs. No one ever said, 'You got a great report card' or 'You look pretty today.' Their attitude was 'If you give a child a compliment, you'll spoil her.' They didn't mean to be unkind. They just thought showing love was improper.

"Marvin's mother and father, on the other hand, were very demonstrative, loving people. I adored visiting them. Marvin's mother would always cook something she knew I liked. I would get a big hug and a lot of compliments. They always made it clear I was loved.

"Marvin was five years older than me, but he always treated me with affection. It was obvious he cared about me. Whenever my mother and my brother and I would go visit his family in Brooklyn, we'd get off the subway, and if it was raining, Marvin would always be standing there to meet us with an umbrella.

"Later, Marvin joined the Merchant Marine, and he'd come to visit me. He was eighteen and I was thirteen, and I was very impressed with his uniform. He'd bring me gifts and take me for walks. He treated me as if I were special, and I never forgot it."

A Parting of the Ways

Beth and Marvin grew up, and their lives followed similar paths. In 1950, they married within weeks of each other, Marvin to a woman who resembled Beth in many ways. Beth chose for her husband a navy man who, like Marvin, loved the sea.

When Marvin was in his forties, his father died of lung cancer. During his final illness, Marvin wanted to get him a private nurse and offered to pay for it. His mother wouldn't agree until she consulted with her son-in-law, who was an optometrist. Marvin's feelings were deeply hurt by his mother's lack of confidence in him. Judgments accrued on both sides, and ultimately, Marvin broke off his relationship with his mother.

For a few years after that, Marvin stayed in touch with his

aunts and cousins, but since he worked nights and weekends, he was rarely available for family gatherings. Gradually, he withdrew from the family, and he and Beth fell out of touch. "Marvin believed that everyone in the family sided with his mother and didn't think much of him. That wasn't true, but Marvin felt so misunderstood and rejected that he didn't want to be involved with us. He got an unlisted number. Then I sent him an invitation for a family event, and it was returned 'addressee unknown.'

"I always missed Marvin, but like everyone else, I took the path of least resistance. In our family, there was this attitude: 'If he won't make the first overture, I won't either.' I went along with that. Also, it was such a busy time in my own life. I had young children, I went back to college, and I started working. I had too much on my plate to pursue Marvin. So years went by, and I just let him go."

Searching for Marvin

In June 1994, Beth retired. Her health was failing; she had quintuple bypass surgery and, later, a heart attack. For two years, she was extremely ill. When she got back on her feet, one of the first things she decided to do was find Marvin. "Being so sick made me realize how short life could be. I told myself, 'If I'm going to get in touch with Marvin, I have to do it now.'

"At that point in my life, my husband was dead, my son lived in California, and my daughters were very involved in their own lives. I was basically alone, and I think I was looking for people to love me. I set out to find Marvin because I craved the caring and affection I'd always associated with him."

Marvin wasn't in the phone book, so Beth had to get resourceful. "I thought Marvin might have retired to Florida. His last name is unusual, so I went to the library and looked up Treach in all the phone books for Dade County, Ft. Lauderdale, and Miami. Then I looked in the phone books for all five boroughs of New York, Westchester, and Long Island, but I found nothing."

Beth's search stalled when she hit this wall. Then one afternoon a couple of years later, she was watching Oprah Winfrey on TV when an ad flashed on the screen: "U.S. Search Company. We will find anyone for $29.95." Beth knew it might be a scam, but she figured it was worth thirty dollars; she called and asked the firm to look for Marvin.

A few weeks later, an employee from U.S. Search Company called back saying that Marvin's uncle, Arty, had been found. "They tracked him down in upstate New York, where he was on vacation. I called the number they gave me, and this ancient man answered the phone. He must have been well into his eighties. He said, 'Yes, I have a nephew like that, but I haven't been in touch with him in forty years.' Arty barely remembered Marvin's name but said, 'Call me in three months when I'm back in Florida. I might have a phone number for him.'"

Three months later, Beth called. Arty did have a number for Marvin in Brooklyn but told Beth he thought Marvin had moved. But then he added, "He had a son-in-law. I think he used to live on Staten Island."

With that scrap of information, Beth went back through her old photos and discovered Marvin's daughter's wedding invitation, which she had saved for twenty years. On it, she found Linda's married name. "I called Staten Island information and asked if they had any Malkoffs, and they did. So I called this son-in-law and said, 'I'm looking for my cousin, Marvin Treach. Is he your father-in-law?'

"The son-in-law said yes. I told him I really wanted to talk to Marvin and asked for his phone number. At first the son-in-law was suspicious—he thought I was trying to sell something—but ten minutes later, my phone rang, and Marvin was on the line.

"He said, 'I'm so happy to hear from you. How did you know where I was?' I told him the whole process I went through, and he said, 'I can't believe you went through all that to find me.'

"I replied immediately, 'You're worth it.'"

I Didn't Want to Push Him

Beth and Marvin talked for a long time that day. During the course of the conversation, they both cried. "We're old now, and it was comforting to see that we still cared about each other. Then I spoke to Marvin's wife, and she said: 'It's so wonderful to hear from you again. It's been really lonely. We just have one child and one grandson, and we always felt we had no other family. When my grandson was bar mitzvahed, we didn't have anybody to invite.'

"It was on the tip of my tongue to say, 'Well, I've lived in the same house for thirty-seven years. You knew where to find me.' But I held my tongue.

"Then very generously, Marvin's wife said, 'Please come see us. Marvin doesn't drive anymore because his eyes are not good, but we would love to have you visit.'

"So I went to Staten Island. My heart was in my mouth. I didn't know if Marvin felt the same way about our reunion as I did, but when I got to the apartment building and started walking toward the entrance, Marvin was standing there in the rain, holding up an umbrella.

"Marvin walked me upstairs, and we spent hours reminiscing. He said he had stayed away from the family for so many years because his feelings had been so hurt."

Neither that day nor in any of their subsequent contact did Beth press for details about what had happened between Marvin and his mother. "I could see that it was very hard for Marvin to talk about it. For me to say, 'What did your mother say to you thirty years ago and what did you say to her?' would have spoiled our reconciliation. If I'd put him on the spot, he might not have wanted to see me again. Besides, I don't think there's any point in going over something that happened so long ago. All we could do was pick up from today and be friends."

Why Don't You Invite Aunt Yetta?

A few months later, Beth invited Marvin, his wife, his daughter, Linda, his son-in-law, and his grandson over for a visit. "It was really nice. My daughters had never met Linda before. My middle daughter and Linda are both in their early forties, and they took to each other like peas in a pod. They've been calling and visiting each other ever since.

"A couple of weeks ago, Linda moved into a new house, and she invited our family over. Her mother said to her, 'Why don't you invite Aunt Yetta? She's ninety-two years old. It's time to end this.'

"So Linda did. Yetta was thrilled and surprised. She said, 'Of course I'll be there, but I'm ninety-two years old. I can't get there unless my son and daughter bring me.' So they all came. It was quite a crowd.

"Basically these people were all second cousins, most of whom had never met. Aunt Yetta, the last surviving sister, was on the verge of tears the whole afternoon. She got together with each one of us, one after the other, and told us how happy she was to see everybody together again. She said she'd prayed about it for years, but never thought she'd live to see it. It was a wonderful afternoon."

Responses and Rejoinders

In this story, which so clearly has a happy ending, one woman's creative persistence led to the reconciliation of an entire clan. Along the way, she faced numerous obstacles, which in her case centered on finding Marvin. In other instances, finding the person is not the problem—figuring out what to do once we've made contact is.

Much of that depends on the reception we receive. There are circumstances, like Beth's, in which the other person welcomes us with open arms. If we are fortunate enough to get such a loving, warm response, we can move ahead relatively quickly, with confidence.

When the response is unclear or ambivalent, it is probably wise to show restraint. The other person may need time to think, to work through feelings, or to decide how to respond. If we move ahead too quickly or push too hard, we may tip the balance away from the outcome we desire.

The final possibility is that our overtures will be rejected and that we will be met with indifference, hostility, or a door slammed in our face. When that happens, we may feel grief, anger, and disbelief—or perhaps relief that we can finally move on.

Miriam Gladys encountered most of these responses when she sought reconciliation with her children. Miriam's story is a wonderful illustration of determination, flexibility, and persistence over time. It is also a sobering example of how reconciliation does not always happen, despite our honesty and good intentions.

Miriam Gladys: Making Amends to My Children

My work is my redemption because I can't take back what happened in my children's lives. If by sharing what happened in our family, I can help someone else, then at least some good will have come out of it.

—MIRIAM GLADYS

Miriam Gladys is a seventy-two-year-old community educator who has spent the last twenty years working to change attitudes in the Jewish community toward addiction, violence, and sexual abuse. Miriam's commitment to her lifework—and to the path of reconciliation with her children—is rooted in her own experience of raising a family during the 1950s and 1960s. "Unbeknownst to most people around us, my husband, Al, was an alcoholic. He was never a staggering drunk; he was functional. But at home, he was unreliable. Once I tried to leave him. I took the kids to my parents' house and told them what was happening. They said everything was my fault. Then I went to the rabbi, and he explained that Jews aren't alcoholics, so again, everything was my fault. Finally, I went to a psychotherapist, who repeated the same thing: 'Jews don't drink. Therefore, it's all your fault.' I was convinced I was worthless because every time I tried to get help, everything got put back on my shoulders.

"None of the people I went to ever asked me how things were going with the children, and I wish they had. I had five children who were very close in age. They were good kids, but they were kids, and at that time in my life I had a very short fuse. Late afternoons were especially stressful because I grew up in an age where you all ate dinner together, and you didn't snack in the afternoon. By four or five o'clock we were all very hungry, but I never let the kids eat. I was prediabetic and didn't know it, and I needed to eat, too—and when I didn't, I would explode.

"I didn't beat my kids, but I threw things at them. I threw things they treasured, and I broke them. I screamed at them. I tried not to say awful things to them because my mother had done that to me, but once I got triggered, I'd lose the capacity to control myself and I would say terrible things, the worst of which was 'I wish you'd never been born.'

"These rage episodes probably happened once a week. Each time, I knew it was wrong and I'd feel deeply ashamed, but I couldn't stop myself."

Going to Al-Anon

"When my son Isaac was born in 1961, I finally went to Al-Anon. The first thing I learned was that if someone has a drinking problem, it isn't your fault. That was a great relief, and I got deeply involved in the twelve-step program.

"I needed to find a way to make my marriage work because I didn't have any way to earn a living. There were no models in my community of women who left unhappy marriages and made it, so I was determined to stay and make it work.

"By the time the girls were in their teens, I had gotten some control over my behavior. I'd learned that I was prediabetic and started feeding us all in the afternoon. After that, my episodes became much less frequent. By the time the boys were in junior high, there were no more episodes. The boys, who were my last two children, had a very different mother than the girls."

When My Kids Needed Support, They Had This Crazy Mother

Miriam's children grew up, and her husband, Al, was diagnosed with lung cancer. "When Al was dying, we all rallied around him, and the children and I were quite close, even though I had not yet expressed to them my deep dismay about what I had done to them.

"Al died in 1985, and three years later, the girls started having memories that he had sexually abused them. A piece of the terrible remorse I feel comes from the fact that I didn't know. When my kids really needed my support, they had this crazy mother, and the fact that I was raging at them got in the way of them trusting me enough to tell me he was molesting them.

"I went into therapy with one of my daughters, and as we worked through her memories, I began to awaken to the deeper implications of my behavior. I realized I needed to make amends to the children because I could see how damaged they had been."

You Ask for Forgiveness Three Times

By this time, Miriam had begun a lifelong exploration of how twelve-step programs interface with Jewish belief and practice. "I got deeply involved with the concept of *teshuvah*, or turning your life around. *Teshuvah* involves going to the person you've wronged and asking for forgiveness, doing what you need to do to recompense them, and then changing your behavior so you'll respond differently if you're confronted with the same situation again.

"I began to take this very seriously. The Talmud says that if you wrong someone, you go to that person and ask for forgiveness three times. So for three years I wrote letters to my kids, talking about what I had done and asking for forgiveness.

"In the first letter, I wrote about being deeply sorry for what had happened, but it soon became clear that that letter wasn't explicit enough. My youngest daughter, Shelley, with whom I spent a fair amount of time in therapy, said, 'You keep putting it into metaphor. When I want you to say, "I did this and this and this," you're talking about light and shadow. I don't want to hear about light and shadow. I need you to name things.'

"In the second letter, I was more specific about the episodes. And in the third letter, I expressed deep regrets about not protecting them from the incest. The boys felt I was going overboard, asking for forgiveness for things they didn't think were so terrible. Basically they said, 'Don't make me look at this. I don't want to think about it. Everything is fine between us.' So I never really had to reconcile with the boys because they didn't think there was a problem.

"But with my daughters Shelley and Lisa, I definitely did. There was a time when Lisa said to me, 'Being with you triggers a lot of stuff, and coming to the house raises too many issues for me.' So for two years, Lisa and I didn't see each other. We were both in therapy, and at the end of that time, we came together with our therapists and started working together. Now we are very close. There's a lot of honesty and openness between us."

Miriam is grateful that things are out in the open with her children, though the healing process has been wrenching. "The hardest part for me was hearing what their childhoods were like for them and knowing it is their truth. With each of my kids, I hoped that they would get to the point where they also wanted to hear from me. But in the meantime, I had to hear a lot of things I didn't want to know.

"My son Isaac has told me about things I did that I don't remember. When he described them, I could swear I never did them, but I also knew that I had to listen without being defensive. One of the things I told the children was 'There are things I did that I remember in great detail, that you may not remember at all. There are also things I did that you remember in great detail, that I won't remember, because it's who you were and where you were that shapes your memory.' "

She Didn't Want Any Part of It

Miriam has made great strides with four of her children, but working things out with her middle daughter, Ruthie, has been much harder. "When Ruthie got my first letter, she wrote back and said, 'You think you can just write a letter and say you're sorry and that you wish you could take back our childhood?' The other kids were touched by the letter, but she basically said, 'Screw you! It doesn't mean a thing.'

"Ruthie refused to speak to me for a long time. For years, I paid for her therapy and sent her a letter once or twice a year saying, 'I am prepared to come to New York to meet with you. I am prepared to do therapy. I will do whatever is necessary for us to begin to heal.' But she didn't want any part of it.

"A year after our estrangement began, Ruthie had back surgery. I told her I wanted to be with her, and she said, 'I don't want anything to do with you.'

"I replied, 'I know you've given me F— as a mother, but the truth is you are about to have a very difficult surgery and you need to have somebody with you, and I'm the only person available.' So I went and stayed with her until she was able to be up and around. She was grateful because she really needed me, but after I left, she stopped speaking to me again.

"Two years later, Ruthie had to have an ovarian cyst removed, and we didn't know if it was malignant or benign. I went to New York to be with her, but Ruthie told me to leave.

"I was very distraught, and I went for some spiritual counseling with Rabbi Arthur Waskow. He said, 'It's very clear. The Talmud says you go three times, you ask forgiveness, and then you have to let go until that person is ready to reach out to you.' It was enormously comforting to hear that. It helped me get through that terrible time.

"After her surgery, I didn't hear from Ruthie for a long time. Then last year, my youngest son decided to get married. I wrote to Ruthie and said, 'We're both planning to be at the wedding. I'd like to find a way for us to both enjoy that weekend and not bring this toxic energy to the wedding.'

"Ruthie agreed to see me for her brother's sake. I went to New York and met twice with her and her therapist. During the first session, she pulled out this list she had written detailing every single thing that I had ever done to her that was terrible. It was four pages, single-spaced, and she read it all to me. Some of it I was prepared for, but some of it was worse than I thought it would be.

"I'd had a lot of support preparing for the meeting. My therapist had said to me: 'When you go there, remember that you're listening to a four-year-old because this forty-year-old woman that you're seeing is not the one who's talking. The one who's going to talk to you is a little hurt child.' That was really helpful because when Ruthie went through her list, it included things like, 'When I was eight years old and said I wanted to be an artist, you said, "Artists have a very hard life. They have a hard time earning a living." Therefore, I didn't become an artist.' She said I made her fat because I took her to Lane Bryant to buy her clothes. It was a litany of all the ways her bad feelings about herself were my fault.

"When she read the list, I listened and I wasn't defensive. Then I apologized for everything I might have done that hurt her.

"In our second session, we tried to figure out a way to be together at the wedding. Ruthie said she didn't want to hang out with the family because she always felt bad about herself around her siblings. She also said she didn't want me to touch her. I agreed to her conditions, and I think that helped her relax, because when we got to the wedding, she asked me for a hug and spent the entire weekend hanging out with her siblings.

"Since then, Ruthie and I have stayed in touch through

e-mail. Because of a genetic illness, Ruthie has serious health problems. Her body aches constantly. She sleeps for two days at a time, then isn't able to sleep for a week. And she's still struggling psychologically. I suspect Ruthie experienced the worst of the incest with Al. She hasn't been able to work for over a year, so I help financially when I can.

"I've made the decision to treat Ruthie like a sick friend who is very troubled, one who doesn't want advice, but only friendly words, and that seems to be helping. I e-mail her about movies I've seen. I send her books, and we discuss them. I still tiptoe around her a lot, but at least we write to each other frequently. Just recently, Ruthie sent me a belated birthday card, and that was an enormous step forward."

Miriam is grateful for this slow, tentative progress with Ruthie, but she doesn't call it reconciliation. "To me, reconciliation means being able to be together without barriers. As long as there are barriers between us, I don't feel we have achieved reconciliation. We have begun, but I don't think we can get much further until Ruthie is ready to take responsibility for her own life, and so far, she is still blaming the rest of us for her problems.

"I hope there will be an increase in our ability to have a relationship, but there's only so much I can do. I continue to tell her: 'I'm here. I'm willing to do whatever it is you want us to do. I love you, and I'm sorry for what happened.' Then I have to let her take the lead. At this point, whatever change is going to happen will have to come from her. The sad part is I don't know if it'll ever happen. But the way I look at it, reconciling with four out of five isn't bad."

Seeking Help Where You Can Find It

In seeking healing for herself and reconciliation with her children, Miriam utilized a number of resources. She drew deeply on her religious tradition, attended individual therapy, family therapy, and religious counseling; she also participated in Al-Anon and other twelve-step programs. Part of determination is eliciting the support you need.

Help can also rise from within. As a woman who successfully reconciled with an overbearing father once said, "If you take small steps and are honest, the divine presence will take two steps for you. You don't have to have it all together or do it all yourself."

Sometimes a person close to us who is not directly involved in the conflict can serve as a mediator or coach. Elizabeth, who is in the process of reconciling with her brother, recalls:

> My sister-in-law is an incredibly warm, extroverted woman who has an amazing grace around relationships. She came from a family that was very different than the one my brother and I grew up in. She easily traverses tensions and conflicts, whereas my brother's style is to disappear when things get tense—and mine is to get confrontational. My sister-in-law's style is to weave things together; she helps us maintain the continuity of our relationship even when there's tension.

Michael Ortiz Hill, who was determined to create reconciliation in a family that had been torn apart by emotional violence, divorce, and psychosis, found a remarkable ally in his mother.

> Last Thanksgiving, I got together with my siblings and my mother, and we managed to enjoy each other's company without any huge conflagrations, which in our family is quite unusual. Afterward, I wrote a letter to everyone, which said: "A small miracle happened this Thanksgiving. We gave each other a bit of slack, treated each other kindly, and enjoyed ourselves. A door is open here, and I think we should talk about family healing now. What is the work of reconciling with one another given our family's history? How can we move forward as adults?"
>
> My mother responded with an extraordinary letter full of depth and complexity. She spoke of her own concern about family healing. She wrote about the consequences of her divorce and the suffering that it had caused the family. As matriarch of

the family, she acknowledged the fact that our family had gone through hell. With insight and kindness, she honored us as her children. Her response was deeply intelligent and soulful.

My mother and I continued to dialogue back and forth. We discussed my brother's psychosis and the bitterness she still felt toward my father. Listening as attentively as I could, I took in her story.

I am forty-two and my mother is seventy-one, but in many ways, our exchange of letters was an exchange between peers. The quality of our communication and our willingness to be real made it an extraordinary dialogue.

Michael approached his mother with compassion, receptivity, and determination. By personifying those qualities, Michael inspired his mother to find them in herself. She took up Michael's challenge, and the healing synergy she and Michael created radiated out to the rest of the family.

My brother got married recently, and we were all there. The generosity, sweetness, and laughter were amazing. I watched my family organically come together in a way it hadn't in thirty years. Things loosened up. The room was filled with the laughter of my sisters, who have been at each other's throats since I was a child. Far beneath the surface, everything was being altered. I had made efforts to encourage this, but now it was happening quite independent of me. Watching my family come together, I was aware of the interconnectedness of things: I had made gestures to my mother, and my mother had made gestures toward my brother. One thing after another had opened things up, and it altered everything.

Don't Sweat the Small Stuff

When we're rebuilding a relationship, it is important to keep our sights on our higher objective. There may be times we need to sacrifice short-term comfort for the sake of attaining long-term gains. This might mean putting out more than our share of the energy in order to get the ball rolling, holding back on saying all of our "truths" at once, going slower (or sometimes faster) than we might want to, or compromising on issues that are less important to us than others. Miriam Gladys did all of these things with her children. Bruce Stevens also had to do them in order to facilitate a reconciliation between his daughter and his wife.

Bruce Stevens:
Creating Détente in the Family

I had an inner belief that if I worked at it really doggedly, I could bring this reconciliation about.

—BRUCE STEVENS

In his midsixties, Bruce Stevens found himself in the middle of a rift between his new wife, Gail, and his only daughter, Bonnie, who was thirty at the time. Bonnie's mother had died of cancer less than a year before Bruce remarried, and Bonnie felt the marriage happened too soon. As a result, she was extremely rude to Gail when they first met. The relationship between the two women deteriorated further when Bonnie became deeply depressed at the end of a love affair and Gail unkindly told her to "get over it."

For the next year, Bonnie refused to speak to Gail. If Gail answered the phone when she called her father, Bonnie would hang up. She refused to come to her father's home and accused her father of siding with his new wife. The one time Bruce and Gail visited Bonnie, she turned her back on Gail and pretended she wasn't there. Things got increasingly strained, until finally Bruce and his daughter stopped speaking as well.

Six months went by with no contact between them. Finally, Bruce realized that he had to do something. "I didn't know how I was going to do it, but I was determined to bring about some kind of peace between Bonnie and Gail because the situation was untenable. I loved my daughter and wasn't willing to give her up, and I couldn't conceive of being in a marriage where my wife felt nothing but animosity for my daughter. I knew it would eat away at me and destroy our marriage."

Bruce called Bonnie and asked if she would be willing to get together at a neutral place to talk—just the two of them—and Bonnie agreed. Bruce remembers their first meeting. "It was very difficult for Bonnie to see me. She needed to talk to me about a lot of old stuff between us, dating all the way back to childhood. I really tried to listen and validate her feelings."

Even though he had strong feelings about Bonnie's self-centeredness and was angry about the problems she was causing in his marriage, Bruce focused on his role as mediator. "My biggest goal was to bring about something approaching normalcy between Gail and Bonnie, so initially I swallowed a lot of things about Bonnie that upset me. I knew there'd be no chance of reconciliation if I started out being completely honest with Bonnie about my personal reactions to what she was doing. In the beginning, she was far too fragile. It's only recently that our relationship has become stable enough to withstand more honesty."

Bruce and his daughter met ten times that year. Each time, Bruce drove three hours each way. Returning home, he'd be exhausted. "Seeing Bonnie required a lot of psychic energy, but I was committed to it. I wasn't going to write off my daughter, and it was clear to me that nothing would change unless I made the effort."

Gradually, as a direct result of Bruce's persistence, Bonnie began acknowledging ways she might have contributed to Gail's hard feelings at the beginning of their relationship. She also became more willing to give Gail the benefit of the doubt, acknowledging that Gail might have had good intentions, even though her response during Bonnie's crisis had been hurtful.

I Have My Daughter Back

After a year, things evolved to the point where Bruce could start talking to Bonnie and Gail about seeing each other again. "At first, Bonnie had a lot of conditions around getting together; she wanted to control everything. Finally, it became clear that nothing Gail or I could do would ever make her feel safe enough; we all had to just bite the bullet and try."

Eventually, Bonnie agreed to a three-way meeting at Bruce and Gail's house. "Bonnie came to the door. Gail opened it and said, 'I'm sorry,' and Bonnie said, 'I'm sorry.' Then they hugged each other and cried. Crossing that threshold and seeing each other was a huge relief. Then Gail apologized, 'Whatever I said to hurt you, I never meant to hurt you.' Bonnie said pretty much the same thing. On both sides, there was a real feeling of 'Let's try to put this behind us.' "

One cathartic evening, however, did not miraculously change things. "There was a letdown afterward. We've had to do a lot of hard work. Eight years later, there are still remnants of hurt feelings. Gail remains guarded around Bonnie, and I think she always will, but she also saw how much energy I put into their détente, and out of respect for that, she's made a real effort to be gracious to Bonnie. And Bonnie realizes that Gail is going to be here for the duration, and she's trying to make the best of that. There are still circumstances that are difficult for us, but I have my daughter back, and my marriage with Gail is growing all of the time."

Expecting the Process to Have Ups and Downs

Reconciliation rarely occurs in one smooth upward spiral. There are breakthroughs, setbacks, moments of grace, and times of sheer grit and determination. As Miriam Gladys puts it, "Reconciliation is ongoing. You have to keep working at the relationships. You have to keep listening and being aware of the impact of your behavior."

We also have to watch for reversals. Leah, who experienced a deep level of reconciliation with her parents, explains:

You can never rest on your laurels. No matter how much you've attained with each other, it's easy to lapse into unconsciousness. On my last visit with my family, we all fell right back into the murky pool of old habits. Before I knew what hit me, we were trapped in an instant replay of all the negative dynamics of the last forty-two years. A series of little events got us spinning in a backward trajectory, and once we got stuck there, it took a lot of talking and thinking and rehashing to get back to a conscious, clear, adult relationship. I felt like this lion tamer with a whip who had to say, "Snap to attention! This is where we are. This is who we are. This is what we just got stuck doing, and now we need to stop."

Jack, who made peace with an opinionated father, recalls a time he almost fell back into fighting over their differences.

The last time I saw my parents, I almost got hooked. They were selling their house, and an interracial couple came to see it. That really upset my parents. When I asked them why, my mother said, "Well, we're racists and we have reason to be." I could feel my hackles rise, but I chose not to engage. Then we started talking about interracial marriage. I asked my parents, "Why do you disapprove of that?" My father said, "Oh, the poor children. They'll always be ostracized. They'll never be black, and they'll never be white. They won't fit in anywhere."

I was stunned that he could still say something like that today. I could imagine believing that in the nineteen-fifties, but now? I sat there thinking about the part of the country I live in—a liberal bastion—and I thought, "My world is so far from the world these people inhabit."

Then I asked myself, "What do you want to do here?" and what I wanted to do was *not* get into a fight about it. So instead of getting in an argument, I just said, "You know, I see it a little differently. Where I'm from, people don't pay much attention to that stuff." I didn't tell my parents that they were wrong. I simply said my experience was different, and that was the end of the conversation. I never could have done that ten years ago.

Deciding to Let Go of the Past

As parents age and die, loyalties and lines of allegiance often shift within a family. The death (or impending death) of a parent can bring siblings together or split them apart. A frequent source of conflict between surviving family members is the inheritance a parent leaves behind. Whether there is a lot of money or simply a few cherished possessions, conflicts over a parent's things can transform long-simmering resentments into open warfare. In this next story, the tale of two siblings caught up in a dispute over a will, one woman's resolve, and her brother's willingness to meet her halfway, transform an extremely troubled relationship.

Kate Gillen: Fighting over My Father's Will

I didn't have any idea how much money was involved—it could have been two cents, or it could have been two hundred thousand dollars. That's not what mattered to me.

—KATE GILLEN

Four years ago, when Kate Gillen was forty-four, she had a fight with her younger brother, Bobby, over their father's estate. It rapidly became clear that a lot more than money was at stake. "Initially, our estrangement was about my father's will, but what it was really about were all the unspoken feelings, differences, and grudges my brother and I been carrying about each other for decades.

"My brother and I had never been friends growing up. My father clearly favored me and gave my brother almost nothing, and as a result, there was tons of jealousy between us. None of it ever got expressed until my father mishandled his will.

"At the time, my brother was a brand-new dad of twins. He was exhausted and overwhelmed, and he started freaking out about money, worrying about how he was going to pay for the boys' college education. I don't have kids, and he knew my financial situation was more than adequate, so he asked my father to restructure his will to shelter some money for his grandchildren.

Rather than look into what that would entail, my father took the easy way out. He told my brother, 'Maybe I should just take the money I was going to give to Kate and give it to your kids.' And my brother replied, 'You'll need to talk to Kate about that.'

"When my father brought it up to me, he made it sound like it had all been Bobby's idea. I was furious, and I called Bobby. He claimed it hadn't been his idea, but I didn't believe him. Even if he had been telling the truth, I was still furious that he would ever agree to such a plan.

"In the middle of the conversation, Bobby hung up on me. He had very little tolerance for my intense reaction because in reality, it had *not* been his idea. He was very upset that I was directing my anger at him, instead of being mad at my father for mishandling and misrepresenting the situation. And the truth was, it was a lot harder for me to get angry with my father than it was to get mad at Bobby.

"After our phone call, all the anger, resentment, and fear I'd ever felt about Bobby came rushing to the surface. I'd always believed if one of our parents died and Bobby got to the apartment first, that he'd take everything and then lie to me about it. As a kid, one of the ways Bobby expressed his resentment was by coming into my room, taking things, and then pretending he hadn't. Of course, that was thirty years ago. Now my brother was forty, and I was still expecting him to act that way.

"The truth was, Bobby had never gotten what he deserved. That was the other thing I had to deal with—the tremendous guilt I felt about how I had treated him. Growing up, I had never been kind to Bobby. Even though I was the favored daughter, there were such meager portions of love handed out in our family that I grabbed on to everything I could get. I didn't share with him; I was not a kind sister. That's something I'd always felt bad about.

"After our phone call, I was embroiled in a lot of old feelings about Bobby. We didn't speak for months, and during that time, I didn't see how things could ever resolve. I realized it was definitely possible that I'd never talk to my brother again."

I Had Nothing to Lose by Reaching Out

Six months into their standoff, Kate spoke with a friend who had gone through a similar struggle with a sibling over a will, and in the course of that conversation, Kate realized she had nothing to lose by reaching out to Bobby. "We were *already* not talking to each other. I was *already* miserable about our estrangement. Things couldn't get any worse, so even though I was still mad, I decided to make an attempt at reconciliation.

"I knew we didn't stand a chance if I didn't level with him, so I wrote Bobby a letter telling him the absolute truth about where I was coming from and what I was feeling. I went back into our history and said things I'd never said before because I'd felt too ashamed. I acknowledged my guilt about how I'd treated him. I talked about the fact that we'd never been friends. I told him how I felt when he took my things as a kid, and acknowledged my fear that he'd take everything when my parents died. I went back thirty years and said everything.

"Even though I was angry, I was careful not to blame him. I was careful to say, 'This is what I feel now. This is what I'm afraid of. This is how I felt as a child.'

"Bobby responded with a similar letter. He wrote, 'You're talking to me through the eyes of an angry eight-year-old sister. According to you I'm a paranoid, lying, dishonest thief.' Then he proceeded to tell me everything he thought about me—basically that I was a spoiled, selfish, bratty kid.

"Then he told me that he had been really upset that no one in the family seemed to care when his kids were born. My father, who said he wanted grandchildren all his life, basically ignored them. My mother moved to Florida a few months after they were born, and I never made any special trips to see them. Bobby told me how devastated he'd been by our lack of interest and support.

"It was a very hard letter to receive. I remember thinking, 'We both have thirty-year-old perceptions of each other, and I don't know if that's going to change. We're living across the country from each other. We don't have a current relationship.' It was hard to imagine what would ever change things. I couldn't envision the next step to take, and I wrote Bobby a note to that effect.

"Things were quiet between us for a while. I needed to let the whole thing settle; I needed to reflect on the things Bobby had said about me. I had to ask myself if they were true, and I realized there were grains of truth in some of them. I needed time to sort those out from his projections and that took time. The whole process was very painful."

The Hatred Was Eating Me Up Inside

During this phase of their estrangement, Kate was still angry, and she fed that anger by getting people on her side. "It was easy to tell friends, 'Look what my brother did to me. Can you believe what an asshole he is?' Then the other person would join right in: 'Yes, he did you wrong. You have every right to be angry and to stay angry.' Or, 'I can't believe he did that! What a jerk your brother is!'

"On one hand, the validation felt good, but the hatred and animosity were eating me up inside. I was waking up every morning with revenge fantasies. I'd go over things in my head repeatedly: 'I should have said this! I should have said that!' My obsession was consuming me. I couldn't think. My mind was always wandering back to Bobby.

"Finally, I asked myself, 'Is this how I want to live? Is this where I want my energy to go?' And the answer was definitely 'no.' I made a decision that no matter how justified I felt in my anger, staying in that bitter, hardened place was not something I wanted to do. If there was any way to resolve things, I was going to do everything I possibly could to achieve it."

I Made a Conscious Choice

A year and a half ago, Kate had to go back to New York on business and she decided to visit Bobby. "I could have gotten hung up in some kind of false pride: 'Let him call me first.' Or, 'I've been here for ten years, and he's *never* come to visit *me*.' But I put all that aside and said to myself, 'I'm going to New York, and this is an opportunity to change things.'

"I called Bobby and told him I wanted to spend the afternoon with him and his kids. He was really happy I wanted to come. We spent the day together and had a good time. At one point, we had a few minutes alone, and I asked him, 'Is there anything else that needs to be said?' Neither of us had more to say. That's when I realized I wasn't angry anymore.

"Six months ago, I went back to New York. I visited my father, and in the course of our conversation, I told him it would be okay with me if he wanted to change his will to give more money to the twins. It wasn't something I premeditated. It just came out of my mouth, and I was amazed. It made me realize that the issue between Bobby and me had never been the money. The money was a symbol of all the things that stood between us, and now that I'd worked things out with him, I felt full enough to give.

"That night, my brother and I had dinner together, and things were great between us. I felt loving toward him, and I enjoyed talking to him. My brother is the one person in my life who can always make me laugh; I laugh more with my brother than with anybody in the whole world. We can have a look between us, and then he'll start to giggle, and I'll start to giggle, and then we'll collapse in hysterical laughter. It happened that night, and it felt great."

Creating a New Future Together

One of the biggest barriers to reconciliation is staying locked in the past. Until we set aside our anger, bitterness, and blame, we cannot accurately assess a relationship's possibilities.

There's an old story about two celibate monks on a journey. As they reach the banks of a wide, muddy river and are considering the best way to make their way across, they see a woman flailing and struggling against the current. Without hesitating, one of the monks dives in, swims out to her, and pulls her to safety on the opposite shore. In doing so, he saves her life but breaks one of the cardinal vows of his order—never to touch a woman.

The second monk, horrified by what the first monk has done, says nothing. He, too, crosses the river, and the monks continue their journey. Finally, after a full day of traveling, the second monk can no longer hold back his disapproval. He chastises the first monk: "How could you do that? You abandoned the discipline of our order. You swore to never touch a woman."

To which the first monk replies: "I set her down hours ago, back by the side of the river. My brother, I held her for but a few moments. You are the one who has been carrying her all day."

When we've had a painful rift with someone, it is easy to call up a whole litany of past injuries. However, focusing on pain and anger, when our goal is reconciliation, is rarely advantageous. In some cases, like Kate and Bobby's, it is important to air those hurts, but in most cases, when we are determined to seek reconciliation, it is wise to focus on what we can share now. Exploring a common interest or focusing on a positive activity can weave a context of connection that makes a relationship safe again—or at least manageable. (A thorough discussion of this idea will take place in the next chapter.)

Seventy-year-old Raymond used this approach to create a contemporary relationship with his brother.

For years, I resented my brother, Eddie; it had to do with this set of turquoise cuff links my father had. After my father died, Eddie took them without discussing it with anyone. My father had very little he left behind—just those cuff links and a picture of himself as a young man back in Italy—and Eddie took both of those things. I guess he felt he deserved it because at the end of my father's life, he lived closest to my father and did most of the caretaking. The fact is, he might have been entitled to keep them—if he had discussed it with the rest of us. But Eddie never did, and that made me mad. I didn't realize how furious I was until we had a big blowup at our cousin's funeral. I accused Eddie of being greedy and self-centered; he said some horrible things about me, too.

Three months went by, and we didn't speak. Finally, I wrote Eddie a letter in which I basically said that we had differences, but that we were still family. Not too long after that, he and I, on our own, arranged to spend the day together at the Pike Street Market in Seattle. We didn't talk about the issues between us, but we walked through the shops there and had lunch at this nice outdoor place.

I remember the day sensually—what I saw, what I smelled, the kind of music we heard. We built into our relationship a little present history that was enjoyable. That was twenty years ago, but I still remember it fondly. We both made a real effort at reconciliation, and it paid off.

We've hardly spent any time alone since. When we see each other, it's usually at a big family event. Occasionally, we go to a ball game together, but mostly we're in a crowd. But that one day we spent together—just the two of us—really did make a difference.

Establishing New Ways to Connect

Reconciliation deals with matters of the heart, and the human heart has amazing capabilities. When the arteries leading to and from the heart are blocked, our body does an incredible thing—it creates new tributaries through which our blood can flow. These new capillaries, which actually did not exist before, have the ability to bypass the old, nonfunctional arteries and provide our bodies with the blood we need to stay alive. In much the same way, we can create new pathways in our relationships—discovering new routes of connection that will help us create contemporary, healthy bonds.

Nancy and her mother were estranged for a dozen years. Several years into their reconciliation, Nancy's mother took up yoga. Nancy recalls:

I'd been a yoga student for many years. When my mom started doing yoga, it helped us form another language for communicating about joy and pain. There's something about being stretched out over my legs in a forward bend and looking over and seeing my mom do the same thing. She's working on staying with the pain of the stretch, and I think, "That is so cool!"

Sometimes yoga feels good, sometimes it hurts, and sometimes it wipes us out physically or emotionally. By doing it together, we get to tell each other, "That pushed me over the edge," or "I got scared."

Yoga has become an important part of our friendship. When we go to family gatherings and are surrounded by relatives and memories of the past, we always pause in the middle of everything and stretch together. I really like that.

Creating something new together can really move a reconciliation along. Fathers and grown daughters have made peace while designing skateboard ramps for the grandkids. Former friends have worked side by side in neighborhood cleanup campaigns. Geographically distant relatives have sent audiocassettes and videotapes to each other, posted photos on the Internet, and created family Web sites. And in Denise Potter's family, an unusual "acceptance retreat" helped a tentative reconciliation coalesce.

Denise's family had been estranged for years. After her father's death, Denise invited her mother and her sisters to something she dubbed an "acceptance retreat." "I told them that the important thing for me was that we begin to accept each other as adult women without all the baggage from the past."

Denise's mother and sisters liked the idea, so they all arranged to meet for a weekend at a lake. Everyone helped organize the retreat. Denise arranged for a massage therapist to give them all massages, two sisters brought drums, and a third brought supplies for facials. Everyone brought candles. Denise's mother brought food, extra blankets, and other "motherly things."

Although some of the activities suggested by one family member were unfamiliar to others, they agreed to be good sports and try everything. So Denise's mother got her first massage, Denise got her first facial, and they all meditated and played drums together.

Denise considers the weekend a tremendous success.

> The place we rented had two huge fireplaces, and we got them going as soon as we arrived. Then we took out a big piece of paper, and everyone wrote down what they wanted to get out of the weekend. Our list included: acceptance, love, bonds, patience, respect, honor, joy, peace, strength, healing, openness, compassion, play, tolerance, kindness, spirituality, understanding, fun, drumming, closeness, individuality, togetherness, and music.

In front of the fireplace that first night, the Potter women talked. They passed around a talking stick, taking turns listening and being heard. The next day, they got their massages, ate out, shopped, and talked some more. They got to know each other in the present. They laughed and had a great time.

On their last morning together, they decided to go to Howard Johnson's for breakfast. Denise remembers:

> That's when the ugly stuff started to rear its head again. My sisters started fighting. I grabbed a spoon off the table and said, "Okay, this is a talking spoon. You can only talk when you're holding it." My sisters were sobbing, but they took turns with the spoon. We hung in there and got through it. In the end, everyone hugged and kissed and said they'd had a great time. But I'm sure the waitresses were pretty confused, trying to figure out what we were doing with that spoon. It was being passed back and forth with a lot of vehemence.

For Denise's family, the acceptance retreat marked a definite turning point. "It was the beginning of a real healing," she says, "which was very fortunate because my mother needed surgery this past fall, and my sister and I were able to share in her care and rehabilitation. We would never have been able to do that if we hadn't spent that time together last year."

Bridging Distance, Getting Closer

For years, my mother talked about the way geography impedes reconciliation. For my entire adult life, she and I have lived three thousand miles away from each other. Until recently, our visits have been limited to two weeks a year, and as she so aptly pointed out, that placed an incredible amount of pressure on us. When we saw each other for such compressed periods of time, the air was thick with expectations and heavy with unmet needs. There was little time for spontaneity or the casual, daily stuff of life—a walk at sunset, a dinner picked fresh from the garden, a spontaneous jaunt to the movies, a child's birthday party.

When there is deep, unresolved conflict in a relationship, as my mother and I have had, it is often harder to work it out long distance. In our case, it was impossible until recently for us to move our relationship into the present because we were so rarely together. Geography prevented us from creating a new history—leaving us stuck in a relationship in which a troubled past was the main thing we shared.

My mother decided to change all that. She wanted us to build a relationship as two adult women in the here and now, and she wanted her grandchildren to know her—not just as a once-a-year grandma but as a real person who matters in their lives. So she took the risk to come and stay here, not as our houseguest, but in a place of her own.

In the winter of 2000, my mother flew out to California and moved into a tiny apartment six minutes from where we live. Her choice—to make an extended visit to her daughter's family—might seem like a natural thing a grandmother might do, but with our long history of separation and estrangement, it represents nothing short of a miracle.

For two and a half months, Temme lived her life just two miles away from us. She picked the kids up from school, walked with Lizzy on the beach, went out on the pier with Eli, and attended Grandparent's Day at Eli's school. One night when we were replacing the linoleum in our kitchen, we all slept at her house to escape the fumes, snuggling on the Murphy bed that magically pulled down from her closet door.

When I think back to past visits—times we fought and stormed off to separate rooms, times I couched my invitations with caveats and ground rules, times I refused to invite her here at all, or the infamous time she traveled across the country and left feeling unloved and unwelcome—I know it took tremendous courage for her to span the geographic barrier between us and plant herself here—willing and open—in the midst of our busy lives. What a profound and powerful gift she brought us.

Honoring Everybody Involved

My mother's visit was successful because the circumstances and the timing were right. Five years earlier, such a visit would never have happened or would have ended in disaster. But my mother and I had come far enough in our reconciliation that spending this kind of time together made sense. My mother initiated the visit, but she did not act alone. We were in sync, aligned in purpose, united around a common goal.

Joyce Winn, who worked in residential treatment with adolescents in Hawaii, has come up with a simple yet elegant guideline for mediating disputes: *the solution has to honor everybody involved, and it has to work.*

The same criteria can be applied to reconciliation. When we're considering a particular course of action, it can be helpful to ask: "Does this action I'm about to take honor everyone involved?" "Am I saying this in a way that respects both of our positions?" "Am I choosing a strategy that's likely to be effective?" "Has the groundwork been laid?" "Is this something we're both ready for?" If the answer to those questions is "yes," harness your determination and give it a try.

Spiritual Strength Leads to Determination

I want to end this discussion of determination with the story of a remarkable alliance between the father of a murder victim and the grandfather of his son's killer. The unusual reconciliation of these two men demonstrates how spiritual strength and forgiveness can transform the worst kind of tragedy. It also shows how "right action"—using our pain to create needed change in the world—can be a powerful antidote to grief and despair.

Azim Khamisa and Ples Felix: Victims on Both Sides of the Gun

I knew that the rest of my life would depend on how I reacted to this calamity. When something like this happens, you can't just sweep it under the rug. You have to deal with it. So I studied the choices I had. I could become consumed with anger and revenge. I could end my own life. And the third option was to go on with my life. Well, how the hell was I supposed to do that?

—AZIM KHAMISA

On January 21, 1995, a twenty-year-old college student at San Diego State University named Tariq Khamisa was earning some extra money delivering pizzas. He responded to a bogus order from members of a teenage street gang that called itself "the Black Mob." It was Saturday night, and after an evening of partying, the gang was high and hungry. They phoned in an order for two large pizzas and gave a fake address. Their plan was to ambush the driver, demand the pizza, and walk away with a free late-night snack. But what started as a simple robbery ended in murder. When they confronted Tariq, he refused to turn over the pizzas, and the gang's leader ordered Tony Hicks, a fourteen-year-old eighth-grader, to shoot him. Tony did as he was told. He held a 9-mm semiautomatic handgun up to the driver's-side window, shot once, and killed Tariq Khamisa.

Because of $27.24 worth of pizza, one boy's life was over and another's would never be the same.

There Were Victims on Both Sides of the Gun

On the night of Tariq's murder, Azim Khamisa was flying home to San Diego after a trip to Mexico City. His best friends, Dan Pearson and Kit Goldman, picked him up at the airport, and the three of them went out together. "Dan, Kit, and I went to a party and got home at one in the morning," Azim recalls. "We were in a happy mood. I went to bed at two. I had no idea my son was already dead less than five miles away."

Azim didn't find out about Tariq's murder until the following morning. "The police came to my house at four in the morning, but I didn't hear the bell. They left a card tucked into the screen door. My maid came at eight-thirty the next morning and brought the card in. On one side it said: Sergeant Lampert. San Diego Police. Homicide Division. On the back was a hand-written note: 'We are trying to reach Tariq Khamisa's family.' I called the number on the card, and the woman who answered the phone told me that Tariq had been killed.

"The first thing that went through my mind was 'They must have made a big mistake.' I frantically called Tariq's number because he had just moved in with his fiancée, Jennifer, three weeks before. When Jennifer answered the phone, she was crying so hard, she couldn't speak. That's when I knew it was true.

"When it hit me, it was like a nuclear bomb going off inside my body. I was blown into millions of smithereens that I knew would never come back together. Life drained out of my body from my head down. The pain was so severe, I went into the hands of my Maker and left my body altogether.

"When I came back, I knew I had to call Tariq's mother. She, of course, collapsed to the floor with a shriek I can still hear. Then I called my daughter, Tasreen, and my mother. We couldn't tell my father because he'd had open-heart surgery just a few days before.

"I called my friend Dan. He said, 'Don't do anything. Kit and I will be right over.' Then I started praying. I am a Muslim Sufi, and we have a chant we do in times of hardship, and I kept repeating that chant.

"When Dan got there, one of the first things he said to me was, 'Whoever the kids are that did this, I hope they fry in hell.'

I responded, 'I don't feel that way at all. I see victims at both ends of the gun.' That response—that there were victims on both sides of the gun—was immediate for me. I had compassion for my son's killer right away. From day one, I recognized that kids are not born as gangsters.

"Dan broke down and started to cry. He said, 'Where do you get the strength to say that?'

"I said to him, 'If this ever happened to you, and I pray that it never does, you would find the spiritual strength to deal with it.'

"He said, 'I don't think so.' "

A Hole I Could Never Fill

As the days passed, Azim grappled with the enormity of his loss. "The first five months I felt like I had a hole the size of the Grand Canyon in my heart. I lost all motivation to go forward.

"For a life to have quality, it must have a sense of purpose. After Tariq's death, I lost my sense of purpose. As an international investment banker, I was used to hundred-hour weeks. I could jump planes all over the world, come back, take a shower, and get on the next plane. Now, it took almost all of my willpower just to climb out of bed.

"I spent a lot of time reading, walking, and working out. I spent time with my family. I prayed a lot, and I wouldn't have survived without my daily practice of meditation. There were nights I meditated longer than I slept.

"The low point for me came on a business trip I had to take to Bulgaria, just three weeks after Tariq was killed. I was there for five days, and it felt like three years. It was February, and it was very cold. I couldn't meditate. I couldn't eat. I couldn't sleep. Every night, I walked for hours to exhaust myself. Eventually, I would take a taxi back to my hotel, chilled to the bone. I felt totally lost and helpless. I thought about suicide. Finally, the hellish trip ended, and I flew back home."

Creating Spiritual Currency

The biggest thing that enabled Azim to survive during those first weeks following the murder was his faith. "I grew up in a very religious family. My mother gets up at three every morning and opens the mosque. She's been doing that for fifty years. Her spiritual practice is extremely well established, and she passed that on to me.

"According to the Sufi faith, prayers are recited at the funeral, then ten days after the funeral, at forty days, three months, six months, nine months, and every year thereafter. The soul stays in the presence of his loved ones for the first forty days, which are allocated for grieving. After the forty-day prayers, the soul moves to a new consciousness in preparation for its forward journey.

"My spiritual teacher explained to me that excessive grieving after forty days impedes the soul's forward journey. He said to me, 'Rather than grieving, you're better off doing a good deed, because compassionate deeds are spiritual currency which are transferred to the departed's soul and help fuel the soul's journey. If you want Tariq's soul to continue its journey, do a good deed.' "

What Can I Do for Him Now?

Ten weeks after Tariq's death, Azim went on a solo retreat in the Mammoth Mountains in an attempt to come to terms with the horror of losing his only son. During his days in the mountains, Azim skied and walked, read and thought. Over and over he came back to one question: "I couldn't save my son that night. What can I do for him now? What kept playing through my mind was the wisdom I had gotten from my spiritual teacher."

Azim began to ask himself, "What if I became a foe, not of the boy who killed my son but of the forces which led him to kill my son? What if I reached out as far as I possibly could and devoted myself to fighting the plague of youth violence?

"I began to think about the idea of starting a foundation in Tariq's memory, dedicated to stopping kids from killing other kids. That could do a lot of good deeds and create a lot of spiritual currency and maybe help him finish his journey in a rocket or a Learjet. As I thought about it more, I realized that fighting against the forces that took Tariq's life would give purpose to my own life. It would be worthwhile for Tariq, for me, and for my country. It seemed like a win, win, win situation."

I Knew That Revenge Was Not the Answer

In the years since Tariq's death, Azim has been asked countless times what enabled him to choose the path of compassion and activism, rather than the path of bitterness and despair. From the beginning, Azim knew that revenge was not the answer. "When something bad happens to you, it's natural to want revenge, but you cannot cure violence with violence. It's like Gandhi says, 'An eye for an eye makes everybody blind.' When you continue to act violently, your pain and sorrow never go away. All that anger and hatred blocks out love and joy, and it can destroy you.

"I thank the good Lord and my mother that I could transcend all that and get to a place of forgiveness. I'm a passionate person, and if I'd gone the other way, I probably would have ruined my own life and the lives of my family. But by finding compassion, I was able to reach out to the family of my son's killer and develop this foundation."*

Meeting Tony's Grandfather

On October 26, 1995, nine months after Tariq's death, the Tariq Khamisa Foundation held its first organizational meeting.

---

*The mission of the Tariq Khamisa Foundation is "to create safer communities, stop children killing children, foster nonviolent choices, and to cultivate personal responsibility through critical thinking and awareness." The foundation takes its Violence Impact Forum into schools, where fourth- to sixth-graders are told the tragic story of Tony and Tariq, so they can understand how anyone can make a series of poor choices when they're driven by hatred, anger, fear, or the need to be loved. More than forty thousand children have had Violence Impact Forums brought to their schools, and more are being exposed to this rich and life-changing curriculum every day. For information or to make a contribution, contact: The Tariq Khamisa Foundation, 2550 Fifth Avenue, Suite 65, San Diego, CA 92103; (619) 525-0062; fax: (619) 525-0068; e-mail: info@tkf.org. The foundation also has a toll-free number: (888) 435-7853.

Afterward, Azim decided he wanted to meet Ples Felix, Tony's grandfather. Ples had been Tony's guardian for the five years leading up to the murder.

The meeting took place in the office of Tony's defense attorney. Azim recalls: "Ples sat down, and I sat next to him. I told him I wasn't angry with him or his grandson, and that the way I see it we as a country are not doing enough for our children, because children are not born as gangsters. He was very quick to take my hand of forgiveness. He offered his condolences. He said, 'You and your family have been in my prayers and daily meditations ever since this happened.' Then we talked about the foundation. I invited him to our second meeting, and he agreed to come."

Mike Reynolds, a writer and filmmaker who has been deeply involved with the foundation, was there when Azim and Ples first met. "The second Azim walked into the room and he and Ples looked at each other, the hair on the back of my neck stood up. There was such power in that moment. A circuit closed, and somehow two positive forces were poised to flow from a terrible tragedy. To witness Ples and Azim shaking hands was amazing. The father of a slain child shaking hands with the grandfather of the killer? It doesn't happen. To have these two men come together was a spiritual moment like nothing I've ever experienced."*

Ples also remembers the significance of that meeting. "When I first became aware that my loving fourteen-year-old grandson was responsible for the death of another person, I immediately began to pray that there would be an opportunity for me to meet his person's family face-to-face. I wanted to offer them my condolences and commit to doing anything I could to support them in their time of loss.

"I was very pleased when I heard that Azim wanted to meet me. I was thankful to God and to Azim. From what I'd read about him in the paper, I knew that Azim didn't want to seek revenge, but I still had some trepidation about meeting him. But

---

*Quoted in Azim Khamisa, *Azim's Bardo* (Los Altos: Rising Star Press, 1998), p. 87.

as soon as we looked into each other's eyes, I recognized that Azim, like me, was a God-spirited person who only wanted the very best to come out of this for his family, my family, and society. All Azim wanted to do was find out whether I was willing to assist him in doing that. It was an answer to my prayers."

Ples attended the foundation's second meeting and spoke in front of Azim's entire family. Azim remembers: "It was a gutsy thing for him to do. He met everybody, and he's been with us ever since."

He Is the Older Brother I Never Had

In addition to their shared commitment to the foundation, Azim and Ples have developed a personal bond. Azim explains: "We're about the same age. Ples is a strong believer in God, and our spirituality resonated. He is also a tough guy. He did two tours in Vietnam. He is a very clear and ethical person. This thing has become as much a ministry for him as it has for me.

"Ples and I often meet for dinner and go for walks. We talk about the foundation, but also we talk about books and food, life and spirituality. We're both single, and sometimes we talk about women. We discuss Tony.

"Ples and I have a special bond, and we probably always will. I believe we were destined to be together, yet if it were not for this tragedy, we would never have met. We are from such different backgrounds. I'm Persian and emigrated here from Kenya. Ples is African-American and grew up in the ghetto. He's earned a master's degree in urban development and works for the city of San Diego.

"In our foundation work, we complement each other very well. Ples understands the plight of the young African-American. He knows how to speak to the Tonys of the world. From me, the kids learn grace and forgiveness. They see the impact of the pain. They learn that there are nonviolent ways to respond to violence. Together, we make a great team."

Ples couldn't agree more: "Azim is not only a colleague. He's the older brother I never had. In the aftermath of the tremendous trauma that was visited on our families, our relationship continues to grow and contribute to our healing."

Restoring the Perpetrator

Tony Hicks was fourteen years, three months old when he shot and killed Tariq Khamisa. Under a controversial California law that had just been passed, he was tried in adult court and sentenced to twenty-five years to life. He will not be eligible for parole until he is thirty-seven years old. Yet if he could, Azim would reduce Tony's sentence. "I don't think the criminal justice system delivers justice. To me, you can only have justice if three things happen: one, you make the victim whole; two, you restore the perpetrator so that he can become a contributing member of society; and three, you achieve these ends with compassion and nonviolence.

"Tony's story is far from over. He'll be in jail until he's thirty-seven. After all those years in prison, he may only come out a better criminal. My hope is that Tony won't go that route and that, instead, he'll join us in going to schools to talk about what he did. As a result of his experiences, Tony could save a lot of children from joining gangs and killing.

"Right now, Tony is nineteen. He has been in prison for five years. Every morning, he gets up and goes to study for his GED. He wants to continue his education so he can become a child psychologist when he gets out of prison, and I pray that he succeeds.

"I will continue to do whatever I can to give Tony hope and to encourage him to stay on the path, so he can be restored and become a productive contributor to society. Tony killed my son. Still, I pray that his life may yet bring value to others and to himself."

Reconciliation Is a Choice

Azim Khamisa and Ples Felix share more than a tragedy; they share an abiding sense of purpose. They have rallied around a single goal: stopping youth violence. Their commitment to this goal, as well as their spiritual strength, has profoundly influenced their families, their communities, and the hundreds of young people served by their programs each year. The relationship between these two exceptional men epitomizes the essence of reconciliation.

Reconciliation is a choice. Azim Khamisa and Ples Felix could have chosen to hate each other, and no one would have questioned their right to do so. But fortunately for them, and the rest of us, they made a different choice. At a critical juncture in their lives, Azim and Ples chose to see each other as human beings, and they left the crossroad arm in arm.

In our daily struggles to reconcile relationships, we face choices, too. And when our intention is reconciliation, we continually make choices that lead in that direction. Baseball manager Tommy Lasorda once remarked, "The difference between the impossible and the possible lies in determination." When we are resolute about finding a path that leads to healing, possibilities emerge. Pursuing them doggedly, with the fierce determination to succeed, is what reconciliation is all about.

PART THREE

Opening the Heart

CHAPTER 6

Communication That Furthers Closeness: The Role of Listening and Honesty

When the truth is told lovingly, with insight and compassion, you can say anything. And when someone listens to you in a compassionate way that allows you to fully embrace your experience, you can survive everything. You can reconcile with any aspect of your life and let it go, when your story can be truly and deeply told.

—SHAWNEE UNDELL

When I began writing this book, I was certain that reconciliation required the kind of honest sharing that Shawnee is describing. I was sure that at the core of every reconciliation story there would be a cathartic sharing of the Truth, a moment of reckoning in which hurt feelings would be exposed, anger would be expressed, assumptions would be unmasked, miscommunications would be unraveled, compassion would flower, and love would prevail. I imagined two estranged people courageously sitting across from each other at a table, next to each other on a couch, or walking slowly through a meadow—untangling old history one knotted thread at a time.

For me, the notion that relationships could be healed without talking everything through violated all of my beliefs about honesty, integrity, and closeness. But it turns out that I was wrong. In my own life, and in the lives of the people I have met, I saw numerous examples of reconciliation in which talking about the past was not what brought people back together again. Conversely, I spoke to a great number of people for whom talking about what happened was not only necessary but essential to reconciliation.

It Was Better Not to Talk About It

I'd like to begin this chapter with the story of Barbara Newman, a woman who contacted her brother after not having spoken to him for thirty years. In the course of their rapprochement, Barbara came to the conclusion that it was better not to share too deeply or express too much.

Barbara Newman: E-Mailing My Brother After Thirty Years

> *My family was very cut off. There was no room for communi-cation. If you got angry with someone, you didn't argue. You went to your room and slammed the door. A typical weekend would be each of us in our own room with a closed door.*
>
> —BARBARA NEWMAN

Barbara Newman grew up in a family where estrangement from siblings was passed down from generation to generation. Her father had twelve brothers and sisters. Growing up, Barbara watched him cut off ten of his siblings, one at a time, for either rumored offenses or no reason at all. Barbara's father never checked out the truth of the rumors he had heard or let his siblings know that they had been cast out of his life. The offending siblings simply ceased to exist.

Barbara was horrified by her father's actions, but she grew up and became estranged from her brother, Larry, for no apparent reason. "I don't know how to explain it, but Larry just stopped speaking to me. We'd be at my parents for Thanksgiving, and he wouldn't speak to me. Mostly, he grunted. When I asked him about it, he'd turn his back on me. I couldn't get any more out of him than that. Eventually I stopped trying."

Initially, Barbara was hurt by Larry's rejection, but she soon stopped caring. "To tell you the truth, it didn't seem all that weird. Coming from such a cut-off family, it felt normal to me."

Yes, I Think It's Time

Three decades passed, and the two siblings rarely thought of each other. On opposite sides of the country, they developed careers, married, and had children. Then two years ago, when Barbara was fifty, she decided to contact Larry. Her children were growing up, they had never known their uncle, and she didn't want them to repeat the family pattern of sibling estrangement. So she got Larry's e-mail address and wrote him a note: "Do you think it's time we talked?"

He e-mailed back the same day: "Yes, I think it's time."

Like many people, Barbara and her brother found the Internet a safe place to begin a reconciliation. With e-mail, they did not have to see each other, hear each other's voices, respond to emotions, or answer spontaneous questions. E-mail didn't require any real commitment; they could each sit safely in their own world, fingers on the keyboard, and not risk much at all.

Eventually, Barbara and Larry expanded their contact to phone calls. Later, Barbara had an opportunity to travel to Pittsburgh for business. She called Larry, and he agreed to meet her for breakfast. "Seeing my brother after thirty years wasn't as dramatic as you might imagine," she later told me. "The weird thing was that I absolutely did not recognize him. I spent a lot of the time just staring at him trying to connect this person I was speaking with to the brother I'd grown up with. I kept looking for some resemblance. He seemed to know he was my brother.

He knew things about our past, but there was nothing about him that was familiar to me. We could have been sitting next to each other on a bus, and it would never have occurred to me that I knew him, never mind that he was my brother.

"Over breakfast, Larry and I talked about what it was like growing up in our family and how we were doing things differently with our kids. Then we bitched about our parents."

Although Barbara is glad to be in touch with Larry, their reconciliation remains tentative. "We've danced around the topic of our estrangement, saying it felt too painful to connect with anyone in the family until we healed ourselves enough to be sure that we wouldn't get sucked back into that mess, but we've never talked specifically about what happened between us. Maybe in five years, I'll be able to ask him, but I don't feel like it's safe to talk about it now. And that's okay with me. It's not a burning need."

The Relationship Between Honesty and Discernment

Knowing when to bring up the past, and when not to, requires an inner sense of discernment. Vicki Shook, who's done extensive cross-cultural research on conflict-resolution practices, believes this kind of self-awareness is fundamental to effective communication. "When we are in a clear state of attention and awareness, we pay close attention to our own body sensations and thoughts, moment by moment. This capacity—to see what we are up to on the inside—profoundly affects our ability to choose the right words and the right tone, and enhances our capacity to listen as well."

This is discernment at the level of interpersonal communication; it's the awareness that lets us know when to speak, how to speak, and what to say. It is the capacity to read another person's cues so we can know whether or not it is wise to proceed with a particular thread of communication. It's being able to read a situation and, in the moment, adjust our course: "How honest should I be here, now, at this time?"

Nurturing this kind of self-awareness enables us to bypass habitual responses to conflict. Shook explains:

Americans are biased toward laying their cards out on the table: "Let's talk about it. Let's get it all out." There's value in that, but it can also be destructive. Talking isn't always the best solution— and it's not a question of how articulate we are. If our articulateness is based on an incomplete understanding of the problem, it's not going to move things forward. In fact, it can make things worse.

When I've tried to talk through a dispute and it hasn't worked out, it wasn't because I lacked the requisite communication skills, but because I failed to understand something critical about the situation. Either my self-awareness was limited, or my awareness of the other person was clouded. Maybe I wasn't aware of parts of my history that kept me from seeing the situation clearly, or I carried judgments that kept me from envisioning the most elegant, effective solution. Or perhaps I hadn't been able to put myself in the other person's shoes long enough to comprehend what she felt or needed. And because I lacked self-awareness, clarity, or compassion, I failed to choose the best approach.

Choosing to Focus on What You Have Now

Such attentiveness is crucial to moving reconciliations forward. Rachel Thomas, the teacher who flew to see her ailing sister Vivian, had the chance to practice this kind of self-awareness recently.

During their first few years of reconciliation, neither Rachel nor Vivian felt the need to talk about the past. But then Vivian flew out to visit Rachel, and their last day together, the two sisters decided to compare notes about the circumstances that had led up to their estrangement. Rachel recalls:

When I first learned that our versions of what had happened were so different, I had this sinking feeling inside. I felt ashamed. It threw me back into the experience of being the "crazy one" in my family, but I decided not to get stuck in that place.

I thought about my version of what had happened, and I realized, "I experienced that. It was very real to me." But that didn't have to mean that I was "right" or that Vivian was "wrong." I had to let go of all of that; it would have gotten us right back into the dynamics that had led to our estrangement in the first place. So I really tried to listen to Vivian with an open mind and an open heart.

Listening to her version of events nudged my memory, and I could vaguely remember the incidents she recalled. Ultimately, I realized we *both* were right. We *both* had our own truth—and the bottom line is we both felt hurt and angry enough to break off our relationship.

Rachel and Vivian talked right up until Rachel dropped Vivian off at the airport. The whole time, Rachel worked hard to stay centered in the present.

Periodically this morass of old feelings would come up—not being believed, not feeling valued, feeling humiliated. I saw them for what they were—old feelings. They don't exist in my relationship with Vivian today, so I was able to observe them and let them go. I chose to stay focused on what we have now, and I kept inviting her to share more. The fact that I could do that felt wonderful.

Mindfulness and Honesty

What Rachel practiced in this conversation was mindfulness—continually noticing her perceptions, feelings, and sensations in the moment. This kind of inner awareness, which seems simple, is actually very difficult to achieve. Most of us spend much of our lives ruminating on the past or planning the future. This is particularly true during difficult conversations, when we are often so busy reacting or planning our next retort that we don't really listen to the other person. Yet it is only in the present moment that reconciliation occurs.

Paul Howerton teaches mindfulness meditation to people in all situations: business executives, cancer patients, grieving widows and widowers, children, doctors, and stressed-out office workers. In this next story, you will see how he drew on these skills to determine the level of honesty that would best serve his attempts to reconcile with his father.

Paul Howerton:
Deciding Not to Talk to My Father

We learn wisdom from falling down on our face a whole bunch of times.

—PAUL HOWERTON

Paul Howerton is a forty-six-year-old father of two who teaches stress-reduction classes in Eugene, Oregon. Ever since he was a young adult, Paul has had a challenging relationship with his father, Martin. Their estrangement arose from the chasm that existed between their personalities, values, and lifestyles. "My father is a very loud, opinionated man who has an answer for everything," Paul explains. "Whenever we'd be out driving, he'd yell at people on the road, calling them assholes. My dad also makes global judgments about whole classes of people. Any time I ever tried to insert another point of view, he'd get very argumentative. Hearing his gross judgments of other people was always very painful to me, yet there was never any room for us to talk about it.

"My father also has a drinking problem. Every day after work, he'd come home and have a couple of martinis, and his personality would change. He could be very mean at times, and when he was drinking, he'd make people feel bad about themselves. He often put my mother down in front of us, and that was always extremely painful for me."

There was nothing about his father that Paul wanted to emulate, and as time went on, the philosophical and spiritual gap between them widened. As a child of the 1960s, Paul rebelled against Western culture and the materialistic world. His father, who grew up during the depression, vehemently defended nuclear energy, capitalism, and conventional thinking.

When he was twenty-six, Paul entered a Buddhist monastery devoted to practices of humility and understanding the human psyche; he stayed there for nine years. "I was deeply involved in meditation and reflection, a very different path from the one my father was traveling as a person committed to the business world. I appreciated the fact that my father had always supported his family, but he lacked a contemplative way of looking at life. He never understood the sensitivities or subtleties of interpersonal communication, and I've spent much of my life cultivating those abilities."

I Needed to Let Martin Be Martin

When Paul was thirty-five, he began volunteering at a nursing home, providing physical and emotional support to people who were ill. There he met Elise, a nurse, and he left the monastery to marry her. Elise and Paul had two children, and as Paul watched his father interact with them, he grew increasingly unhappy. "Every time we'd visit my parents, my father would pick us up at the airport and start right in swearing at people on the road who were driving too slowly. He'd make sarcastic comments to Elise and me; he'd start arguments just to be argumentative. He said a lot of things in front of the kids that I wished they didn't have to hear."

Paul also felt distressed about his own lack of connection with his father. "I didn't know who he was, and he didn't know who I was. I felt like we had nothing in common except the fact that we were related by blood."

Paul's sense of dissatisfaction grew, but he took no action. "I stewed on it for several years. Finally, it got to the point where my feelings about my father were keeping me up at night. I decided I had to talk to him about it. I figured if I was honest with him, he might be able to change.

"I imagined the two of us sitting down and me saying, 'Dad, I don't know if you're aware of this, but I feel a lot of pain about our relationship. I don't like it when you drink and become mean. I don't want to hear you put Mom down. I want to have a deeper, more meaningful relationship with you.' Yet I was hesitant to initiate such a conversation because my dad isn't the kind of person who works to improve his relationships.

"Several years ago, I was visiting my parents, and things came to a head; it felt like the pain of our relationship was destroying me inside. I knew I needed to talk to my father. I went to my room to meditate on how to best approach him, and I had a flash of insight. I realized that this big conversation I'd been yearning for was not the best way to resolve the situation. In fact, I saw that it would only make things worse. My father didn't have the skills to deal with the feelings and information I wanted to share with him, so the odds were that he would get defensive or shut down more. Talking to him wouldn't bridge a gap; it would only create more separation and misunderstanding.

"Up until that moment, I'd been on this trajectory of trying to change my father. When I reflected deeply, I saw that the thing that was going to heal me was not changing him, but internally acknowledging how painful it was for me to have him as my father. I needed to feel my own fear, pain, and sadness, and I needed to let Martin be Martin.

"In that instant, our relationship transformed. Before, my anger and sadness seeped into every conversation with my father. The words might have been 'How is the weather?' but the subtext was 'How's the weather? And by the way, do you realize what a jerk you are?' It was all there in my tone of voice, in the way I gestured, in the sense of sadness and apathy I brought to all of our daily interactions. My father picked up on that, even though nothing was ever said.

"After I went through my internal shift, I no longer had that intonation in my voice. The chip I had on my shoulder, the antagonism I carried, the fact that I was not proud of him—all of that was gone. There was a fresher, lighter quality to my interactions with him. I went through a cellular shift, and my father felt it. We never discussed it, but I'm sure he no longer felt looked down upon. That enabled him to feel less defensive and more natural when he was around me, and as a result, our relationship got softer and we became closer friends."

My Feelings About Him Still Rise and Fall

Despite Paul's epiphany, there are still times when it is painful for him to be around his father. "Sometimes he still ticks me off, and I think to myself, 'Oh, he's just pulling a big Martin again.' The last time I saw him he was putting down my mother, and it was very difficult for me. I'd have to say my feelings about him still rise and fall, but there's a lot more spaciousness within me to let him be who he is. I've come to see that he's actually a pretty wise man, and there are things I actually can learn from him.

"I started my own business a few years ago, and my dad has shared some of his wisdom with me. He deeply appreciates that we finally have an arena in which we can meet; I'm able to receive his teachings, and he's very happy to impart them to me. It doesn't take away our differences, but it's made a marked change in our relationship."

Interestingly, it's only now, four years later, that Paul feels he could actually have that honest talk with his father. "Because I'm not coming from that deep, painful place anymore, I could probably say, 'You know, Dad, there was this time a few years back when I felt I needed to say something to you, but I couldn't.' He might be able to hear that now because our relationship is so different. But to tell you the truth, I don't know if it's relevant anymore."

Hearing My Mother's Story

At times, honesty *is* what's called for, though not right away. Sometimes, it's appropriate for honesty to come later, after a reconciliation has been firmly cemented. That's how it was for my mother and me. We were seven years into our reconciliation before we talked honestly about the forces that had driven us apart. That conversation took place on a quiet fall morning in November of 1999.

My mother and I are sitting across from each other on my living room couch. The springs are shot from children jumping on them, so we both sink down a little beyond the point where it's comfortable. The fabric on one of the arms is frayed. I am sure my mother notices, but she doesn't say anything. There is a tape recorder between us and a microphone on a stand.

My mother knows that I've been working on this book about reconciliation, and I've invited her to tell our story from her point of view. I explain that I am going to talk and respond as an interviewer, rather than as a daughter. I assure her that if we need to talk things through, we can do so later.

I ask my mother to tell her story in the third person, as if she is talking about an imaginary daughter, rather than me, believing that might make things easier for both of us. When I am about to begin, I look up, sensing my mother's reluctance. "You've hurt me in print before," she says. "I want you to promise that you'll let me read everything you want to say about me."

"Okay, Mom," I tell her, and I mean it. I don't want this interview—or what I write about her—to undermine the progress we've made toward reconciliation. I've grown to care deeply about how my mother feels, and I have learned painful lessons about the power of words, so I reassure my mother, "Yes, you can read it, and if there are parts you don't like, we'll work it out together."

My mother hesitates and shifts uncomfortably on the couch. I sense her inward struggle. Part of her believes me; part of her is not so sure. Finally, she decides to trust me; I see the change in her eyes. Tentatively, and then with increasing candor, she starts telling our story from her point of view. "For a very long time, starting when she was a teenager, I felt like my daughter hated me, and I really couldn't figure out why. I always saw myself as a loving mother.

"It was extremely painful for me because I was at a very vulnerable time in

my life. I was trying to find my way on my own after my husband left me, I was worried about my son who was away at college experimenting with drugs. And the only person I was living with was this daughter who was angry at me all the time. There was nothing I could do to please her. I tried everything in my power to support her after her father left us. I hoped her anger was just teenage rebellion, her reaction to me as the custodial parent who tried to set the limits. But she just kept drifting farther and farther away from me—living her life in total opposition to how I hoped she would live. At sixteen, she turned down a full scholarship to Wellesley College. She became involved with a guru. She moved far away from me. But the worst part wasn't what she was doing; it was how much she distanced herself from me.

"As the years went by, we had less and less in common. There was less we could talk about, less that might bring us together. Things went from bad to worse. I just about accepted one decision of hers when I'd be confronted with another disappointment and then another and another. Then came the final blow. She called to tell me that my father had sexually abused her. When in my shock, I reacted to that—granted, not in the best way—she got mad and wouldn't talk to me.

"My daughter wrote a very popular book in which I felt personally attacked and humiliated. It put me in a position of being torn between my caring about her and my original family, and it almost destroyed me.

"After that blow, my daughter and I both made efforts to come together, but our lives had diverged so much that it was hard. There were so many things we couldn't talk about.

"At one point, I flew across the country to go to therapy with her, and I felt like she and the therapist ganged up against me. They expected me to grovel and say, 'I'm sorry, everything I did was wrong,' but I couldn't do that. Instead of making it better, therapy only made things worse.

"My daughter and I tried to talk a few other times, but we could never make any progress. Finally, we both came to the conclusion that these efforts to get validation from each other weren't going to work, so we decided to leave the unresolved stuff sitting there.

"We've never been able to talk about the force that drove us apart the most—the accusations of sexual abuse. I've had to accept that my relationship with my daughter cannot include her memories of my father."

My mother's voice is intense with feeling. She is reliving every bit of the pain. She turns to me, her eyes vulnerable and filled with tears. I hand her a tissue. Our hands touch, and I take her hand in mine. There is a pause. For a minute, I am her daughter again.

Then the moment passes, and I slide back into my other role. I ask my mother what finally enabled her to accept "the elephant in the room"—the fact that I am sure her father abused me and she is sure he did not.

"I don't know if I should tell you this," she says. "I'm not sure you'll be able to handle it."

"It's okay, Mom," I say. "Go ahead. I don't think you're going to say anything I haven't heard before."

Haltingly, she goes on. This time she is talking directly to me. The third-person stuff has gone out the window. "I tried to believe the accusations, but I never could. I have searched my memory, and I've come to the conclusion that my father could never have done that to you.

"Then I read a lot of literature from the False Memory Syndrome Foundation. They described a profile of the typical survivor with false memories, and you fit it one thousand percent. That was a big turning point for me. Instead of seeing you as my tormentor, I saw you as a person who was under the influence of people who had convinced you that these memories were true. That helped me stop feeling that I had to protect myself and my family against you."

I am flabbergasted! This was not what I expected her to say. But at the same time, I am delighted by my mother's resourcefulness in finding a way to live with the unspeakable. Though I don't agree with her analysis, I feel no need to correct her. Instead, I say, "That's amazing—the False Memory Syndrome Foundation helped you make peace with me!"

"It did," she continues. "And then there was another incident that helped me see where my loyalties lay. I went to a False Memory Syndrome Foundation meeting. Someone got up and started attacking you and [your book] The Courage to Heal, *and I immediately wanted to get up and punch the guy. No one there knew I was your mother, but I wanted to shout, 'How dare you say that about my daughter!' In that moment, I realized I felt much more loyal to you than I was to them. I picked up my pocketbook and left."*

This time, I start laughing—imagining my mother at a False Memory meeting, revealing her identity as my mother and defending me to people who consider me their worst enemy. I am tickled by the idea and touched by her loyalty. "That's great, Mom," I say. "You should have let him have it!"

It's quiet for a while. We are both enjoying the moment, relishing the extra space she has just created with her honesty. Then my mother asks, "How about if I turn the tables on you a little? Tell me, how have you come to accept the fact that I don't believe you?"

Being in this role is not as comfortable for me, but I know she has earned it, so I make my own attempt at setting the record straight. "I did a lot of hard work, Mom. I was in therapy for years. Then I moved here. I fell in love and had children. I got happier, and incest was no longer at the forefront of my life. It receded in importance, and I no longer needed you to believe me." I hesitate, knowing the next part is harder to say. "What it really came down to was that I looked at your life and realized that you couldn't afford to believe me. You grew up with him. He was your father. You loved him, and you needed to remember him as a good man. I guess I finally accepted that."

I don't say more, and she doesn't ask. We look at each other, more love in our eyes now than there has been in years. We chat a little longer, I ask a few more questions, but the heart of our talk is over.

In our idiosyncratic ways, my mother and I each found a way to accept the unacceptable in each other. We have agreed to disagree. There are things we don't talk about, but we don't need to anymore. Around the elephant in the room, we have stretched out our hands, and our fingers are lightly touching.

We Needed to Talk About It

My mother and I needed to wait until our reconciliation was solid before we could have this talk, but there are other circumstances in which reconciliation is only possible when there is complete honesty from the start. Kate Howard and her siblings needed to unravel their tangled history before they could begin to form contemporary relationships with each other. And they did so in a most creative way.

Kate Howard: Creating a New History

We got together and decided that the sum of the parts was more than the hole it came from and that we were all going to do what we needed to do to grow as human beings.

—KATE HOWARD

Kate Howard is a social worker and the mother of three adult children. She grew up in a big family full of craziness and chaos. "There were seven kids in my family, one mother, and three fathers. The questions 'Who are you?' 'Who are your relatives?' and 'What kind of a family is this?' created a lot of conflict between us.

"Because of the big age spread, the oldest and the youngest kids grew up in very different worlds. When I was little, we had this constrained Catholic upbringing where you couldn't say shit if you had a mouthful of it. Then when I was thirteen, my mother ended her relationship with my stepfather and got involved in civil rights. It was her time of rebellion. She pulled up the carpets in our house and established a flophouse for anyone who wanted to stay with us.

"It was a completely chaotic environment. My mom had lots of affairs. My youngest sister, who was nine, was sexually abused for four years, and nobody knew it. My eleven-year-old sister was 'in a relationship' with a thirty-year-old man. It was crazy.

"My four youngest siblings grew up with no structure and no morality. They were raised in a completely different world than those of us who were older, and that led to some major breakdowns in the way we could relate to each other."

I Thought It Was Time for Us to Come Together

As Kate and her siblings grew up and left home, they each found a way to make sense of their crazy upbringing. But they were still basically disconnected from each other. Criticism and judgment ran heavy between them, petty misunderstandings arose, and unspoken resentments smoldered. "None of us had an updated idea about each other as adults," Kate reports. "We were all still inhabiting the world we'd shared as children. It took all of us twenty years of healing to even *want* to know what was happening to the others."

That shift happened for Kate when she was forty-four. "I graduated from social work school and did my own therapy. I thought, 'I'm different now. I wonder if my brothers and sisters have changed as well.' I starting feeling it would be nice for us to get closer.

"I called my sister Lynne and said, 'What would you think about getting together for a family reunion—just us kids, with no parents—but with a focus? What if we did two days of therapy together?'

"I envisioned a time when we could get together without my mother and ask ourselves, 'What's good about us? What's positive in our relationship with each other? What legacy are we leaving our children?'

"My sister thought it sounded like a good idea, and so did everyone else. And our kids all wanted to come—they were eager to see their cousins and meet some of the aunts and uncles they had heard so much about.

"My sister found a therapist. We split the cost seven ways, so it was affordable. Then we all traveled to the Midwest with our families.

"The first day, the seven of us met at the therapist's house. We sat in a circle, and the therapist said: 'I want you to go around the room and say a couple of things about an issue you want to talk to one or more of your siblings about. This is not about your mother, so get her out of the middle of the circle. You've come here for each other, and we're going to focus on the work you can actually do with each other.'

"We all came prepared to work on real issues, and I'd have to say that eighty percent of the major sources of pain we had with each other were resolved in those two days. We talked about our anger and felt heard. We expressed feelings and shared stories. We laughed and said how much we loved each other. As we brought painful pieces of our history in front of the whole group, we realized that none of us knew very much about each other; things had happened to each of us that nobody else knew about. In turn, we'd ask, 'Didn't you know that was happening to me?' The other six would answer, 'No, we were too busy trying to save our own asses to notice.'

"In the course of those two days, our biggest realization was that the major source of our pain was not us. We'd been taught a way of being with each other that we no longer believed in, and in those two days we got to think about how we wanted to be with each other in the future.

"A lot of miscommunication had been set up by the ways we habitually communicated. Everything had always been channeled through our mother, and that had set up all kinds of misunderstandings between us. In order to trust each other, we needed to clarify the lines of communication. If I wanted to know what my sister thought about something, I needed to go directly to her. If I wanted to know why my brother said something about me, I needed to call him on the phone and ask him. During those two days, we all made a conscious decision to communicate directly with each other, and that has made a world of difference."

At the end of their final session, the siblings planned a picnic with their families, but when they reached their cars, one of their truck batteries was dead. Kate recalls: "We all got behind the truck and pushed it, and we took pictures of us pushing it. It reinforced for us what we had just spent two days learning: that working together, we had the force to resolve all sorts of things.

"That afternoon, we had a great picnic. Our spouses and kids joined in. We talked, played music, and took family photos. My kids said to me, 'Hey, your sister Susie has a really great sense of humor. How come you never told us?' And I said, 'I never knew!' "

As a Family, We Are Changing Together

In the four years since their family session, Kate and her relatives have had five more family circles. The ground rules are always the same: One person talks at a time, and no one comments on what anyone else has said. People can ask questions for clarification, but they are basically expected to listen respectfully until each person indicates that he or she is done. Generally, as people talk, there is a lot of physical sharing—people leaning on each other, sitting in laps, giving back rubs. "Each circle has its own unique character. This year at Christmas, we passed around a sock, and the rule was you could only talk when you had the sock. Everyone spoke about how they were doing with the goals they had set at the last circle. We discussed what was changing emotionally for us and what we were doing with our creativity. Last Thanksgiving, we focused on what we felt grateful for. When my daughter and son-in-law got married, we talked about hope, new babies, the future, and how our family can support a couple in having a good relationship."

Despite the fact that they are working with a parent who has not changed or healed as they have, Kate feels there are enough siblings in her generation to set the family on a new course. "As grown-up siblings, we are the adults. We are the people everyone sees as 'the family.' That gives us the power to redefine who we are as a clan of human beings. Through our circles, we have transformed the story of our family."

LEARNING TO LISTEN

In a culture that honors "doing," multitasking, and filling in all the empty spaces in the day, the art of listening has been all but lost. Even in the best of circumstances, listening is hard, and when people feel angry, hurt, or cornered, the difficulty magnifies.

Fortunately, you don't have to be good at listening in order to become better at it. Listening is a discipline. Like playing scales on a piano, the more you work at it, the better you become. All it takes is a clear intention and the willingness to practice.

It's best to start with conversations in which you don't have a lot at stake—a neighbor you're chatting with over the fence or an old friend you bump into at the grocery store. Observe where your mind goes when you are supposedly listening. Pay attention to how frequently you think of the past or the future, how often you are busy planning your next sentence rather than hearing what is being said. Notice how quickly and incorrigibly your mind hops away. At first, this can be disconcerting—when you realize for the first time how infrequently you actually listen.

Once you have become familiar with the erratic ramblings of your mind, practice reining your mind back in. Every time you notice your attention drifting, gently bring it back. Don't judge yourself. Just notice that your mind has wandered off again, and refocus it on listening.

The object of these exercises is not perfection. It is to gradually increase your ability to concentrate, your capacity to listen, and your awareness of your own unique and idiosyncratic mind.

When you've gotten the hang of this (at least on a rudimentary level), try it in a conversation where you have a little more at stake. Practice listening when you feel stressed or upset. Try it with your boss or with your children when they are screaming at you. See if you can listen then.

When you attempt to listen to someone with whom you have had a conflict, it's normal for a myriad of feelings to emerge. Anger, surprise, sadness, fear, defensiveness, fury, optimism, hopelessness, confusion, or numbness may all arise within a short span of time. As the other person talks, it's likely that your brain will fill with a rapid succession of judgments, thoughts, and ideas: "I cannot believe she said that!" "Why does he always have to go on and on like that?" "I don't want to hear this crap anymore!" Your mind may busily churn out a dozen rebuttals: "But I remember when you said . . ." "That's not the way it happened! You're wrong!" "You think you had it bad, what about the time you . . ."

If your goal is to listen, rather than to escalate or prolong a conflict, notice these thoughts, judgments, and admonitions, but do not get waylaid by them. Instead, let them pass through your awareness and bring your mind back to your deeper intention. Every time a voice in your head says, "Why should I even bother talking to her?" remind yourself, "My job right now is to listen." Every time your mind wanders, come back to the thing you truly desire: "I want to discern the truth of this situation." "I want to understand the core of this human being."

An Opening of Doors

True listening is at the heart of reconciliation. Listening is the willingness to take in what another person is saying, even when it is painful to hear. It is the acknowledgment of truth as it is, rather than as we wish it to be. Listening entails slowing down enough to discern the deep rhythms that resonate under the surface of what another human being is saying. It means stopping our mind long enough to take in another person's truth, without judgment, defense, or rebuttal.

Although listening sometimes verifies our worst fears or confirms that reconciliation is impossible, far more often deep listening leads to an opening of doors. When our objective is to get to know another person, rather than to win, listening can lead to increased compassion, understanding, and kindness.

Michael Ortiz Hill has practiced meditation for more than twenty years, and it shows in his capacity to listen. Michael deeply desired reconciliation with one of his sisters, who still carried a lot of hurt feelings from childhood. Knowing this, Michael dedicated himself to listening to her without expecting anything in return.

My sister has a remarkable memory for small incidents that happened twenty-five years ago. She can still express deep bitterness over who I was as a confused adolescent. I had to come clean with her and patiently eat her shadow. I couldn't be reactive. I couldn't expect reciprocation. Her sense of being exiled from the family was deep, and she needed to be heard.

The way Michael listened to his sister was thoughtful and unique:

> When I received letters from my sister, I would record them on a tape recorder and listen to them a couple of dozen times as I drove around doing errands. I'd really get into the deep textures of what she said before responding because my first response was always reactive. If I responded from that place, it only would have thickened the chaos; it would not have resolved it. So I waited until I could respond intentionally in a way that served kindness and reconciliation.

When we truly learn to listen, as Michael did, amazing transformations can occur. Shawnee Undell experienced this when she discovered the deeper textures of listening in the course of reconnecting with her mother.

Shawnee Undell: Receiving My Mother's Story

My history is a gift, like my body—it's what I am made of.
—SHAWNEE UNDELL

Shawnee Undell is a twenty-eight-year-old writer and performance artist who spent the first four years of her life living with her mother, who was a struggling single parent. "It took everything my mother had to find a way to pay the rent and put food on the table. As an extremely empathetic child, feeling the extent of my mother's pain was excruciating.

"When I was four years old, my mom went to India for three months, while I stayed with my godmother, whom I'd met once before. When we picked my mom up from the airport, she didn't recognize me. Later that night, she took me to a satsang meeting.* A man we met there offered to give us a ride home. I didn't

---

*Satsang is spiritual discourse. It means, literally, "in the company of truth."

want to get in the car with him. A sense of dread washed over me when I realized I didn't have any choice. He drove us home and never left. My mother married him three months later. Ten months after that, my little brother was born.

"My mother had always been passionate, but now her rage became explosive. She was intensely loving and could fly into a screaming rage at the drop of a pin.

"It was a nightmare. My stepfather was depressed. He slept in the living room all day. He either ignored me or treated me like I was special in a really creepy way. His depression and her rage filled every corner of the house. I felt trapped, and I held my mom responsible. I stopped trusting her or confiding in her.

"When I was in elementary school, I walked home as slowly as I possibly could, because I dreaded going home. I counted the days until I'd turn eighteen. My love for my little brother sustained me, and I shielded him as long as I could. When he was six and I was twelve, I looked at him and realized that staying was hurting me more than it was helping him. I couldn't stand it anymore. I just had to get out."

The next day, Shawnee left home for good. She stayed with friends and lived on a Christian Bible School commune with her father. After a suicide attempt at thirteen, Shawnee moved in with her godmother, and ultimately, into a foster home. During these years, contact with her mother was minimal. "My mother called and visited me occasionally, but I shared nothing of my life with her other than the obligatory 'I'm alive.' I wanted nothing to do with her.

"Then, for my seventeenth birthday, my mother gave me a gift certificate for unlimited collect phone calls to her, which I thought was hilarious since I wasn't speaking to her. I had just gone through a custody battle with her, I was under a lot of pressure at school, and I was living in a very conservative town that made no sense to me culturally. Although my foster family was very loving and stable, I still felt like a total stranger. So I took my mom up on her offer and started to call her when I felt desperate. I remember sitting on the floor, feeling the texture of the carpet, thinking, 'I can't believe I'm talking to my mom.' The flip side of this was 'I can't believe she's listening to me.' And she was.

"I realize what incredible strength it must have taken for her to hear how unhappy I was, knowing she was powerless to do anything—except listen. That was the only role I'd let her play in my life, and she offered that to me with incredible grace.

"Slowly, over the next few years, we developed a new relationship. The phone had a lot to do with it, because our relationship was too volatile in person. It got to the point where we could talk about anything and laugh about it. My mother could make me laugh more than anyone I've ever known."

I Decided to Interview My Mother

When she was nineteen, one of Shawnee's college professors spoke about the experience of being silenced. She said something that Shawnee never forgot: "Silence is only heard in the moment it is broken."

That insight led to a chain of events that transformed Shawnee's life, and it began with an idea for a class project. "I decided to interview my mother about her experience of being raped at seventeen while she was hitchhiking. It was a story I'd heard repeatedly while I was growing up, a story of incredible suffering in which she felt blamed for the crime she had endured. Even though my mother had often spoken to me of the rape and its aftermath, I realized that I had never really heard her.

"I have a vivid memory of our interview. We sat on my mother's bed, and I turned on the tape recorder. I can remember the wool blanket we were sitting on, the way the light was coming through the window, the scratchy hum of the tape recorder, and my mom telling her story. Together, we created a sacred atmosphere, one that was profoundly healing for both of us.

"During the hour and a half she took to tell her story, I discovered a completely different way of listening. Asking questions felt like an intrusion. Instead of being a young woman who wanted to change her mother's story because I didn't like the way it turned out, I simply listened. And because I listened without judgment, it took our conversation to an entirely different realm. Something broke open, and for the first time, I realized 'That could have been me,' a truth I'd never wanted to acknowledge before.

"As I listened, I knew I was apprenticing myself to her. My mother told her story vividly, accurately, and without shame, and in doing so, she set the standard for honesty. She taught me the value of being real and telling your truth, and about the importance of being a witness to your own life.

"I began to really see my mother for the first time. Until then, I'd felt ashamed of how messy and difficult her life had been. But over the next four years, as I explored her history and the lives of my grandmother and my great-grandmother, I began to have a whole new appreciation for who she was and what she'd been through. I gained a sense of compassion for her that I'd never felt before."

The experience of being deeply heard changed Shawnee's mother, too. "For the rest of her life, she never told the story of the rape again. She didn't need to. It was as if something profoundly wounded in her had found some kind of release, and that changed everything between us."

She's Still Listening to Me

When Shawnee was twenty-two, she moved to New York City to study theater. "I'd just auditioned and been accepted into the Actor's Studio M.F.A. program when I got a call telling me my mother was dead. She had died that morning of causes that were never discovered. She was forty-three years old.

"My mother's death was a complete shock to me. Yet I'd

spent the last four years of her life dedicated to healing our relationship. Somewhere inside of me, I must have sensed that I wouldn't have the opportunity to wait until she was eighty to be interested in her story.

"My mother and I reconciled a relationship that had seemed insurmountable. We'd cleared away so much garbage that we couldn't bump into anything that would irreparably change our relationship.

"There's a certain delight in being with someone you've been through that much with. I cherish that kind of connection. It's rich and delicious, and I miss it terribly. Yet the transformation I experienced with her is a deep, sustaining resource for me. I know it's possible to face anything if I'm willing to be changed."

The Marriage of Authenticity and Kindness

Talking honestly, as Shawnee and her mother did, requires trust and intimacy. In order for it to bring two people closer, it has to be something they *both* want to do. When one person insists on "setting the record straight" at the other person's expense, honesty becomes a weapon that can magnify hurt, intensify anger, and increase separation.

I grew up hearing the adage "Honesty is the best policy," but there have been many times I have taken it too far. I spent years in the slash-and-burn school of communication; I felt justified in putting out the truth, regardless of how it was communicated. I did not really care about the outcome of a given dialogue; all that mattered was 'telling it like it is.' I valued honesty over compassion and was full of righteous indignation about what I had to say and my right to say it. If I was confronted on my insensitivity or accused of verbal cruelty, I defended myself indignantly, "Well, I was just being honest!"

I wish I had known earlier that my style of communication was so abrasive.

For years, I was not capable of seeing the complexity of any given situation; I did not know how to take into account the feelings or responses of the people I was so determined to confront. I think now, if

I had been able to approach tough subjects in a different way, I might have avoided quite a number of alienated relationships and stepped on far fewer toes. I would have learned more about building allies and less about making enemies; I might not have wasted years in long, protracted estrangements.

Reconciliation requires both honesty *and* kindness. Kindness without honesty is not enough, and honesty, without the tempering of compassion, is not sufficient either. It is the marriage of the two that makes deep healing possible.

Richard Hoffman decided to confront his father, not because he wanted to punish him but because he wanted them to build a more meaningful relationship. The results of Richard's honesty were quite dramatic and went far beyond anything he anticipated when he decided to share his truth.

Richard Hoffman: Half the House

> *Going in there, guns blazing, "Listen you asshole," is not going to get you where you need to go. It's really important to figure out why you're confronting someone. I was doing it because I loved my father, but I didn't have much of him left. I thought there was potential there, and if I wanted to awaken that potential, then the primary thing for me to bring with me was not my anger.*
>
> —RICHARD HOFFMAN

Richard Hoffman is a teacher, father, and the author of *Half the House*, a gripping memoir about his boyhood in Allentown, Pennsylvania.* Richard's story of redemption and reconnection—in which he and his father come to terms with a shared legacy of silence—illustrates the interrelationship of accountability, justice, and reconciliation. In it, we see one man's courage to demand a more honest relationship with his father, and another man's willingness to rise to that challenge.

---

*Richard Hoffman, *Half the House* (New York: Harcourt, Brace, 1995).

Richard was the first of four sons born to Richard and Dolly Hoffman. His father was a brewery worker; his mother, a housewife. Two of his brothers, Bob and Michael, suffered from a degenerative form of muscular dystrophy that ultimately killed them, Michael at thirteen, and Bob at twenty-one. Caring for two terminally ill children pushed the family to its limits, and their deaths left the survivors devastated. Richard remembers: "There would be a funeral, a burial, and then my brothers were never mentioned again. We didn't know how to grieve in my family. And as more and more topics were deemed too painful for my father and me to talk about, our relationship began to rely entirely on a kind of father-son cartoon: 'How are those Red Sox doing?' 'Boy, did you see that Celtics game last night?'

"I never talked to my father about the reality of my boyhood, what it was like living in his house and growing up with his set of values. And I never told him about the boyhood rape I suffered at the hands of my childhood coach, Tom Feifel."

In 1993, a series of circumstances led Richard to seek a more honest relationship with his father. The first was his mother's death. "When she died, I realized that my relationship with her had been unreal ever since I was ten, when Feifel raped me. I never told my parents about it. With two very sick brothers who needed a lot of care, I became the model son. I brought home A's on my report card. I was a star athlete. I pretended to be this sunny newspaper boy my mother never had to worry about, when in fact I was devastated inside. My mother had never really known me, and I didn't want the same thing to happen with my father."

The other thing that motivated Richard to level with his father was becoming a parent himself. "My father, my son, and I would be driving around Allentown, and my father would point out all these places where my worst nightmares took place. He'd tell my son, 'That's where your Daddy played baseball. There's where your Daddy played football.' He talked about Allentown as if it were a wonderland and I'd had a terrific childhood. Hearing him say those things made me realize how many untruths there were in our relationship. They had been accruing for a long time.

"I finally realized there was nothing to lose and everything to gain. We could either break through to some mutually acknowledged truth and build a relationship based on that, or we were going to continue to have this charade of a father-son relationship."

I Was Angry About a Set of Values He Represented

Before approaching his father, Richard took the time to get clear about the ways he felt proud of his father and the areas in which they still had some reckoning to do. "My father grew up in the depression, the youngest in a family of seven. He always wanted to be a baseball player, and he got a tryout with the St. Louis Cardinals. But then he was drafted, and he became a paratrooper and a combat soldier instead. When the war ended, they sent him home from Europe and gave him a parade. He got a job in a brewery, married my mother, and started a family. The next thing he knows, he's got two kids who are fatally ill. My brothers' care was very expensive. My father was always working more than one job to make ends meet. He pulled that wagon for a long time, and I admire him for that. I really respect him for sticking it out.

"But at the same time, my father was unable to deal with anything he couldn't control. He was an autocrat at a time when he thought that's what was expected of him. He could turn violent on a dime because his rage was so close to the surface. I got the tar beat out of me a lot.

"Mostly I could accept all of that. What I needed to reckon with him about was the fact that he hadn't protected me as a kid. I was angry about a set of values he represented that he had never bothered to examine: ideas about the relationship between parents and children, misogyny, homophobia, racism, a lack of respect for anything interior or contemplative, ideas about sports and victory, and a contempt for 'weakness.' He embodied all of those 'masculine' ideas so destructive to men's souls. That set of ideas, still very much alive in our culture, blinded him to my experience as a boy. Even his own violence toward me—the beatings I suffered—was chalked up to discipline and was supposed to make me tough.

"I found these attitudes appalling, and I saw them as an impediment to our having a real relationship. I wanted to call him on all of that and see if it was possible for us to move ahead in an honest way."

We Need to Get Some Things Straight

In June of 1990, Richard left his wife and children in Boston and drove to his father's house alone. It was his first time back in Allentown since his mother's funeral, five years earlier. "I worried that confronting my father was going to kill him. I had this image of him keeling over from a heart attack. I thought he might kill himself. I also knew he might throw me out, saying, 'How dare you come here and disturb my life with all this stuff? It happened a long time ago. Leave me alone!'

"The truth of the matter is, I needn't have worried. My father is a combat veteran. He raised a family working three jobs at a time to make ends meet. He lost his wife. Two of his kids were dead. And I thought I was going to say something that was going to give him a heart attack? I had an inflated view of my own importance."

Richard walked into his father's kitchen carrying a set of props in a black vinyl gym bag: three AA medallions representing three years of sobriety, a picture of himself as an eight-year-old wearing suspenders and a clip-on bow tie, and a metal spatula. "I unzipped the black bag and pulled out the medallions. I asked my father if he knew what they were, and he didn't. That was the first shock for him—that he had a kid in AA. Then I took out the picture of myself and put it on the table. I asked him what he remembered about that kid. He started telling me all kinds of wonderful things, all of which were true. Then I started to fill in the other side of that story. I didn't tell him that his memories of that boy or that time were wrong, just that they were incomplete, and he was able to hear that.

"The more difficult thing was to take the metal spatula out of the bag. I asked him if he remembered hitting me with it. He said, 'I probably threatened you with it once or twice.'

"I said, 'No, you hit me with this thing. Now I have a little boy, and I can't imagine what would possess somebody to take this metal instrument and hit a child's soft bottom with it. What were you thinking?'

"At first he tried to minimize it. 'So I spanked you. That's what we did in those days.'

"I replied, 'You didn't spank us. You beat the shit out of us. You chased us around with a belt when you came home drunk from the brewery. I was scared to death of you.' "

Richard's father began to cry. As a grandfather, he couldn't imagine hitting his grandson like that. Finally, he turned to Richard and said, "You're right. I don't know what the hell I was thinking."

We Were Meeting in a New Place

That simple acknowledgment profoundly shifted things. "From then on, we were meeting in a new place. My father was no longer committed to defending his past behavior, and I was no longer committed to rubbing his nose in it. At one point he told me, 'Since your mother died, I've been trying to get my life squared away with the man upstairs. I thought I had my accounts pretty well figured out, but I guess I was wrong.'

"Then I told my father about Tom Feifel. Once he knew about the rape, he understood the tremendous amount of pain that I was bringing to the table, and he was also able to recognize how his values and the all-boy macho sports world had set me up for that kind of abuse."

As more truth was revealed between them, the dynamic between Richard and his father began to change. "What started as a battle turned into a tug of war, and then it became a dance. My father and I both wanted to tell the truth, but now we wanted to take care of each other, too. My goal had never been to punish my father; I hadn't come to make him grovel. I knew how devastating it was for him to go back and look at his life in this light. So when I saw him move into a place of self-loathing, 'Oh my God! You're telling me this is who I was,' I'd try to balance it: 'Wait a minute! I didn't come here to trash you, so don't trash yourself either. You did a lot of things right. I just want to get this picture clear.' "

But Richard and his father were skating on thin ice, and at times, Richard's father balked: "Wait a minute, here! Jesus! You're telling me stuff that happened thirty years ago. What the hell do you want me to do?"

And Richard's response was, "I'm not telling you what happened to me thirty years ago. I'm telling you what's been happening to me *for* thirty years. I'm trying to stop the rage and the shame, to stop hating myself."

Finally, Richard's father was able to see that Richard had not initiated this conversation to punish him. "He recognized that there was work we needed to do, and that if he was willing to do it, I was willing to do it. Together, we made a commitment to fix things.

"What I saw that weekend is that my father is someone who steps up to the plate. He always has been. His response to me that weekend was not inconsistent with the greater part of him. Family means a great deal to him, and that includes me. My father has a strong ethical sense; he believes in accountability. That's why he said to me, 'I don't want to lose you. Where do we go from here? How do we fix this thing?' That willingness enabled us to work things out over the course of that weekend. If he hadn't taken that attitude, I wouldn't have stayed more than an hour."

As it was, Richard stayed for three days—the three most intense, emotional days of his life. "In between walking the dog and watching sports on TV, we talked about everything: the rape, my brothers' deaths, my mother's death, my father's experiences in the war, my father's family, all of it. Then we went out to the cemetery together, something we'd never done before."

Years later, in *Half the House*, Richard described the work of that weekend this way: "The lies that estranged us from each other were not conscious ones; they were made of shame and silence and fear, and blame was irrelevant. Our tasks were different. Mine was to shed the props and poses I'd found necessary to come this far, not only the black bag of talismans that insisted I'd been wronged, but the handful of postures—the good son, the college-educated-but-never-forgot-his-roots son, the always-there-in-a-pinch son, the father-of-the-grandchildren son, the healthy you-don't-need-to-worry-about-me son, and others—that had defined me to him for so many years. His task, I imagine, was to muster the courage to face who he'd sometimes been as a young father, without going on to condemn himself on the one hand or rationalize his behavior on the other. What we were building together as we walked his dog through Jordan Park, as we visited the family plot at the cemetery, as we sat in our stocking feet and watched a ball game on TV, was trust."*

I'm Never Going to Read It

In the fall of 1994, Richard got a book contract for *Half the House*, the memoir he had written about his childhood. When he first told his father about the book, his father blanched. He said he'd never stand in Richard's way, but that he would never read it.

Richard told him, "It's certainly no hatchet job on you. It's the story of our family from my point of view. Whether you agree with it or not, there's nothing vindictive about it. I dedicated the book to you."

---

*Hoffman, *Half the House*, p. 126.

Richard's father repeated, "That's fine, but I'm not going to read it. You and I have worked out this stuff, and I like things the way they are. I don't think I can go back and look at everything through your eyes. I've been sorting it out for myself ever since we talked."

Right before the book went to press, the publisher's lawyers read the manuscript and asked Richard to get releases from the people he had written about. Among those named were his father, his aunt, and his one surviving brother. His father signed, saying he had been given the opportunity to read the manuscript and had declined, but that he had no objection to the book's publication. What he told Richard was, "I hope it sells a million copies and helps a lot of people, but I'm not going to read it."

Richard's eighty-two-year-old aunt Kitty read the release and asked, "Why the hell do they want me to sign this thing?"

Richard replied, "Because you're in the book."

And Kitty said, "It's a book. If I don't like it, I can close it."

After the book came out, Kitty wrote her nephew a letter. "She said she'd stayed up all night in her bedroom reading it, remembering, and crying. It was the most beautiful letter I ever received. Forget the *New York Times Book Review*. Aunt Kitty liked it!"

Then Richard's father called. Their conversation went something like this: "Wow, you've got a big fan down here."

"Yeah, I just got a letter from Aunt Kitty."

"She really loves your book."

"She was very clear about that in her letter, and I was very moved."

"I read your book, too."

"And . . . ?"

"Well, I might argue about whether something happened in the summer or in the fall, but I would say you got the truth of things down pretty well. I'm proud of you." Then he hung up quickly, before Richard could respond.

Richard waited until the next day to call his father back. "We talked a little more. He said he'd been really moved by the book; it brought my brothers and my mother back to life for him."

There's This Guy Feifel

Several weeks passed. Unbeknownst to Richard, his father had taken copies of *Half the House* and handed them around to a number of people involved in youth sports in Allentown. Each time, he'd say, "There's this guy Feifel here in this book. Do you ever hear about him anymore? Where is he?"

Feifel was in another part of town, still coaching. The police found him, searched his home, and discovered extensive pornography and sex paraphernalia. Then detectives talked to the boys Feifel was currently coaching, and found more than a dozen recent or current victims.

When Richard's father called to tell him that Feifel was about to be arrested, Richard was stunned. He had assumed Feifel was dead or long gone. Unfortunately, that couldn't have been further from the truth. Feifel was still raping ten-year-old boys, and in fact had been doing so for more than forty years. In his house, police found a card file full of three-by-five cards arranged chronologically, beginning prior to Richard's involvement in Allentown youth sports. Each card had a picture of a kid on the front, with his name, address, and telephone number, height, weight, and parents' names. And on the back were dates, times, places, and descriptions of sex acts Feifel had performed on each child.

Richard had a chance to see these cards, years later, after Feifel died in prison. "It was a long stack of cards, anywhere between five hundred and a thousand. As I flipped through them, I started to recognize names of guys a little older than me, then my teammates. Then I found my card. There it was with my picture on the front, and on the back documentation of all the times I'd been to his house, times he'd abused me in the gym, in the bathroom, all of it. It was all right there."

We Were Comrades in Arms

When Richard learned about the role his father had played in Feifel's arrest, he was deeply moved. "Suddenly, we were comrades in arms. My father was saying things like, 'Suppose you hadn't moved away. Then Robert would be playing on one of those teams, and did I want that snake getting a crack at the next generation, too? Not if I could help it.'

"I said to my father, 'To have gone through everything we've gone through and to have you read the book and like it and accept it was already more than I could dream of. And now to think that we're doing this together, I can hardly grasp it.'

"And he shouted into the phone, 'You? I feel fifty years younger!' "

It Happened to Me, Too

Tom Feifel was arrested and brought to trial. Four boys he was currently abusing testified against him. The district attorney led off the trial with Richard's book. The story went out over the AP wire. Phone calls started coming in from all over the country from men in their twenties, thirties, and forties who had grown up in Allentown, all saying that Feifel had abused them, too. More than four hundred calls were logged by the police, and, of course, they represented only the men who read the story and called in.

It was an extraordinary time. Richard recalls, "My father and I went through this whole thing together. It was a tremendous piece of healing for both of us. We both felt we couldn't be doing anything more important." *

---

*Tom Feifel was sixty-eight at the time of his arrest, and he was sentenced to eight to twenty-two years in prison. It was expected that he would serve out the maximum amount of time, but soon after he was incarcerated, *Dateline NBC* did a story on *Half the House*, Feifel's arrest, and the trial. Two days after it ran, Richard got a call from the detective who had arrested Feifel, saying he had died in the prison

Far More than an Apology

In Richard's case, the decision to identify Tom Feifel by name, and not protect him with a pseudonym, stopped a sexual predator from devastating the lives of a new generation of boys. And Richard's decision to tell his father the hard and painful truth about his life led to a profound reconciliation between them.

Unfortunately, honesty like Richard's does not always lead to justice or reconciliation. Few of us have family members—or friends—who can "step up to the plate" the way Richard's father did. Far too often, when people try to bring more truth into a relationship, they are met with denial and anger or are told they lack compassion.

The ironic thing in Richard's case is that he has always felt deep compassion for his father. "I've always seen him as a guy who didn't have the tools to deal with an array of emotions. There was work. There was rest. There was anger. There was calm. Forget any of the colors of the spectrum in between. Forget any of the emotional fine motor skills you might need to create satisfying relationships in a family. He didn't have them. Or if he did, they were blown out of him somewhere in Europe in 1944.

"I always had that kind of compassion for my father, and I used that awareness of how hard his life had been as an excuse for not holding him accountable. I could have easily kept letting him off the hook, but that was really just a way of patronizing him. By not holding him up to a higher standard, I didn't challenge him to reach for a richness of life he'd been missing, and I just couldn't bear to do that anymore."

Richard's honesty brought him a real father—and a lot more. "I got more than a sloppy apology from my father. He took

---

hospital. Richard will probably never know exactly how Feifel died, but he has his suspicions. "I've done volunteer work in prison, and I know what goes on there. Guys watch TV, and they lift weights, and they victimize pedophiles. I tried to find out how it actually happened, but all the Commonwealth of Pennsylvania will say is that he died of heart failure."

responsibility without making excuses, and he did what he could do to correct things. My father took up arms with me to ensure justice. In the process my father underwent a kind of rebirth. He shed a great deal of shame. He began to feel—reembracing accountability, grief, love, sadness, pity, and joy—instead of being shut down, defensive, circumspect, and seething. I got my father back. I got the assurance that hadn't been there when I was a little boy—that he would fight for me, stand by me, protect me. I gained an ally I sorely needed and then watched with respect as he acted to protect other children. The fact that he is my father only made me prouder."

Another Profound Truth

When two people come to the table with authenticity and kindness—and a deep willingness to listen to each other—neither comes out of the interaction unchanged. Although both people may enter the conversation believing they have the corner on the truth, they rarely emerge the same way. As the Danish physicist Niels Bohr said, "The opposite of a correct statement is a false statement. But the opposite of a profound truth may well be another profound truth."

This principle holds true in interpersonal relationships as well as in the larger world. However, when estrangements are rooted in religious, cultural, and political differences, it can be extremely difficult for people to listen to each other with an open mind. But when adversaries enter into a dialogue with a basic respect for differing points of view and ground rules that make conversation possible, alliances can be built even across the most intransigent lines.

Building Peace is a unique summer camp that brings Palestinian and Israeli teenagers together. The Building Peace program uses communication workshops to break down the traditional hatred that exists between warring groups in the Middle East.

Melodye Feldman: Bringing Palestinian and Israeli Girls Together

If we are to reach real peace in this world and if we are to carry on a real war against war, we shall have to start with the children.

—MAHATMA GANDHI

Each summer, Building Peace brings together fifty high school girls for a three-week institute in Denver, Colorado. The majority are flown in from the Middle East. Half are Palestinian Arabs, the other half Israeli Jews.* The girls are recruited to represent the broadest possible diversity in terms of race, culture, socioeconomic background, politics, and religion. The group is rounded out with a diverse mix of American girls. When they first meet, these kids know very little about each other, except that they are sworn enemies.

Melodye Feldman, founder and director of Building Peace, explains: "When the girls come off the plane, I take the Palestinians and the Israelis aside and say, 'Tell me what you think the other side looks like.' They come up with lists that include: 'Big heads. Made of steel. Made of armor. Ugly. Malformed faces. Big hands made of metal. Grotesque looking.' If I had an artist to draw what they described, she would be drawing monsters.

"Both groups say similar things about each other. The Palestinians see the Israelis as invincible monsters that 'bombs couldn't kill.' Even if bombs could kill them, they'd keep coming back. For the Israelis, it's pretty much the same. They visualize huge armies coming from outside of Israel. They see the Palestinians as uncivilized and demonic."

When they first arrive, each girl is paired up with a girl from a similar background and placed in the home of a host family. The Christian and Muslim kids are put into Jewish homes and the

---

*For the purpose of this story, "Israeli" indicates a Jew who lives in Israel, and "Palestinian" connotes Arabs who live in Israel or in the West Bank and Gaza.

Jewish girls into non-Jewish homes. In a safe setting, they start to build relationships with people who are different from them.

The girls are asked about their goals: "Why are you here?" "What do you want to learn?" "What are some things you want to teach?" "What's your responsibility?" Ground rules are established, including no physical violence and no name-calling. The girls are told they can get angry or storm out of a room—and still remain friends.

Major aspects of the program—movement, art, and communication—are introduced in an opening session. The girls are taught the basic listening skills at the core of the Building Peace program: mirroring, validating, and summarizing.

Then the girls are taken to camp. Melodye explains: "We've gone from living in people's homes with a girl they feel comfortable with, to camp, where they live in integrated cabins. This is a big deal for Palestinians and Israelis. It's not something they've ever done before. I've had kids ask me to check under the bed for knives and weapons. I've had kids refuse to sleep in the same cabin as an Israeli or a Palestinian."

Then the girls participate in an all-day ropes course. "To go on the high ropes, you have to trust those on the ground belaying you. It's really amazing when you see a Palestinian holding a rope, who literally has an Israeli's life in her hands. Then you hear her yell up, 'I'm here to support you.'

"This summer we had a man named Saad with us, who had escorted the girls over from Palestine. Saad is forty-two years old and was a political prisoner in Israeli jails for eight years. At one time, he was a coordinator of the Palestinian Uprising, but later he decided to work toward building peace with the Israelis.

"He was on the ropes course working with a seventeen-year-old Israeli girl. As he held the rope, he looked up at her and asked, 'Do you trust me?' She said, 'Yes, I trust you,' and they made eye contact. When she came down, Saad walked over to her and said, 'Will you trust me when we are living together back in our land?' She replied, 'I will trust you when we are back living together in our land,' and he burst out crying.''

Heart to Heart

The girls participate in a daily program that begins with an intensive communication workshop each morning. After lunch, they get together in small, integrated groups for discussion. Often these groups deal with direct conflicts between Palestinians and Israelis.

Like any other camp, there is hiking, sports, and art. Every year the girls each make a square for a peace quilt and fold a thousand origami cranes for peace. In the evenings, they discuss identity and culture and learn about women's capacity to work for peace.

Halfway through the program, the stakes are raised again. "We take the kids on a strenuous overnight where they have to rely on each other. Then we set up four-person tents, and we put two Israelis and two Palestinians in each tent. I tell them to discuss three things: 'Share three things you fear most about the conflict.' 'Share your hopes in relation to the conflict.' 'List some of the things that you and your tentmates have in common.'

"The next morning, we do an exercise called Heart-to-Heart. I ask each girl to look for the person in the group that she knows the least or who is the least like her. Then I ask the girls to find the pulse on each other's wrist. Then I have them ask for permission to find the pulse in the other person's neck. If they feel really comfortable, I ask them to go to the breastbone and feel the pulse in the person's breast. I ask them to look each other in the eye. All this is done silently.

"When we talk about it later, the girls say things like, 'I've never touched my enemy before. She feels warm like I do.' 'Her heart beats just like mine.' 'Inside, she's just like me.' 'I could see her soul when I looked in her eyes. I could see myself looking back.' ''

I Understand What Makes You Afraid

Listening and being heard are at the core of the Building Peace program. "In our communication workshops, the girls can talk about anything. So one girl will say, 'I have something to talk about. Will you listen?' And because we're dealing with Israelis and Palestinians, the issues that come up are about the conflict: a brother who is in prison, a cousin who was shot, a girl who lost a friend or a family member on a bus that was blown up.

"One year, when we got to camp, two of the girls got into a heated argument about Israeli checkpoints on the road between Jerusalem and the West Bank. The Israeli girl came up to me and said, 'I want to leave tomorrow morning.' I said, 'You can't leave tomorrow. What's the issue?' She said, 'I just got into an argument with one of the Palestinian girls. There's no way we're going to be able to get through this camp.'

"I said to her, 'You're not leaving. Look around you. It's beautiful here. I recommend you find this girl and take a walk with her. Talk about anything else but the conflict. Find out the things you have in common.'

"The next morning this same girl ran over to me and said, 'I found her, and we talked most of the night. We talked about our parents. We talked about our siblings, about boys, school, and clothes. Then we talked about the roadblock.'

"I asked her what they'd said to each other. What the Palestinian told the Israeli was, 'Whenever I come to that border, and I have to pass back and forth to get to my school in Jerusalem, I feel less than human. I never know when the Israeli soldiers are going to search me, be cruel, or forbid me to go in, even when I have all my paperwork. I never know how I'm going to be treated, and it feels awful. I hate the people who sit there and have the power to treat me like that.'

"What the Israeli said back to her was, 'I want that security roadblock there because when I wake up in the morning and have to get on the bus, I don't know if I'm going to make it back home at the end of the day. There are people out there who want to kill me, and I never know when there's going to be a terrorist attack. I feel more secure when that soldier is at that roadblock.'

"She went on to say, 'I want that roadblock to be there, but now I understand that I have a friend on the other side of that roadblock, and when she comes there, she's not going to be treated nicely. If I were you, I would feel the exact same way you feel.'

"And the Palestinian was able to say to the Israeli, 'Now I understand that that roadblock is your security and that you're petrified that you're not going to be able to return home at the end of the day because there might be a bomb on your bus.'

"Taking it even further, the Israeli said, 'If I was a Palestinian, and I was growing up in a refugee camp and I had no hope of ever becoming anything and was regularly treated as less than human, why wouldn't I strap bombs on my body, go into a crowded marketplace in Israel, and blow myself up? At least that way, I would die a martyr.' She said, 'I'll never condone terrorist attacks and violence, but I'm beginning to understand what could motivate a person to do that.'

"The Palestinian replied, 'I'm not a terrorist. I don't believe in that. I hate the Israelis for what they're doing to me, but you are my friend and I care about what makes you afraid.' Then the conversation went even deeper, and the Palestinian was able to ask, 'When you grow up and become an Israeli soldier, how are you going to act?' "

In Each Girl, There Is Peace

Incredible bonds are formed at camp, but after three weeks, the kids have to go home. Although Building Peace runs a yearlong follow-up program in the United States and in the Middle East, these girls must return to countries where prejudice, dehumanization, and hatred are the norm. They're teenagers. They are not politicians with the power to change things. How can they possibly integrate what they have learned with the reality they face at home? For many of the girls, a kind of cognitive dissonance sets in. Melodye explains: "When the kids become friends with each other, they often come to me and say, 'You've screwed me up because I don't *want* to like them. I don't like what they've done. Yet I do like this *one*. Now what am I supposed to do?'

"I ask them, 'Can you go home and say, "All Palestinians are terrorists?" ' and they say, 'No.' I ask, 'Can you go back and say all Israelis agree with their government?' and they say, 'No.' Then they have to go home and begin the lifelong struggle of figuring out how to deal with the fact that they've changed."

Despite the difficulty of this task, Melodye believes this kind of peace building is critical. "These girls are doing something so powerful. They're listening to each other. They're giving each other faces and names. They're starting to exist in each other's minds, and that's the beginning of reconciliation." *

When Honesty Changes the World

Listening deeply to another human being—whether it be a friend, an enemy, a person who has wronged us, or someone we have wronged—is a radical and powerful commitment to reconciliation. When we couple that commitment with the optimistic belief that people can change, we give ourselves, and the people we are struggling with, the opportunity to grow, to heal old wounds, and to make peace.

---

*For more information on Building Peace, contact: Seeking Common Ground, P.O. Box 101958, Denver, CO 80250; (303) 698-9368; fax: (303) 698-9764; e-mail: *bhfpeace@aol.com* or on the Web: www.buildingpeace.org.

CHAPTER 7

Recognizing Our Shared Humanity: Finding Compassion

The mind creates the abyss and the heart crosses it.

—NISARGADATTA MAHARAJ, JNANA YOGA MASTER

It is a blessedly quiet afternoon. I have picked Lizzy up from preschool and drawn her a warm, relaxing bath. She is singing softly to herself in the water, talking to her rubber ducks, immersed in a fantasy about unicorn-penguins. Eli is not home from school yet. We are having leftovers tonight; I cooked enough stew yesterday to last three nights. All I have to do is set the table and make some toast.

It is 4:30 P.M., this wet winter day is drawing to a close, and everything is still. Instead of the normal predinner chaos, kids fighting and screaming that they are hungry, there is a lovely and luxurious lull.

I walk over to the dryer and open the door. I pull out a big unwieldy pile of dry things, carry them into the living room, and unceremoniously plop them on the floor. The load is full of sheets and towels my mother dropped off earlier today. I begin to smooth and fold the soft cotton, turning big rectangles into littler and littler ones, until they are thick and neat and small enough to stack. Some of the sheets are familiar—like the old paisley set I loaned her when she arrived in Santa Cruz.

I like folding my mother's laundry. I like the fact that she is living just a few minutes away. I am glad that her apartment did not come equipped with a washer and dryer; it gives her a reason to stop by unannounced. She is out of underwear. She needs socks. Her nightgown is dirty. I enjoy knowing my mother's clothes are swishing around in my washer. I like taking a break from my day to lift them, wet and heavy, and heave them into the dryer. It warms me to know that a little piece of her is tumbling around in the dry heat as I write in the other room. I cherish being part of my mother's daily life in such a mundane, ordinary way—and I never would have known that if she hadn't brought her laundry over. Such intimacy is new and tender for both of us.

As I stretch my arms wide, sheet corners clutched in either hand, I think about all the clothes my mother folded for me: the tiny cotton diapers, the stretchy infant playsuits, the sparkly leotards and tights I wore at four, the beautiful red dress (with the pocket) that she sewed for me in second grade, the navy blue sailor dress I wore for my fifth-grade picture, the blue jeans and T-shirts that were my uniform in high school.

Smoothing the wrinkles out of a towel, I imagine her much younger, her belly full of me, standing over a small white dresser, folding and refolding tiny baby clothes, caressing each little sleeve, wondering who I might be. I picture her face soft and open, a young mother, savoring the smell of the bleach, enjoying the creamy nap of the cotton. Maybe she pressed my tiny jammies up to her cheek, thinking of me. Now, more than forty years later, I press her top sheet up to my face, thinking of her. It is in the privacy of these small daily moments that I am reweaving my love for her.

Discernment with Heart

Compassion is discernment with heart. It is the ability to see another person clearly, without illusion, from a place of loving-kindness. Compassion enables us to understand why our brother hurt us and to simultaneously care about his hurt, to recognize our father's history and feel sad about what he, too, had to endure. Discernment teaches us why it's so hard for our partner to admit her mistakes; compassion is what makes it possible for us to encourage rather than condemn her.

Compassion enables us to recognize our shared humanity, move beyond who was right and who was wrong, and lift reconciliation to a new level—one where keeping score, who did what to whom, and "whose turn it is" lose their meaning. It is the inner quality that enables us to care more about what we have to offer than what the other person has to give. It is the place where heart and mind come together, where a tenuous reconciliation grows from a negotiated settlement into a loving relationship.

Compassion is a powerful and transformative force that grows from the spaciousness that is created inside us as we move through our own healing process. It is a capacity that lies dormant within each of us until it is awakened. We can be open to it and we can nurture it, but it is not something we can force ourselves to feel.

Donna Jenson has given this matter a great deal of thought.

> Compassion is promoted all the time. Every religion in the world tells us to be compassionate, but getting to the place where we actually feel compassion is a perplexing thing. We work hard to get there, and then something happens. I call it grace. I've had moments when my resentments were just washed away, when I could stand with my arms open wide. That kind of grace is very mysterious, but if I'm open and available to it, it comes.

Most of us have had moments such as Donna is describing—when we rise above our own self-interest and care deeply about another person's pain. Then the moment fades, and our own desires, obsessions, and feelings predominate once again. But just because we have not evolved sufficiently for compassion to flow from us like a steady stream does not mean we cannot move toward it through our intentions, choices, and actions in the world.

Antonio de la Peña: Washing My Mother's Hair

After years of therapy, I was finally able to understand where my mother was coming from. She didn't know how to deal with me being gay; she didn't know how to be my mother. Once I

understood that she did the best she could, there was no need for
me to be angry at her anymore.

—ANTONIO DE LA PEÑA

Antonio de la Peña grew up in a large Latin extended family that was conservative and Catholic. As one of the youngest of seven siblings, he rarely got to spend time with his mother. She was always far too busy. When Antonio was eight, his grandfather died, and Antonio went to live with his grandmother, who raised him.

While with his grandmother, Antonio began to understand that he was not like other boys. "I'd always known I was different, but I didn't know why. When I was fourteen, I realized I was gay. Being gay is not okay in the Latin culture. My grandmother and I never discussed it, but it was clear that she knew. One day she said to me, 'When you finish your schooling, you must go very far away and learn as much as you can because your life is not going to be easy.' So I left as soon as I could. I was seventeen."

After his grandmother died, the rest of the family ignored Antonio. But despite their lack of warmth or acceptance, Antonio faithfully stayed in touch with his mother. "In the Latin culture, you love and respect your mother, and I always have. All my life, I've called my mother every Sunday. I still do. No matter where I am—in Europe, South America, or New York—I call my mother every weekend.

"But for twenty years, my mother never asked about my life. Since I didn't have a wife or children, there was nothing for us to talk about. So I asked her about her problems. I comforted her. I told myself, 'Who else is going to listen to her?'

"Out of respect, my partner, Paul, and I went to visit my mother once a year. We'd sit in her living room, and everyone would ignore us. They'd watch the tennis game on TV, talk to the children, or leave and go in the other room. After ten minutes, things would start feeling really bad. Paul and I would look at our watches and say, 'It's time to go,' and we'd spend the rest of the weekend with our friends."

For more than twenty years, Antonio's relationship with his mother consisted of a one-sided weekly phone call and a ten-minute visit once a year. But as Antonio neared fifty, and his mother turned seventy-five, he started wanting more. "My mother was getting older. I said to myself, 'If she dies, I won't be able to talk to her, so I might as well get everything out in the open now. If she doesn't accept me, it'll hurt, but at least I'll know.' "

I'd Never Been Alone with My Mother Before

Antonio waited for the right opportunity. It came when his mother and sister arrived to visit his brother, who lived near Antonio's hair salon. "I knew they'd stop by the salon to see me. I told my sister, 'Let me have two hours alone with my mother. After that, she'll be yours. You can have her as before for the rest of your life.'

"I told my mom, 'I'd like to spend a few hours with you. I'll fix your hair. We'll have a good time, and we can go out to lunch.' My mother agreed, but she didn't really understand that we were going to be alone. I was forty-seven years old, and I had never been alone with my mother before.

"My sister brought her to the salon and left. I could see the fear in my mother's face as soon as she realized that my sister was leaving. I was nervous, too.

"I sat my mother down. I washed and conditioned her hair. I massaged her head. I made her really comfortable. Then I started cutting her hair. When she got relaxed, I said, 'Mom, we need to talk.' I hugged her and said, 'Nothing bad is going to happen. I'm not going to scream at you. I won't put you down because of the past. We need to talk about the past, but just this one time. You're my mother, and I love you very much.' Then I gave her a nice long hug.

"I said, 'I'd like to hear in your own voice how you feel about me. I want to know if you want to be my friend. I know you're my mother, but we have never really talked before. This is a time we can be very close to each other, but only if you want to. If you don't, I'll respect your feelings and always wish you the best.' "

Antonio promised himself that he was going to say everything he had on his mind, so he continued, "I don't want to have this pain in my heart, thinking you don't care for me. If you don't want to be with me, I'll just get on with my life, but I need to know. Good or bad, I will understand. Now, I'd like to hear from you. Do you accept me as your son and your friend?'

"My mother started to cry and said, 'I love you. You are my son. I want to be your friend.' Then we hugged each other. I started feeling better, and I could tell she did, too.

"I said to her, 'Let's not talk about the past anymore. No matter what you did, you did your best, and I don't feel bad about it anymore. I forgive you and respect you. Let's move forward and be closer.'

"She agreed. Then she said, 'I'm sorry. . . .'

"I said, 'Don't be sorry. It's over. The main thing is we love each other and you're my mom.'

"She seemed to relax then. She said, 'Finish my hair; then let's go out to lunch and have a good time.' And that's how it ended."

Compassion Begins with Acceptance

When we accept another person's inadequacies, compassion arises. Rather than see their weaknesses as something malicious directed at us, we begin to recognize them for what they are—human frailties.

Whenever I have reconciled with someone, I've had to go through an internal process of accepting things about the person that I don't like: it might be neediness, self-centeredness, or lack of responsibility around money. Rather than hold up an impossible standard, I strive to see the other person as human. When someone does something I don't like, I remind myself, "Oh yeah, I remember. This is one of those foibles." Rather than judge flaws, I strive to "appreciate quirks" instead, and that's a shift in perspective I can make without ever discussing it with the other person.

Our capacity to accept other people's failings grows as we learn about their lives. Shawnee Undell interviewed three generations of her family as part of a college assignment. Learning about her family's history softened her judgments considerably. "Hearing my mother, my grandfather, and my great-grandmother tell their stories really changed me. It gave me compassion for the ways things just occur in life and you respond to them, and you do the best you can."

Even when the wrongs committed against us are severe, it is still possible to gain this sense of perspective and, with it, compassion. Maggie is a thirty-six-year-old doctor who was sexually abused by her father. In the course of healing from the incest, Maggie experienced severe depression, attempted suicide four times, and underwent numerous hospitalizations.

Eight years ago, with the support of her psychiatrist and her husband, Maggie confronted her father. "He denied everything, told me I was from Satan, and that I had worms in my brain. I told him to never contact me again, and we haven't spoken since."

Last year, Maggie began to explore her family's history, and it has had a profound impact on her ability to come to terms with her past.

Learning about my father's specific history has really helped me. I'd always known that he was an alcoholic and a Valium addict, but I never understood why. Then my mother started telling me more about his life. They'd grown up together on the same street so she was able to tell me a lot of details about his parents. I found out that my grandfather was an atrocious drunk who would disappear for weeks at a time, then come home and fly into horrible fits of rage. He molested every one of his kids, just as *his* father had molested him.

My father's mother was abusive as well. She'd been raised strict Southern Baptist, and she used to drag Dad all over the house by his ears. She stuffed bars of soap in his mouth and belittled him constantly. As a boy, my father had all kinds of emotional problems and often set fires in the neighborhood.

My mother told me that when she gave birth to me, she was hospitalized for severe postpartum depression. When she got out of the hospital, she went to see a psychiatrist with Dad. After one session, the doctor said he could practically guarantee that my father was schizophrenic. That one session is the only therapy Dad ever got. He never had any help for his problems.

After my mom told me all of this, I started digging into the histories of some of our great-aunts, and from them I discovered that incest, alcoholism, and mental illness had been in our family for generations.

Finding out what had really happened in our family felt like a lightbulb going on. It answered so many of my lingering questions: "Why did my father do such heinous things? What made him act so crazy?" When I learned about his untreated mental illness, I finally understood. I realize now that my father probably endured as much pain as I did. I started to feel compassion for what he suffered as a child, and for the amount of pain I know he's still in.

Diane DeVito was also sexually abused, and as a result she, too, is cut off from her father. Yet despite their estrangement, Diane has found a way to view her father with tenderness.

When he was a boy, my father played with an antique tea set my grandmother had—a little teapot with tiny little cups. I have kept that little tea set on my shelf, and it means more to me than anything. I look at it every day because I can see the innocence of my father in those teacups. I see the side of him that wasn't corrupted or tainted, the side that was naive and playful. I imagine him in the corner with this tea set, wearing shorts like they wore in those days, pretending to have tea with people. I imagine his simple goodness, just a child having fun, not wanting to hurt anybody. That's what makes that tea set so precious to me. If there were a fire, it's the first thing I would save.

Unfortunately, Diane's family circumstances make it unlikely that her feelings of compassion will ever lead to a direct reconciliation with her father. But even when empathy does not lead to reconnection, just feeling it—letting the love well up in our soul—makes us more open-hearted and magnanimous.

Learning to Live with a Broken Heart

Anna French is a therapist who was estranged from her mother for two decades. In the ten years since Anna invited her mother back into her life, their reconciliation has deepened primarily because Anna's level of compassion has grown.

> My reconciliation with my mother is more inside myself than a heart-to-heart reconciliation with her. I accept my mother and her limitations. I don't rule out the possibility of a deeper, more reciprocal reconciliation between us, but I'm not naive about her limitations. She is quite ill, and you never know what surprises people will come up with when they are facing death. There are always wild cards, but I'm not holding my breath waiting for a dramatic change. I accept things as they are.
>
> I have deep compassion for my mother's pain. She's living alone. Her health is failing, and she's going blind. She's contemplating suicide. She's old and frail and won't be here much longer. I feel compassion for her life—and her end. She won't die surrounded by loved ones. She will kill herself quietly one night and not wake up.
>
> My mother is not going to say, "I'm sorry I took my rage out on you." Or, "I'm sorry I didn't mother you the way you needed to be mothered." She'd have to have a pretty profound spiritual epiphany in her final days to ever say those things. It is possible, but I don't expect it or hope for it, and that's okay with me. Reconciliation means learning to live with a broken heart.
>
> Underneath the anger and rage and drugs and sex and wild lives we've lived is a small child with a broken heart. I've gotten to the point where I'm much more comfortable feeling that broken heart in relation to my mother. The next time I see her, I expect that we'll talk about her suicide, and then I'll just sit there with a broken heart because I'll never have the mother I wanted.

It is one of those wounds that has shaped me, and it has made me as fine a therapist and a mother as I am. It's like a subtle limp. There's no cosmetic surgery that takes those kinds of scars away. I will always have the imprint of her as my mother, but what I choose to do with that is my business.

Facing Mistakes with Love

In order to care deeply about another person's pain, we must first care about our own. Until Anna French was willing to sit with her grief, she could not feel compassion for the emptiness at the core of her mother's life.

Facing our own pain—and our own failings—deepens our capacity for compassion. Acknowledging our own imperfections can lessen our propensity to judge and lead to greater empathy for the weaknesses of others.

However, it is crucial that we face our flaws with kindness. Constantly chastising ourselves for our deficiencies blocks the flow of compassion. Yet acknowledging our weaknesses with caring is difficult to do.

Many of us have harsh voices in our heads that condemn us for our failings. Creating an alternative voice—one that forgives errors, supports growth, and loves us despite our flaws—takes a lot of hard work but is extremely worthwhile.

Jeanette is an alcoholic who grossly neglected her daughters. When she got sober, and began to recall the kind of mother she had been, Jeanette was overwhelmed with guilt. She apologized to her children repeatedly and offered to do anything she could to help them, but she could never shake the deep self-loathing she felt.

I couldn't get past the fact that I had ruined my daughters' lives. That loomed so large in my consciousness that I couldn't think of anything else. For years, whenever I saw my children, I was filled with shame and regret. Finally, my sponsor pointed out that wallowing in my remorse was a way that I was keeping the focus on me, rather than on my children. She suggested that my self-loathing might be placing a burden on my kids, and that rather than continuing to focus on my failings, I should concentrate on how I could be a better parent now.

That conversation was a wake-up call for me. My sponsor was right—I was no longer the negligent drunk I had once been. So I stopped identifying so strongly with my failure as a mother. As soon as I did that, my daughters came more clearly into focus. Rather than continuing to see them as hurt and wounded children, I was able to recognize them as the struggling, beautiful young women they were. I was able to notice what they needed *now*, and in small, appropriate ways, I began to give that to them. I may have been a terrible parent when they were growing up, but once I accepted that I was human and that I could change, I was able to become a better mother to them in the present.

As we learn to love ourselves despite our imperfections, we soften and become more accessible. From that place of openness, the potential for reconciliation expands considerably. As one man put it, "When I finally accepted the fact that I could screw up and still be okay, it made everyone else's screw-ups a lot more tolerable."

Compassion Comes from a Place of Wholeness

Our capacity for compassion is often directly proportional to the amount of satisfaction we are experiencing in our lives. When we're thriving, it's a lot easier to say, "My father is seventy-five, and he is not going to change," or, "My sister is having a hard time right now. I think I'll call her today."

Barry is a fifty-year-old architect who designs cooperative housing developments all over the world. He has been able to rebuild his relationship with parents who were extremely critical of him, largely because the rest of his life is going so well.

How do you reconcile? You live well. You develop spiritual and human richness in your life so you can have the abundance you need to reconcile. Without reserves, you can't engage with people you find challenging.

I'm at a place in my life where I can afford to be generous. I may have gotten shortchanged on parents, but I have so much richness in terms of my wife, my children, and my friends. My life is full of love. I live in a beautiful place where I look out at the mountains every day. I travel all over the world. I do incredibly interesting work. I can go through the list of all the spiritual things I've done to put salve on this wound and become whole. That abundance, more than anything, gives me the capacity to reach out to my parents.

Sometimes it is by giving people what we wished we had received that we find a path to reconciliation. Jessica, whose immigrant mother was too overwhelmed to meet her basic needs, recalls:

My whole life, I wanted a mother who would take me shopping at the mall and buy me lunch, who would call and ask me, "How are you today?" and really listen. Instead I have a mother who I call and ask, "How are you today?" And she says, "Oh, things are very bad. I don't even have any underwear." So I take her to the mall, buy her underwear, and take her out to lunch—and she's happy. For years, I resented it, but I've finally reached the place where I'm glad I have the money to take her.

Sometimes Just a Little Is Enough

Cultivating a sense of gratitude can make it possible to appreciate, rather than resent, a circumscribed relationship. Colleen Carroll experienced this when she made peace with her father, a shut-down man with little to give.

My father isn't the kind of grandfather who plays with his grandson. The time he spends with Sam is taxing for him. I've had to grieve that loss, but I'm also aware it could be worse. My father isn't an alcoholic. He's not crazy. He's in good health. He takes care of himself. Although he doesn't help me out in my life, he's not making my life hard, either.

Right now, I'm much more thankful for what I do have. I used to spend all my time focusing on what wasn't right. Now, I'm in a place of seeing the glass half full, rather than half empty.

What changed my perspective was Sam. Sam almost died when he was born, and I've never stopped being grateful for the fact that he's here at all. Since his birth, I've also had the experience of having my career, which I thought would provide well for me, take a downturn because of changes I had no control over. Those two things have made me more thankful for simple things like sleep, a meal that isn't cold, and the opportunity to watch my child grow.

Before my son was born, I ate at the finest restaurants, bought nice clothes, and took trips to various parts of the world a couple of times a year. I took all of that for granted. Now, I can't do any of that, but I've learned to appreciate the simple things. Rather than saying, "Gee, I don't have a nice car," I say to myself, "I'm grateful I have a car that's still running."

I could focus on the fact that Sam doesn't have a grandfather who dotes on him or takes care of him, but I don't. I'm glad that my father is healthy and that he's alive. He buys Sam birthday and Christmas presents and occasionally, when he goes on a trip, he brings him something. It's not what a lot of kids have, but it's something. Sam has a grandfather he's getting to know, and I'm thankful for that.

Compassion as a Choice

In every relationship, particularly in those that have been estranged, feelings about the other person are mixed. We love our mother but are angry at what she denied us. We cherish our son but resent the years of hell he put us through. We love our friend's sense of humor but balk at her vanity. It is rare to have a single, clear-cut feeling about someone with whom we have shared a difficult history. Yet despite conflicting feelings, we can still choose to act with compassion.

This is true in interpersonal relationships and also in the larger world. When the person we are estranged from is not a family member or a friend, but rather a former enemy, we are faced with a choice—

whether to follow the path of hatred and prejudice or to consciously choose a different path, where compassion overrides malice and understanding outweighs fear.

Marc Levy, a Vietnam veteran, chose the latter path when he reached out to Bao Ninh, a former North Vietnamese soldier. Marc's story demonstrates a basic truth about relationships: it is harder to sustain hatred for a group of people once you learn to care deeply about one of its members.

Marc Levy: Understanding "The Sorrow of War"

Any soldier who has been in combat knows that there comes a time after the battle, when the smoke has blown away and the dust has settled, when you must lean over and give your foe a hand. For in that moment of generosity, the war is truly over.
—FREDERICK DOWNS JR., VIETNAM: MY ENEMY, MY BROTHER

Marc Levy was highly decorated for his service as a medic in the Vietnam War. Since he left active duty late in 1971, Marc has suffered from anxiety, depression, flashbacks, and nightmares—hallmarks of post-traumatic stress disorder (PTSD). For thirty years, Marc has struggled to cope with the aftereffects of the war. He made the rounds of VA psychiatrists, took a variety of medications, spent time on a psychiatric ward, attended veterans' groups, worked as a social worker, collected disability, and drifted. He also traveled extensively through Central America, Asia, and Indonesia, later returning to Vietnam and Cambodia, where he had had his most traumatic war experiences. Of all his attempts to reconcile his experiences in Vietnam, one of the most significant began with a book. "In 1994, I was living in New Zealand and I read Bao Ninh's book, *The Sorrow of War.* It was the first book I'd read about the war in twenty years. Bao Ninh spent six years fighting, and he portrayed the war from the point of view of a North Vietnamese soldier. He had an amazing ability to describe the sustained level of violence that the Americans unleashed on the Vietnamese. I felt like I was there with the constant bombing and the planes. Seeing the war through Bao Ninh's eyes, I learned about the Vietnamese people, who had always been a mystery to me. For the first time ever I saw the enemy as human.

"I was completely taken by Bao Ninh's ability to re-create the war, to convey both its horrors and his own humanity. I wanted to meet him.

"When I got back to the States, I wrote Bao Ninh a letter. I said, 'You are a great and good man and your book moved me.' In 1997, he wrote back, thanked me for writing to him, said he hoped to meet me someday, and wished me peace. I was stunned by his graceful letter.

"In 1998, I applied to attend the William Joiner Center's Writers' Conference, and I was accepted.* The orientation session was held in a big auditorium. I looked to my right, and not ten feet from me was a delegation of five Vietnamese writers who had come to work with us. They were lined up against the wall, waiting to be introduced. One of them was Bao Ninh, whom I recognized from his book jacket photo. I nearly jumped out of my seat.

"After the introductions were completed, the Vietnamese started to leave, walking single file, as if through the jungle. I bolted up, climbing over the people in my way. I was about five meters behind Bao Ninh. Just before he left the room, I yelled, 'Bao Ninh!'

---

*The William Joiner Center for the Study of War and its Social Consequences at the University of Massachusetts at Boston was founded in October 1982 to provide educational and other services to veterans. The William Joiner Center conducts research, makes policy recommendations on issues relating to veterans, and encourages teaching and scholarship on the Vietnam War and its social consequences. The center sponsors an annual writers' workshop for Vietnam-era writers, which brings together American and Vietnamese writers. For more information, contact: William Joiner Center, Healey Library 10-27A, 100 Morrissey Boulevard, Boston, MA 02125-3393; (617) 287-5850; fax: (617) 287-5855; Web site: http://omega.cc.umb.edu/~joiner/index.html.

"He whipped around like a top because he wanted to know why an American was calling his name. I said, 'My name is Marc Levy.' He looked at me, eyebrows shooting upward, eyes nearly popping out of his head. Then he spoke my name, and we rushed at each other and shook hands. It was a stunning convergence.

"Even though I didn't speak Vietnamese and he didn't speak English, we were communicating in another language. After shaking hands, I opened my arms in a gesture of an embrace, and Bao Ninh scooped me up in his arms. Now he's only five six and I'm six feet tall, but he was strong. He brought me to him in a thick bear hug and started clapping me on the back. And then it happened. All this emotion started welling up inside me, and I broke down in his arms. I started sobbing uncontrollably.

"Bao Ninh held me for a couple of seconds and then gestured for me to sit down. Once I regained my composure, an American writer, who lives in Vietnam, translated for us. Bao Ninh agreed to meet me the next day."

"I Now Understand Something of Your Losses"

The day after their emotional encounter, Marc and Bao Ninh met and spoke for three hours through a translator. Marc recalls: "I'd been commissioned to write an article about how the Vietnamese fought, and I tried to get Bao Ninh to talk about war. He repeatedly declined or sidestepped my questions, saying he didn't want to talk about that. But we talked for three hours anyway. Toward the end of our time together, I said, 'Are there any things you want to tell me that I haven't asked you?'

"He said, 'Yes. Tell your friends we were not robots. We were human beings.'

"Before we parted that day, I gave Bao Ninh a wallet-sized picture of my platoon that I have always carried with me. He studied it long and hard, then asked, 'How many are dead?'

"I told him the truth. 'Most of them were wounded. We didn't have bad casualties like you.' Then I wrote on the back of the picture: 'For Bao Ninh. These men meant as much to me as your men meant to you. I now understand something of your losses.' "

Jack Daniel's

Several days later, Marc had a final opportunity to spend time with Bao Ninh—this time in a Boston bar. "Toward the end of the conference, the Vietnamese delegation and a bunch of Vietnam vets decided to get together and spend the night drinking. The Vietnamese were all famous writers in their country. We sat and talked and it was pleasant, but underneath we were all aware that we would have been at each other's throats thirty years ago.

"I sat next to Bao Ninh. Everyone got drunk. I don't drink, so I just sat and observed. At one point, I left and bought some liquor. One was a bottle of Jack Daniel's, specifically for Bao Ninh, since I heard that's what he liked to drink. I had the bottles gift-wrapped and came back in. As the evening wore down, I brought the bottles out and gave one to the head of the Vietnamese delegation. I said, 'I'm so glad you came. Reconciliation means so much to all of us.' I gave him the bottle of wine, and he was very happy.

"Then I set the bottle of Jack Daniel's down in front of Bao Ninh. He was knocking back whiskey and chain-smoking cigarettes. I gestured to him, 'Open it.' He slowly peeled the wrapping paper back, and when he saw it was Jack Daniel's, he jumped up out of his seat, like a Jack-in-the-box catapulted by a triple-thick steel spring, and shouted, in perfect English, 'Jack Daniel's.' Then he came over and bear-hugged me three times because I was giving him the equivalent of one hundred hits of Valium; Jack Daniel's helps him deal with his trauma."

Everyone Lost in That War

Meeting Bao Ninh changed Marc's life and strengthened his sense that the Vietnamese were people he could, and should, care about. That's not an idea he had ever gotten support for before. "When I was hospitalized, and later, in all the veterans' groups I attended, whenever I said the Vietnamese were human beings, everyone got pissed off. They'd either ignore me or glare at me. I'd wonder, 'Is there something wrong with thinking this way?'

"Meeting Bao Ninh convinced me I was right. Before I met him, I only knew that it was my war and that the Americans had lost. My level of trauma was fairly deep, but my perspective on it was selfish and superficial. Now I know that everyone lost in that war and everybody suffered."

The Light That Wasn't There Before

Although his encounter with Bao Ninh affected Marc profoundly, he still struggles with PTSD and sleeps with a machete next to his bed. As he puts it, "Reconciliation is imperfect."

There are days he can live up to his vision and other days when the war grips him and the enemy seems as real as it did thirty years ago. "How I talk about the war depends on who I'm talking to. There are times I feel a deep sense of forgiveness and compassion, and other times I get together with a bunch of vets and start right in: 'Oh, the fucking gooks!' I can choose to go in that direction and talk that talk, but when I speak that way now, I feel I've done something wrong. It's getting harder to do it, and I'm glad.

"I've attained a certain level of freedom I didn't have before. It's not perfect, but I'm no longer living in a desolate lunar landscape. Meeting Bao Ninh wore down some of the rough edges that were anchors on my soul."

Bringing Together the Ultimate Enemies

For many people, children of Holocaust survivors and children of Nazis represent the archetypal enemies. Yet it is the lifework of Armand Volkas, an Oakland-based drama therapist, to bring these two groups together so they can transform their legacies of pain, shame, and violation into a deep empathy for one another. This chapter's final story explores the building blocks of compassion between people who have no historical reason to trust each other.

Armand Volkas: Bringing Together Children of Holocaust Survivors and Children of Nazis

Whenever a Jew and a German meet, millions of dead lie between them. *

—ARMAND VOLKAS

Armand Volkas's parents were resistance fighters who met in the Auschwitz concentration camp. His father was part of the underground there. His mother was on Block 10, where Josef Mengele authorized the use of women as human guinea pigs for experimental surgeries.

Miraculously, both of Armand's parents survived the war, and they later immigrated to the United States. Armand grew up in southern California trying to make sense of his parents' horror stories about the Holocaust.

---

*Although for the sake of brevity, Armand speaks here (and throughout this story) using the terms "Germans" when he's referring to children of Holocaust perpetrators and "Jews" when he's referring to children of Holocaust survivors, this terminology is not always accurate. Germans and Jews are not mutually exclusive groups. Jews have lived in Germany for two millennia. Jews have been German citizens, spoken German, and fought in wars for Germany for centuries. It has only been through anti-Semitism and Nazism that Jews have been defined as "not German." Also, there were many German gentiles who were victims of the Holocaust because of their resistance, political beliefs, homosexuality, or disabilities. So although differentiating the two groups as "Germans" and "Jews" is expedient, it would be more correct to say "children of Holocaust perpetrators" and "Jewish children of Holocaust survivors" each time these words appear.

When he was a senior in high school, Armand met someone who would play a significant role in his future. "My high school had a German foreign exchange student named Emeran Mayer, whose father had been a foot soldier in the war. He was the first German I had ever met. We became friends, and I brought him home to meet my family. My friendship with Emeran was my first act of reconciliation."

When asked what made it possible for him to even consider bringing a German into his parents' home, Armand said: "At the end of the war, my father was in a soup line at Buchenwald; he looked like one of those skinny people you see in the newsreels of the camps. German political prisoners ran Buchenwald at the time, and one of them recognized my father. He put him in the infirmary and saved his life. So in my home growing up, there was always a distinction between a German and a Nazi. The fact that Emeran was German was not a problem for my parents."

Inside the Mind of a Perpetrator

After high school, Armand became interested in theater and pursued his passion for acting and directing in college. He graduated with a master's degree in fine arts in theater from UCLA, produced a groundbreaking play about the legacy of the Holocaust, and later created an experimental Jewish theater company.

During this same period, Armand started meeting with other children of Holocaust survivors. "In support groups, we discovered common themes in our lives: lack of trust, depression, an enmeshment with our survivor parents, feelings that the world isn't safe. I got involved in all of that, but after a while, I started to feel that people were holding on to the victimization. I began asking myself, 'Why am I organizing my life around this event?' Instead of just remembering the Holocaust, I wanted to transform it.

"When I got together with Jewish children of survivors, they acted as if the Holocaust had happened only to Jews. Yet the Holocaust belonged to everyone. I found myself becoming curious about what had happened to the children of the Nazis. I wondered, 'Do they suffer like I do? Are they having nightmares? Do they know their parents' stories the way I know mine?' That was the genesis of my idea to bring Germans and Jews together."

It would be eight years before Armand realized his vision and offered the first Acts of Reconciliation workshop. During those years, three things happened that deepened his resolve. The first was his decision to study drama therapy. The second had to do with his old friend Emeran. "He and I had lost touch for twelve years, but then we ran into each other on a hiking trail in the Santa Monica Mountains. In catching up with each other, I learned that Emeran had become a gastroenterologist and was teaching at UCLA. After our chance meeting, we renewed our friendship. Once again, fate stepped in to weave our lives together.

"My mother began to develop Alzheimer's disease. At the time of her diagnosis, Emeran became our family doctor and adviser. It was as if a strange circle had been drawn. German doctors at Auschwitz had operated on my mother, and here was a young German doctor from the next generation who was now in a nurturing and healing role. An act of reconciliation took place in my family around my mother's illness, and I felt the need to take that healing out into the world."

The third pivotal event for Armand involved a legal case. "In 1986, I was asked by a public defender to work with a twenty-one-year-old man who had murdered two adults and an eighteen-month-old child with a knife. Over the course of a year, I worked intimately with this man and, in doing so, immersed myself in the mind of a perpetrator. Using drama therapy, I went with him into that moment when he took that knife and stuck it in the bodies of his victims. It was extremely draining work for me emotionally, but I was driven by a need to understand him. I needed to know how someone could dehumanize other people enough to torture them, rape them, and kill them.

"After working with this man for more than a year, I felt compelled to continue my work with perpetrators. It was almost a spiritual need. I felt driven to understand the evil behind the Holocaust, and I knew that the closest I could get to working with Nazis was to work with their children, who knew them intimately."

I Am a German, and I Feel Ashamed

In 1989, Armand invited seven children of Holocaust survivors and seven children of the Third Reich to spend several days together exploring the legacy they carried from the war. He began by asking pairs of children of Holocaust survivors and children of perpetrators to interview each other about their history, why they came to the workshop, and what they wanted the group to know about them. Then they were asked to introduce themselves, speaking as if they *were* their partners. So a child of a survivor might stand up and say, "My name is Hans Volmer. My father was a Nazi officer, and I feel shame." A child of a perpetrator might stand up and say, "My name is Rachel Levinsky. My father was shot and killed by the side of the road outside of the Warsaw ghetto." Right from the beginning, Armand had the group participants walking in each other's shoes.

Over the next three days, Armand led the group through a series of exercises in which they enacted each other's stories and dreams, explored specific memories and dilemmas, and created rituals to help each other find some closure with particularly painful experiences. Armand recalls: "We argued. We yelled at each other. We drew and painted. We created poetry. We created characters. We grieved. We held each other. We played together, reclaiming childhoods that had been lived in the shadow of the war.

"At the end of the workshop, what struck me most were the

deep bonds that had been formed. Something profound and transformative had taken place. There was a feeling of redemption. I realized this work was very powerful and that I could make a real impact with it."

Armand had found his life's work.

Choosing Reconciliation

People come to Armand's workshops because they are tired of carrying the burden of the war. They want relief from their pain. But children of survivors and children of perpetrators arrive at the workshop carrying two very different histories. "Germans come to the workshops feeling tremendous guilt, rage, and shame. They resent the Jews for making them feel that way: 'Haven't we paid enough reparations? When is it ever going to be enough?' 'Do we have to grovel?' 'What's the point? You'll never let go of it!'

"On the Jewish side, there's rage and a desire for vengeance: 'I'm not going to buy your products.' 'You haven't even begun to deal with it.' 'You're not sorry enough.' 'I hate you.' 'You can't suffer enough.' "

In the course of the workshop, the Jews feel safe enough to express their rage directly at the Germans, something their parents never got to do. Once they get the opportunity to express it, they begin to move past their victimization. "Initially, Germans come to the workshop afraid of hearing Jewish rage and Jewish pain, but ultimately, they find it's a relief to hear it, rather than just imagine it.

"Once the Jews have been able to express their pain and their rage, I help the Germans express theirs: 'It's unfair of you to lay this on me! I wasn't even born. Both of us have been given this legacy, and none of us asked for it.' "

Jews witness and empathize with what the Germans have experienced, and a catharsis happens. They feel tremendous compassion, and from that, understanding is born. "The workshops create a double bind for people. By showing the humanity of the perpetrator, victims have to face the question, 'How can I hate this person and have compassion for him at the same time?' They have to resolve that conflict, and when they do, it's palpable in the room. It's the moment the Jews make the choice: I'm going with this feeling of compassion, and I'm putting these other feelings aside. Once they do that, they've cleared the emotional path to reconciliation."

Recognizing the Potential Perpetrator Within

After empathy has been established, another critical piece of the work remains: recognizing the potential perpetrator within. One of the ways Armand evokes this understanding is by pairing up the child of a survivor and the child of a perpetrator and asking them to take turns being master and slave.

Although not all workshop participants choose to participate in this exercise, it is profound for many who do. Liz Rosner, a Jewish child of survivors, recalls: "When I was a master with a German as my slave, I stood above her and had her crouch down below me. Anytime she tried to raise her head and look at me, I barked at her that she was not entitled to look at me.

"Dehumanizing her like that was emblematic of my power over her. I was keeping her in an animal state of shame and inferiority. It was really disturbing to feel my own capacity to be so oppressive and cruel. Yet that was very much at the heart of what Armand was trying to teach us—that Jews do not own the role of the victim, and the Germans do not own the role of oppressor. Tragically, these human potentials are in all of us, and the only way we are ever going to heal from the nightmare of the Holocaust is to recognize that. As long as Jews persist in seeing cruelty as a German characteristic, we are going to be capable of that kind of cruelty ourselves."

For Liz Rosner, feeling compassion for the Germans in the room was not as hard as recognizing her own potential for cruelty. "I *wanted* to see myself as compassionate. There's something noble in recognizing that all human beings suffer, but taking on the less appetizing part, that we, too, are capable of cruelty, was much more of a challenge.

"That doesn't mean I had to identify with evil in the extreme sense. You don't have to envision yourself as Eichmann. When you try to do that, you're going to bump up against a wall because it's too hard to see yourself as a pure monster. But all of us have mistreated human beings in our lives. And the Holocaust happened not because there were a few monsters, but because there were so many ordinary human beings willing to participate in a system that was designed by monsters. The crux of this work for me was that I had to recognize that evil is a continuum and that it was possible for me to locate myself somewhere on that continuum.

"As human beings we are capable of angelic behaviors and evil behaviors and that's as true for my enemy as it is for me. Integrating that reality—that we are all capable of the entire range of human behavior—increases our capacity to live in a peaceful world. I believe this is a path toward peace."

Integrating a History of Perpetration

People who do this work have the opportunity to transform the feelings they have inherited so that they are no longer imprisoned by them. The cycle of rage, shame, and guilt is broken. People feel less burdened and depressed, more able to manage difficult cross-cultural interactions in the world. Very deep bonds are forged.

The transformations that occur profoundly affect the participants, but their influence doesn't stop there. The work also provides social therapy for the larger community. As Armand explains, it ripples out, changing perceptions and providing a powerful model for dealing with racial injustice, cultural hatred, and genocide. "There's been no model in history of how to integrate a history of perpetration. When these things happen, people get entrenched in hatred and a desire for vengeance. There aren't models for how to hear each other, work through rage, or access goodwill when you still want revenge. No one has taught us how to reach out, to grieve, and to remember. Yet if we don't work through these deep hurts and tame the potential perpetrator in all of us, the human race is doomed to destruction. If we don't learn how to do this kind of healing, then conflicts such as Kosovo or East Timor will only escalate.

"Part of what we do is bring this work out into the public. We show people, 'This kind of healing *is* possible, and if Germans and Jews can do it, others can, too.' Right now, you might look at Serbs and Kosovars and say, 'Reconciliation would be impossible.' But we're saying it can be done. It is possible to move from being entrenched in hatred to being allies, and these are the emotional steps to do it."

THE ROAD FROM REVENGE TO COMPASSION: SIX STEPS THAT CAN CHANGE ENEMIES INTO ALLIES

As a drama therapist, Armand Volkas believes that the creative arts can help people express and master complex emotions. In his workshops for Jews and Germans who share a historical burden from the Holocaust, he has identified six stages of reconciliation.

1. **Breaking the taboo against speaking to each other.** There is an invisible barrier between children of survivors and children of perpetrators because speaking to the "enemy" is often perceived as a betrayal of the dead. Yet until these two groups engage in honest dialogue, they cannot begin to work through the layers of unresolved feelings they carry about the war and about each other.
2. **Humanizing each other through telling our stories.**

When children of survivors and children of perpetrators listen deeply to each other's stories and hear each other's pain, they begin to care about one another. In spite of their "hatred" for what their parents suffered (or did), these feelings of empathy and friendship become more powerful than the historical imperative to hate each other.

3. **Exploring and owning the potential perpetrator in all of us.** In order to reconcile, people need to acknowledge that, under extreme circumstances, we all have the capacity for cruelty. Accepting this truth levels the playing field: children of survivors can no longer insist that the perpetrator is "over there," and children of perpetrators no longer have to carry the burden of being tainted by an evil that runs in their blood.

4. **Moving deeply into the grief.** Grieving together is essential. People carry their parents' and grandparents' pain, and until that pain is grieved fully, the legacy continues to be passed on to the next generation.

5. **Creating rituals of remembrance.** As part of the workshops, children of survivors and children of perpetrators create commemorative rituals to publicly acknowledge the complex, difficult history they share.

6. **Making commitments to acts of creation or acts of service.** One way to master this kind of legacy is through creativity and service. Children of survivors and children of Nazis need to share their stories, to create poetry, art, and beauty. Or they need to channel their energy into service: working with Kosovo refugees, helping survivors of rape, or doing other work toward ending injustice.

This Work Is About the Future

Armand's work has opened hearts, changed minds, and broken seemingly insurmountable barriers. Because of that, it has also been controversial. While some Jews respect his vision and admire his courage, others have been furious at him. "There is such rage and desire for vengeance on the part of many Jews, even though the Holocaust is now a generation removed. I've had Jews almost spit on me for the work I do. When people say my work is a betrayal of those who died, I tell them, 'The Holocaust is passing into history. This work is about the future. We're going to have to continue to have relations with these people, and if we don't change this energy, it will come back to haunt us.' "

The Burning Fields

In 1995, Armand made a pilgrimage to Auschwitz. "I went and saw the block where my mother had been operated on. I visited the gas chambers. I walked around the camps. In Birkenau, I wandered around the place they call 'the burning fields.'

"At a certain point in the war, there were so many transports bringing in Jews that the gas chambers couldn't kill them fast enough. So they created these huge piles of bodies and burned them for weeks on end. What struck me wandering around the burning fields was the fact that they were alive with the most beautiful wildflowers that I've ever seen. I was struck by the way nature was able to transform such horror into a beautiful aesthetic. The spiritual reality of that motivates my work."*

Acts of Reconciliation: A Sharing of Poetry

Among the acts of reconciliation that have emerged from Armand's workshops are joint poetry readings by children of Holocaust survivors and children of perpetrators. The following poems, by Elizabeth Rosner and Hans Jorg Stahlschmidt, are examples of the body of work that has been created.

---

*Armand Volkas has worked with other polarized groups as well: Palestinians and Israelis, African-Americans and European-Americans, blacks and Jews, as well as members of the deaf and hearing cultures. He has also brought together Japanese, Chinese, and Koreans to work on healing their legacy from World War II. For information about his work, contact: The Acts of Reconciliation Project, P.O. Box 21467, Oakland, CA 94620-1367; e-mail: avolkas@aol.com.

SPEAKING TO ONE OF GERMANY'S SONS

by Elizabeth Rosner

This is not about apology:
what, after all, can possibly
be forgiven between us
when none of it and all of it
belongs here.

In the world where you and I
can face one another like this,
nothing visible to tell us apart,
ghosts hover at our shoulders
whispering in the voices of
our parents and the dead.

If you were a window
and I at the glass
tried to see through you,
wouldn't I be faced
with my own face,
myself in the glass
looking back and through
and beyond?

I'd see your ghosts there too,
in uniforms maybe with dogs
and maybe terrified,
maybe trying to shape
the word Why or even
No.

And if not, if your ghosts
have blood on their hands,
what can I say about that?

Did any of us ask
to be born into this place
or that one?
Could our fathers know
that we would come after them
trying to make our own mistakes
come out right?
Don't our mothers hope
that our sleep is sweet
and untroubled,
that our hands don't tremble
when we stretch them toward
one another?*

GERMANS AND JEWS
Holocaust Commemoration 1996

by Hans Jorg Stahlschmidt

As the sun has to sink and the moon
and all hope far below the horizon
our hearts have to be full of night first
and we have to feel the fear
before we can feel a timid love.

How can I not be heavy
when I am with you
like ancient miners we have to descend
into this dark quarry where bones sleep
restlessly and prayers and screams
are entombed in the earth.

---

*From Elizabeth Rosner's chapbook, *gravity*, Small Poetry Press, P.O. Box 5324, Concord, CA 94524; (925) 798-1411. Poem first published in the journal *Mosaic*. Reprinted by permission of the author.

We have to labor hard to make
the gray coal shine and to find our
faces in this broken stone
we have to be heavy first before we
can find the lightness of the morning rain
and be children again playing in a Bavarian
meadow or on the beach near Tel Aviv.

We have to trust the heaviness as
we trust the sun setting
as we trust falling asleep
as we trust the fever to cure
our sweating dreaming bodies.*

Compassion Moves Out into the World

By identifying the path by which enemies can find compassion for each other, Armand Volkas has given us a tool with great promise. Perceiving enemies as human makes our world safer. Rather than view the world through a lens of fear and negativity, we gain the capacity to choose a more optimistic point of view.

Desmond Tutu, winner of the Nobel Peace Prize and chairman of South Africa's Truth and Reconciliation Commission, spent many months listening to testimony about the atrocities committed under apartheid, but came away still believing in the importance of compassion. In a speech before the National Press Club on October 6, 1999, Tutu said:

> The commission made me realize yes, we have an incredible capacity for evil, but we also have an incredible capacity for good. We are remarkable people. . . . We are made for the transcendent. . . . We are made for gentleness, compassion, and caring. After peering into the abyss of evil, the paradox I come away

---

*Hans Jorg Stahlschmidt from *Wetlands*, Small Poetry Press, P.O. Box 5342, Concord, CA 94524; (925) 798-1411. Reprinted by permission of the author.

with is that we're on the eve of a new millennium. And the thing about us human beings is that we are good.

This perspective—that people are worthy of compassion—comes within our grasp when we heal sufficiently to know that a meaningful life is possible for us. As we reconcile more deeply with our own grief and imperfections, a broad and healing compassion can arise.

In his book *A Year to Live*, Stephen Levine expounds on this idea:

When the suffering has subsided around painful events sufficiently for us to comprehend what they have to teach us, then the past takes on a different meaning. We receive 'the gift within the wound,' the insight and strength, the appreciation of compassion that we need to heal so many other parts of us.*

As human beings, compassion is our birthright. As we regain our wholeness and soften our hearts, we can feel its transformative power in our lives.

---

*Stephen Levine, *A Year to Live* (New York: Bell Tower Books, 1997), p. 75.

PART FOUR

Making Amends

CHAPTER 8

Taking Responsibility: The Role of Humility and Accountability

Human beings love to be right. When a person is willing to give up being right, a whole world of possibilities opens up.

—PETE SALMANSOHN

Years ago, I was suffering through the death throes of a stormy, tumultuous love affair. It was midmorning on a Monday. I was struggling to focus on the work in front of me, but I couldn't. I was too obsessed with the latest injustice my lover had dealt me. I called my friend Barbara in distress and gave her a blow-by-blow of our latest fight. When I was done, she was quiet for a moment and then said, "You know, Laura. I hear how upset you are. Everything you're describing sounds terrible and unfair. I can see why you're angry. But there's one thing I need to tell you: being right is the loneliest place in the world."

Pride is one of the biggest impediments to reconciliation. When we keep a score sheet in relationships and only hit the ball when it is "in our court," we set up an impenetrable barrier between ourselves and other people. People who have been hurt by someone often say, "It was all my sister's fault. I'm not going to make the first move." Or, "It's Javier's turn to call me. I called him last time."

It is natural to want things to be fair; it is natural to want to be right. But reconciliation has very little to do with being right. It has everything to do with staying focused on the larger, overriding goal of mutual healing and reconnection. When our aim is to reconcile, and not to win, keeping score becomes unimportant. As author Charles Klein puts it, "Where love is strong, blame becomes very insignificant."*

The Price of Pride

Garrett Barry died last year at the age of eighty-seven. He was a retired railroad engineer, a deacon in the Baptist church, a husband, the father of seven, grandfather of twenty-one, great-grandfather of fifty-three, and great-great-grandfather of twelve. He was a man who took tremendous pleasure in family. He was famous for his storytelling, his skill at horseshoes, his excellent barbecue, and his deep bass voice, which filled the rafters of his church every Sunday. Garrett Barry was a good man, an honest man, a stubborn man. He was well loved by everybody, but it was hard for him ever to admit he was wrong.

Garrett died without meeting four of his grandchildren, eight of his great-grandchildren, and five of his great-great-grandchildren. When Garrett's second son, Walter, was seventeen and about to graduate from high school, he fell in love with a fellow senior, Ana, who came from a large Mexican-American family. Garrett and his wife, Emma, did not want their son marrying a Mexican, particularly a Catholic, and they did everything they could to force the couple apart. They forbade their son to date Ana. They yelled. They cajoled. They threatened. Two years later, when Walter was still dating Ana, Garrett told his son, "If you marry that girl, I'll never speak to you again."

Walter, driven to choose between his family and the girl he loved, married Ana. He moved in with her family, a mile away, and got a job in the local mill. He worked there for forty-five years, fathered four children, and never spoke to his father again. When they ran into each other at the hardware store, Garrett would turn away or look through

---

*Charles Klein, *How to Forgive When You Can't Forget*, p. 25.

his son as if he weren't there. Emma, whose heart was softer, secretly visited Walter and Ana, stealing a few moments when she was headed for the store or returning from a church social.

Later, when Walter and Ana had their first child, Emma took a stand against her husband, saying, "Nothing is going to keep me from my grandbabies." And nothing did. Every Thursday, for the rest of her life, she walked to Walter's house to have dinner with her son and his family. But neither Walter nor Ana, nor any of their children or grandchildren, ever set foot in Garrett's house again.

Years passed, times changed, and intermarriage became more common. Mixed-race couples were more accepted in the world. But Garrett never changed. For him, it was as though the boy who played the trumpet, ran a four-and-a-half-minute mile, and loved cherry pie was gone. For Garrett Barry, backing down was out of the question, saying he had been wrong, impossible. Garrett's stubbornness and pride cut him off from three generations of love. Then he grew old and died.

All of us have known Garretts in our life—people who let anger and pride keep them separated from the people they love. It is tragic for them and tragic for those they've shut out of their lives.

Acknowledging Your Own Weaknesses

When people are in a conflict that is strong enough to end a relationship, they are usually too busy blaming the other person to see their own behavior objectively. As relationships become increasingly polarized, there are fewer opportunities to say, "Maybe in this way, I was wrong." Acknowledging mistakes becomes a sign of weakness, rather than a sign of strength and maturity.

When relationships reach the breaking point, the predominant feelings are usually self-righteousness, outrage, and hurt: "How could she do this to me!" "I can't believe he . . . ," or "I'm not going to let him get away with this!" These are the intense feelings that propel people to say, "That's it! This is the end." They are also the feelings that we must overcome to achieve reconciliation.

Rather than blame the other person for the failure of the relationship, we might ask ourselves, "What could I have done differently?" "How have I contributed to this impasse?" "How am I still being rigid, unyielding, or judgmental?" The answers to these questions can help us ascertain the ways we may be responsible, at least in part, for where things stand.

Taking Stock, Looking Within

When we honestly inventory our own intentions, actions, and motives, we sometimes realize that we behaved honorably and did the best we could under the circumstances. Other times, our self-assessment leads us to face painful faults. Sometimes the mistakes we made have less to do with what we did at the time of an estrangement (where perhaps the other person *was* more at fault) and more to do with how we have responded since then. That was the case for Celia Sommer in her estrangement from her sister.

Celia Sommer: Letting Go of Being Wronged

I set myself up as this poster girl for having a homophobic sister and I milked it for all it was worth.

—CELIA SOMMER

Celia Sommer and her sister, Ellen Fine, were not particularly close growing up, and as they got older, their choices in life drew them farther apart. Ellen, the older sister, moved to Israel for seven years, then returned to the United States and became an Orthodox Jew. Celia, who is five years younger, came out as a lesbian.

The big rift between the sisters happened at a Chanukah party at Ellen's house, when Celia was twenty-four. Celia remembers it this way: "Right in the middle of the party, I went up to Ellen and said, 'I want you to accept me for who I am.'

"She said, 'I love you, but I don't accept you.'

"I said, 'How can you love me and not accept me? If you do

that, you do not love all of me, because who I am is a woman who loves women.'

"Ellen replied, 'But I can't accept that about you. If you were homeless and had nowhere to stay, I could not in good conscience have you and your partner sleep in my house.'

"My voice really rose at that point. 'If we were homeless, you wouldn't let us stay here? You wouldn't let your own sister sleep in your house? What kind of religion is that?' We started screaming at each other, and my mother came over to quiet us down. I turned to Ellen and said, 'Well, I won't stay in your house. I am who I am!' Then I went out to my car and sobbed for the rest of the party."

For more than a decade, the sisters remained stuck at this impasse. They refused to speak and avoided each other at family gatherings. During these years, Ellen gave birth to four sons and Celia met her life partner, Lena. Celia loved her nephews dearly but was only allowed to see them on her sister's terms. "I wanted my nephews to come and stay with us, but my sister's husband said they couldn't. They saw our community as a real Sodom and Gomorrah."

Children Create a Common Ground

Things softened when Celia got pregnant with her son, David. Celia recalls, "Even before he was born, Ellen viewed him as a potential cousin to her sons. That helped open her heart to me."

Celia was seven months pregnant when one her nephews was bar mitzvahed. In a gesture of reconciliation, Ellen invited both Celia and Lena. "It was a big step for her. I don't think it was easy. Ellen didn't introduce us to her friends, but there I was in an Orthodox synagogue, visibly pregnant with no husband."

When David was four months old, Celia brought him to visit his aunt, and Celia experienced a whole new side of her sister. "My sister is a bit of a strident intellectual, but she loves babies and is a wonderful mother. She was so tender and sweet to David right from the start. She embraced him as her nephew without reservation. I often think God gave me a son partly so I could bond with my sister."

Acknowledging My Part in the Estrangement

"I began to realize that I was only going to have one sister in my life, and that started to mean something to me. I started feeling a lot of love for Ellen, and I found myself letting go of the old resentment. I also began to recognize my part in our estrangement—holding on to what Ellen had said fifteen years before. For me, the bottom line in our relationship was always 'I'm gay, and my sister wouldn't let me sleep in her house if I was homeless.' I allowed that one sentence to become a wall separating us. I used it as fuel to see her as wrong and bad, to justify pushing her away.

"Never once in all those years did I ask Ellen, 'Did I hear you right?' 'Was that just something rhetorical you said?' 'Have you changed your mind about that?' 'Do you still feel that Lena and I couldn't stay in your house if we were homeless?' Instead, I held the injury up like a flag.

"Once I spoke at a Jewish lesbian conference about how hard it was for me to reconcile being Jewish with the fact that I had a sister whose Judaism didn't extend to me. I got a lot of attention for being a victim of my sister's prejudice and insensitivity. But talking about it like that ensured that that one interaction remained the defining moment of our relationship. That was my part in our estrangement. She shouldn't have said it, but I shouldn't have reveled in it, either.

"Two summers ago, Ellen allowed one of her boys to spend a weekend with us. This past summer, Ellen and her husband came and slept in our house. And just recently, I e-mailed Ellen to tell her that Lena and I had given each other rings, and that at some point we wanted to have a reception. I asked if she'd come, but I also gave her an out. I said, 'If you can't come or don't want to come, that would be totally fine with me.' As I typed those words, I realized that it really would be okay if she didn't come. Ellen wrote back and said that if we had the reception in the summer, they'd be happy to come. That felt like an incredible breakthrough.

"I haven't forgotten those words Ellen once said, but they're no longer in the foreground. They're part of our history, but I now feel big enough to say, 'Ellen said a stupid, objectionable thing that caused a deep hurt,' and still remember that she loves my son, calls when I'm sick, and sends me great books to read.

"What happened between us has its place on a much bigger canvas, and it would be wrong of me to keep putting it in the center. It's now out on the border of our relationship, and keeping it there opens up the space for healing between us. The injury can't be undone, but it's in the past. Now we get to create a new history."

There's an old saying, "Temper gets you into trouble. Pride is what keeps you there." When we insist on being right, all we get is a lonely seat on the top of the heap. But when we admit our flaws and have compassion for our mistakes, we join the imperfect human race. Ultimately, it is not by insisting that we are right, but rather in admitting that we were wrong, that we gain sustenance, reclaim our dignity, and, when the conditions are right, repair estranged relationships.

Learning to Apologize

Apologies are a powerful tool in relationships. A sincere apology can be healing for the person making the apology, as well as for the person receiving it. As author Stephen Levine once said, "Amends feed the heart and quiet the mind."

Yet it's not easy to apologize. I know there have been times for me when having to say "I was wrong" felt like a death sentence—moments an apology stayed stuck in my throat, not because I did not want to say it but because I did not know how to get it out. Like many people, I find it easier to be humble in retrospect than in the moment.

Even when we do manage to apologize, our apologies are often insincere or inadequate. We apologize for the wrong things or in the wrong way, simultaneously pointing our finger at the other person ("But you did this!") while we take responsibility for our own misdeeds. Other times, we use apologies to manipulate the other person into giving us something we want, whether it be silence, cooperation, or forgiveness.

A genuine apology does not require anything in return. It stands alone, on its own merit, with no strings attached. Genuine apologies are clean and simple; they are unencumbered by rationalizations or self-defense. Elizabeth Menkin, whose family met with the drunk driver who killed her sister, said, "I've grown in terms of my understanding of what makes an apology genuine. It's making an apology without using the same breath to make an excuse."

The Role of Remorse and Respect

Although it is appropriate for remorse to accompany an apology, our regrets should not speak so loudly that they require the person receiving the apology to take care of us. As the person who is apologizing, we should be able to stand firm on our own feet, without needing anything from the other person—and that includes caretaking comments like, "It's okay," "Don't worry," or "There, there, I forgive you."

Conversely, when we're the person who has been wronged, we may believe it would be satisfying for the other person to grovel in front of us, but being the recipient of someone else's guilt and misery is usually more of a burden than a relief. One woman, long estranged from her brother, recalls:

> I always held out the hope that my brother would see how he'd wronged me and come back with his tail between his legs. I thought that would make me feel better, but when he did come to me groveling and beating himself up, it didn't feel good at all. What I realized was that I could never feel truly good when someone else was feeling humiliated and ashamed. There's no way that could feel like a victory.

Even if we hate what someone has done to us or have been waiting a long time for an apology, the other person is still a vulnerable human being who is taking the risk to be accountable. Rather than further chastise him or her ("Oh yeah, and you *also* did this!" or, "You're *always* that way!"), it is usually better to respond with simple acknowledgment: "Thank you, I appreciate that." Then, or at a later time, we can delve into the subject further if it seems appropriate.

Being gracious in the moment does not mean we'll never get another opportunity to talk about how badly we were hurt; it just means that when someone finally comes forth with an apology, it is not the best time to go on the offensive. Attacking during an apology doesn't lead to reconciliation. Unless both people walk away from the encounter with their dignity intact, there will be little basis on which to rebuild trust.

It may be helpful to remember that in most estrangements, both people have hurt each other, and both have things to apologize for. Recognizing this may make it easier to approach a particular "moment of reckoning" with compassion. Although we may be the person receiving the apology this time, next time we may be the one having to apologize.

From Apology to Action

Saying the words—"I'm sorry," "I regret what I did," "I can see how that affected you"—is part of an apology. But words alone are not enough. For an apology to have meaning, it must be accompanied by a consistent change in behavior. When one person in a relationship consistently talks too much, shows up late, breaks promises, fails to listen, or disregards another person's feelings, simply saying "I'm sorry" is not enough. The person who is apologizing needs to learn to hold his or her tongue, arrive on time, keep promises, listen, and demonstrate kindness. He or she doesn't have to do these things perfectly or be transformed overnight, but needs to work at them consistently and sincerely. Without genuine efforts to change, apologies remain hollow.

Pete Salmansohn, a fifty-one-year-old environmental educator who lives in Maine, learned the value of putting an apology into action in his relationship with his father.

Pete Salmansohn:
Choosing to Get Close Again

The quicker you clean up your past, the more possibility and freedom you have to do something new and meaningful in your life.

—PETE SALMANSOHN

"Growing up, I really loved my father. He coached baseball, was a Cub Scout leader, and took us camping and fishing. He was a good dad, and I basically had a good childhood. But as I got older, we drifted apart. I could never really put my finger on why we were estranged, but my father didn't accept my values. It was the late sixties. I was a Vista volunteer. I was against the war in Vietnam. I was in SDS. My father had lived through the depression and been dirt poor. His vision of what would be good for me was a civil service job.

"As I moved into my twenties, my dad and I were increasingly on different wavelengths. I stopped respecting him. I saw him as narrow-minded and penny-pinching. I felt angry and annoyed with him most of the time; our relationship was an argument waiting to happen.

"For twenty years, we were basically stalemated. It bothered me that I didn't like my father, and I worked on it in therapy for years, but therapy never changed anything. I had erected a wall between us.

"When I was forty-one, I signed up to take a seminar designed to help people gain more freedom in their lives. At the end of the second day, the leader was hammering us about how important it was to make peace with our parents. He was saying things like, 'This is costing you your life.'

"What he said really clicked for me. I decided to call my father and do my part in tearing down the wall.

"It was twenty to twelve on a Saturday night. I went out to the lobby and dialed my father's number. I didn't know if he'd be awake or asleep.

"He answered the phone, and I said, 'Pop, I just want to tell you a few things.' I wasn't sure what I was going to say, but my whole body was shaking, my heart was pumping fast, and I was sweating. A huge emotional dam was about to burst.

"I said, 'I want to ask you to forgive me for making you wrong all these years. I've been holding all of these resentments and criticisms against you, all of which I've made up in my head.'

"I started to cry. I told my father I loved him and that I wanted to have a great relationship with him. I said I wanted to get rid of the past. I began sobbing. At that moment, I felt an incredible amount of love for my father.

"My father was wonderful. He listened carefully. At one point, he said, 'Whatever this is you're doing, I approve.' I laughed with joy. Then he told me he loved me. That wasn't something that was ever said much in our family, but from that moment on, saying 'I love you' became much easier.

"I said good-bye to my father and hung up the phone. Then I went out into the parking lot. It was November in New England. It was after midnight. It was dark and cold. As I walked outside, I was still crying, and I felt this empty space open up in my chest, right below my breastbone, all the way down to my stomach. It was very visceral.

"My relationship with my father totally changed from then on. I saw that he was a guy like everybody else—afraid, fumbling his way through life, and doing the best he could. I was able to recognize that he was a person with love in his heart and fear about expressing it. I could see that his insecurities didn't always lead him to make the best decisions. I saw all of that, but I wasn't judging him anymore. Instead, I was able to say, 'We're all in the same boat. Some of us do better than others.'

"During the last six years of my father's life, I saw him more, and I continued to tell him I loved him. I didn't hold back on affection, and in return, I got a big piece of my life back.

"When my father died, I was sad, but there was nothing

unexpressed. If I hadn't had those six years with him, I think I would have felt horrible. But as it was, I was at peace with my father's death.

"I completely subscribe to the philosophy of making peace with your past so it doesn't limit your present life. Since I did that with my father, I've cleaned up almost all of my significant relationships—with my brother, my mother, and a bunch of my friends. It's the most valuable thing I've done in my adult life."

The Accountability Continuum

The role humility plays in a reconciliation varies depending on the nature of the estrangement. When both people have played a role in creating the rift, they *both* need to acknowledge their part in what went wrong. Estrangements based on misunderstanding, judgment, or a stubborn refusal to say "I'm sorry" or "I was wrong" can often be remedied by one or both people relinquishing their pride.

In these instances, "who started it" or "who was the most wrong" does not matter. Getting bogged down in that kind of debate only reinforces feelings of estrangement. What's necessary instead is humility and an attitude of generosity toward the other person. The more quickly (and sincerely) both people admit their mistakes—both internally and to each other—the more favorable their reconciliation will be.

However, when estrangements are rooted in deeper violations, in which one person has committed a terrible wrong against another, the dynamics are different. The victim of interpersonal violence such as incest, abandonment, or battering does not owe the perpetrator anything and does not need to meet the perpetrator halfway. Although we all make mistakes, people who have been on the receiving end of gross mistreatment are not required to cultivate humility in order to mend relationships with the people who have hurt them. Rather, they need to build the courage, strength, and determination necessary to heal and reclaim their lives. Once that arduous task has been achieved, it can be beneficial to nurture the kind of receptivity that would allow a sincere apology from the person who wronged them. But even then, they are not required to welcome that person back into their lives. As my partner, Karyn, once remarked, "Just because someone says they're sorry doesn't make them a hero."

Former perpetrators face a very different task. They need to nurture not only humility but accountability as well—the willingness to own their mistakes, ensure that they will not be repeated, and do all they can to make amends for the hurts they have inflicted. They need to do this not just for the sake of repairing the relationship but also in order to rebuild their own dignity, self-respect, and, if possible, place of worth in the community.

The Courage to Admit a Wrong

Taking responsibility for deeply hurting another human being takes tremendous courage. Being accountable for violent, abusive behavior means curtailing behaviors that may have been rewarding, habitual, or previously unquestioned, and opening the door to ways we may have been violated ourselves. It means shifting the blame to our own shoulders, while giving up our right to rationalize, minimize, or deny our transgressions. Many people don't want to make that leap; they would rather hide behind a wall of control, anger, and intimidation.

It takes great strength to admit that we have perpetrated a great wrong. Franklin Carter found that strength when he took responsibility for the violence he had used to dominate the women in his life.

Franklin Carter: A Violent Man Changes His Life

> *I've had to reconcile with all the women I've been around. To all the ones I've been able to find, I've made overtures of reconciliation. I don't expect to ever be forgiven for the stuff I did to them; I don't expect to ever regain my humanness in their eyes, but I do expect that I will never treat anyone that way again.*
>
> —FRANKLIN CARTER, FORMER BATTERER

"I was the youngest of four children who grew up in a family where we went to church and did all the *Leave It to Beaver* stuff, except we were black. I grew up in the rural South with cows, chickens, and pigs. I drank well water until I was thirteen. We were poor, but we didn't know it because everyone around us was poor, too.

"The big change took place in my family during the years my parents were getting divorced. It was an ugly situation. My father, who was a pillar of the community, battered my mother until we got big enough to stop him.

"Once when I was eight, my father called me outside and showed me a .38 caliber bullet. It was one of those old soft lead bullets. On the head of the bullet was carved B. L. My mother's name was Betty Lou. I didn't know what to think."

How the Hell Am I Going to Raise This Child?

Franklin had his first girlfriend at sixteen. "Audre and I had sex every Friday. We used Emco spermicide religiously, but when I was seventeen, she got pregnant. My teachers offered to pay for an abortion, but Audre would hear nothing of it. I'd just been accepted at Yale, but because of the pregnancy, I couldn't go. I ended up going to a local college instead.

"I turned eighteen right before my daughter, Dinah, was born. Her birth left an indelible impression on me because they wouldn't let me in the birthing room. I sat in the waiting room for thirteen hours. They treated me like a nonperson. Finally, someone came out and said, 'You got a little girl.' I went to the nursery, and the nurse held up this really long, red baby. I remember thinking, 'How the hell am I going to raise this child when I don't know what I'm doing myself?' That's when I started feeling sorry for myself and blaming women for getting knocked up.

"After Dinah was born, I went to college from nine to one and worked in a machine shop from midnight until seven in the morning. It was 1970, and Audre and I decided to get married. By November of that year, we had a son."

I Blamed Her for Everything

When Franklin first dated Audre, he always treated her with respect, but over time that started to change. "I remember the first incident of violence in that relationship. I was studying for an exam. Audre wanted attention from me, and I didn't want to give it to her. I was tired. I wanted her to leave me alone. There was a shouting match, and I easily outshouted her. It was the beginning of a long process of threats and intimidation.

"In my junior year, I couldn't handle working and going to school, so I dropped out. Right then, they started laying off at the machine shop, and I lost my job. Audre and I both did whatever we could to keep food on the table and a roof over our heads. Our apartment cost sixty bucks a month, and it was a rathole. We were barely making it, and I blamed Audre for not getting the bills paid. One day she came home from work and we had a fight, and I shoved her hard in the chest. At the time, I was convinced that I wasn't doing anything wrong; I believed it was all her fault.

"Most of my abuse of Audre was psychological. I never gave her validation or admiration. Instead, I gave her what I call 'the treatment.' I wouldn't speak to her. I refused to relate to her as a person. But coming from where she came from, it didn't seem so horrible. Her old man beat everybody's butt. To her, that was just life.

"Audre and I divorced in 1971. I got custody of the children on the grounds that she was unfit. Sexism being what it was then, if a man asked for his children, he got them. The whole system was stacked in my favor.

"At the time, I had a good job. I was making lots of money. I got myself a bachelor pad and dated heavily. I had so many people helping me with the children that I had the best of both worlds. I had custody, but anytime I needed a baby-sitter, I had one. Having the kids was a great calling card for dating women, because when they found out you had custody of your children, you had an instant halo, and I used that to get sex."

I Had Lots of Ways to Destroy Her

In 1977 Franklin remarried, and pretty soon he started abusing his new wife as well. "I was doing the same kind of stuff. I ignored Natalie, put her down, and screamed at her. Natalie and I had three children together. I told her if she left me that I'd take the kids away from her. I controlled the cash and could stop the flow of the money real quick. I ran everything with an iron fist; I was a real Captain Bligh. We also had physical confrontations; I pulled a gun on her once. I had lots of ways to destroy her.

"I hadn't changed one bit. I could have had fifty girlfriends or fifty wives. It would have happened the same old way.

"Finally, after ten years, Natalie couldn't take it anymore. She went to a lawyer and had me removed from the home. This time, she was the one who got custody.

"When that marriage ended, I started to do some serious thinking. I realized that I'd found something wrong with every woman I had ever been with—and I never found nothing wrong with me. When you start getting up into the teens on relationships with women, whether they're casual, short, or long, you start thinking, 'If these things keep ending, there's one common factor here and I'm it.'

"Still, I was going from one relationship to another. Finally, I met Sharon. Our relationship was platonic for many years. When it finally became romantic, Sharon was the one who asked me to marry her. After thinking about it for a few months, I said yes. She and I had a child together. Fifteen years later, we're still together.

"There's never been any abuse in our relationship. Part of that was maturation on my part, knowing deep down inside that that kind of behavior doesn't work. I knew that the way I'd been was so destructive, it was indescribable, and I didn't want to act that way anymore. The other thing that helped was that Sharon was a very empowered woman who would never be dependent on anybody."

Write Down Your Worst Incident with a Woman

"When Sharon and I got together, I was looking for a new place to volunteer. So I picked up the phone book, and the page it opened up to was No More Violence. It was one of those serendipitous moments.

"I called to volunteer. Every couple of months, they'd call me to stuff envelopes. Usually everybody goes crazy over black, male volunteers but they weren't going crazy over me. That intrigued me. Then they let me come to some of the gigs they were doing. They were talking about homophobia and sexism; I didn't know what the hell they meant.

"At that same time, I decided to go to graduate school and study counseling. A lot of folks go into counseling because they're messed up; that was certainly the case with me.

"When I finished my degree, I joined the yearlong internship program at No More Violence. The first thing I had to do was take their batterer's intervention class. It ran for thirty-six weeks, and I had to attend, not as an intern but just like any other man in the class. The first day, we had to do something called a 'New Man Check-in,' where you write down your worst incident with a woman. The most recent woman I'd been abusive to had been Natalie so I wrote down some of the stuff I'd done to her. Then I had to read it out loud.

"The first time I wrote my New Man Check-in, I left so much out that the other men in the room told me it was not acceptable. They were in the same boat I was in, and they knew I was bullshitting. They said, 'That ain't gonna float, brother.'

"It was the first time I'd ever been confronted about my behavior toward women by other men, and I didn't like it one bit. But I made my revised New Man Check-in longer and more detailed. They told me to keep working on it. They made me rewrite it five times."

For Franklin, the internship was excruciating. "Here I was in a room where men were not going to pat me on the back just because I'd worked and kept the children. They pointed out to me that I had an agenda when I got the children, and it wasn't just their safety—it was bolstering my ego. I hated hearing that, but I kept going back. Part of it was my man thing: 'There ain't nobody gonna wash me out of nothing. I'm gonna finish what I start.' Some of it was a real need deep down inside of my gut: 'I need to know how to stop hurting people.'

Once I got past the shucking and jiving and really started doing the work, I began to see how the battering paradigm is central to many of the maladies we suffer in society today. I started to recognize the part I'd played in it, and the part I could play in its abatement as well.

"In the last weeks of the program, I started asking myself, 'What do I want to do with this material? I've got all this knowledge and all these emotions; I need to do something with it.' Ultimately, I decided to work for No More Violence. I'm still a counselor there today."

We Had to Bring Our Sons to Class

"At the very end of the internship program, I had the opportunity to read my New Man Check-in to my fifteen-year-old son Jerrell. It was one of the requirements of the program. If we had sons, we had to bring them to class. Some of the other men in class refused because they didn't want their sons to know the horrible things they'd done to their mothers. But I wanted to illustrate to Jerrell that he didn't have to follow in my footsteps.

"I didn't prepare him ahead of time because there was no way to soften the blow. I just sat there and read it to him. It was really, really tough. I cried through it, and the other men in class were crying, too. Jerrell hugged me and cried as well. We've talked about it many times since then."

It Was the Difference in Memory Between the Guards and the Prisoners

As an organization, No More Violence doesn't encourage men to apologize to the women they have battered. Franklin explains why: "The theory is this: if I hurt someone and then say 'I'm sorry,' it really doesn't mean anything. Men who batter women have been apologizing for years, and then they turn around and do the same old thing again. I knew I was capable of doing that as well. What I needed to do was change my actions and be consistent in those changes so that when I had the chance to talk to a former spouse I could treat her differently."

Franklin has had those opportunities with Natalie, with whom he still shares parenting. "Natalie and I always had a relationship because of the children. I always paid her child support. Then, eight years ago, when she was having some financial trouble, she asked Sharon and me to take the children. As a result, I started seeing Natalie every two or three days.

"Our relationship was always very strained. Then three years ago, she came over and I read her my New Man Check-in. She cried while I read it, and then she started telling me about all of the stuff that I hadn't put in there. Her memory of what had happened was so different than mine, I was flabbergasted. And she was shocked to hear my version because it was so inaccurate. It was the difference in memory between the guards and the prisoners. The guard remembers, 'I whacked him one time,' and the prisoner remembers, 'This guy beat me half to death.'

"That was a tough conversation, but it was a turning point for us. It was like someone putting a fan on in a room that's full of smoke. Things started to clear up. After that, I felt like I could talk to Natalie about what I was really feeling, and she started feeling safer with me."

In addition to owning up to what he did and changing his behavior in the present, Franklin has found other ways to compensate Natalie for the abuse she suffered at his hands. "I'm a firm believer in restitution. When you hurt people, you should pay them. That's what our whole legal system is about. I can't change Natalie's life, but when there's an opportunity for me to assist her, I'm right there. Right now, she's saving up to buy her freestanding home. Because the place she was in was overcharging her, Sharon and I offered to rent her a vacant condo we owned at a reduced rent. It's larger and nicer than where she was before, and I feel like that's part of my restitution. When I reach retirement and my investments mature, I will pay her from that, too."

We Hugged Each Other and Talked

Franklin has not had as many opportunities to reconcile with his first wife, Audre, but he has had some. "After I got custody of the children, I didn't see Audre for ten years. She never saw the kids or called them. It was hard for her to be around the guy who had her children because of the stigma society placed on her for 'losing her children.' Of course, she didn't lose them at all; I took them away.

"The first time I saw Audre was by chance at a big sporting event. It was good to see her. We hugged each other and talked about how everybody was doing. Then the discussion went deeper. She said she was sorry she hadn't come to see the children. I said, 'I'm sorry, too,' and claimed some of my abuse. It was awkward because she said, 'It wasn't none of your fault. I just messed up.' I insisted, 'No, that's not what happened.'

"It's hard to explain to women who live in this culture that this stuff isn't their fault. It's very much like talking to a slave who says, 'My master treats me real well. He only beats me once a month.' Audre had no power in that relationship, and I had all the institutions backing me up. She didn't stand a chance. Her fathers and her brothers had beaten her; then I came along with more of the same.

"After that chance meeting, Audre and I stayed in touch. Our children are grown, and they take good care of her now. Recently, our oldest boy gave me a birthday party, and once again, Audre and I talked about issues between us. I can honestly say I think she's moved on. I know I have."

Breaking the Generational Cycle

The changes Franklin has gone through since he first walked into No More Violence have freed him. "I don't have to act out that man role anymore. I don't have to be in charge. The only person I have to be in control of is me, and I can definitely do that. It makes life a lot easier for me—and there are definitely rewards. Just recently, my son Jerrell was in a relationship where he got dumped. And he did not attack this young lady; he did not call her a bitch or a whore. He came to my room and said, 'Dad, I've got to talk to you.' So we sat down, and we talked about women and relationships. It was a great conversation. It was worth everything—to see him not do what I would have done when I was nineteen."

The Healing Power of Accountability

When one person finds the courage to be accountable for a great wrong, it can be incredibly significant for the person who was hurt. Reconciliations often leap forward when the truth is finally acknowledged—particularly if the acknowledgment comes without excuses or expectations. Sasha remembers the moment her father owned up to a lifetime of cruelty.

My father was eighty-four when he heard that I had cancer. He called in tears saying he hadn't been able to sleep because he was scared that I'd die and that he'd be punished for having treated me so badly. He said, "I know I have been a brute and a bully to you all through your life. I am sorry for being so horrible to you, for ruining your youth. Please forgive me."

When he apologized, my whole body relaxed. I said to him, "That's all I ever wanted—for you to take responsibility for what you did to me." Then I felt my heart open, and I let it all go. That moment of acknowledgment transformed our whole relationship.

Unfortunately, such acknowledgments are rare. Seventy-two-year-old Miriam Gladys made amends to her children for her rage when they were small, but says that her level of accountability is unusual among her peers.

> I've seen lots of people in my generation excuse their own abusive behavior by saying, "*Everybody* did that to their kids. You don't have to apologize for *that*." I think the shame we feel about what we did to our kids can be so horrendous that we close ourselves off and act as if it was another time and that we were different people, and therefore, what we did has nothing to do with us. We refuse to acknowledge our regrets because that would mean taking responsibility for what we did.

Yet without accountability, there is only so far reconciliation can go. Stephan, whose father beat him as a child, wishes they could reconcile but says it is impossible. "My father's never admitted anything. Until he owns up to what he did, how can I trust him again?"

Accountability Leads to Self-Respect

When perpetrators take responsibility for what they have done, it doesn't guarantee reconciliation, but their accountability gives them back something else they desperately need—a sense of self-respect. Without that, offenders cannot transform their histories of violence and manipulation. Until they face their own grief and pain, acknowledge their wrongs, and take steps to redeem themselves, they stay mired in the shame, guilt, and isolation that lead to repeat violations. While perpetrators cannot control the receptivity of the people they have hurt, it is possible for them to reconcile within themselves, to be accountable for what they have done, and to slowly work their way back into the human community.

CHAPTER 9

The Question of Forgiveness

I feel like forgiveness is a course in which I've only taken the first couple of classes and it runs for two semesters.

—ELIZABETH MENKIN

There is a tremendous amount of confusion in our culture right now over the concept of forgiveness. Forgiveness has expanded beyond its traditional place in religious circles; it has penetrated popular culture and become the subject of talk shows, pop psychology books, and hundreds of articles in the mainstream press.

Religious advocates of forgiveness believe it is our moral duty to forgive; they say forgiveness is necessary for salvation. Secular supporters of forgiveness claim it reduces blood pressure, lowers the risk of heart attack, and boosts self-esteem. Forgiveness has been hailed as a panacea for healing troubled psyches, reuniting estranged families, rebuilding divided communities, and strengthening our national character. Yet despite these claims of grandeur, exactly what is meant by "forgiveness" remains unclear.

The words "reconciliation," "forgiveness," "compassion," and "acceptance" are often used interchangeably, when in fact they are not at all synonymous. People who experience forgiveness invariably feel compassion and acceptance, but don't always choose to reconcile. And people who reconcile experience compassion and acceptance, but don't necessarily forgive.

Certainly, it is necessary to move beyond rage and bitterness to achieve reconciliation, but forgiveness is not the only way to accomplish such healing. As one woman told me, "I don't forgive my father for what he did. I'm just choosing to be around him anyway."

This chapter focuses primarily on forgiveness after grievous wrongs have been committed—incest, vehicular homicide, murder, and genocide—because forgiveness in these circumstances is so difficult to achieve. If people can forgive in such extreme circumstances, it is definitely possible to do so with life's smaller trespasses.

Forgiveness as Something You Work At

There are many divergent ideas about forgiveness, many of which are diametrically opposed. One of the most basic dichotomies is that forgiveness is something we work to achieve, and conversely, that forgiveness is a spiritual gift. The first school of thought suggests that we can attain forgiveness through intention, effort, or prayer.

In her book *Forgiving and Not Forgiving*, Jeanne Safer notes, "Genuine forgiveness demands every mental, moral and spiritual resource you have. . . . Nobody forgives spontaneously; victims must make an effort to move beyond their inevitable shock, rage, grief and desire for revenge."*

Beverly Flanigan, in *Forgiving the Unforgivable*, also describes forgiveness as something to be achieved. "Forgiveness is the accomplishment of mastery over a wound. It is the process through which an injured person first fights off, then embraces, then conquers a situation that has nearly destroyed him." †

Both of these definitions describe a process similar to the one I have

---

*Jeanne Safer, *Forgiving and Not Forgiving* (New York: Avon Books, 1999), p. 43. Reprinted by permission of HarperCollins Publishers, Inc.

---

†Beverly Flanigan, *Forgiving the Unforgivable* (New York: Macmillan, 1992), p. 71.

outlined as necessary for reconciliation; our terminology is different, but the journey we describe is much the same.

People who achieve forgiveness through their own efforts often characterize it as a spiritual pilgrimage. Letty says forgiving her friend Robin was very much an inward journey.

> During the three years I didn't speak to Robin, I meditated every day on my desire to forgive her. Initially, all that came up in my meditation were feelings of rage and betrayal, but over time, feelings of empathy, caring, and forgiveness crept in. If I hadn't made a commitment to that daily meditation practice, I don't think we'd be friends today.

Azim Khamisa, who forgave the boy who murdered his son, worked at forgiveness through meditation and prayer.

> Forgiveness is the place where preparation meets grace. You can't make it happen, but if you continuously pray for it and prepare for it, it will sprout in you and grow into a powerful force. It's a very inward journey. You ask for the strength to forgive. You dig deep for it, and there comes a time when it's the right thing to do. You get up one morning not able to forgive, and the next morning, you're ready. When forgiveness happens to you, you'll know. It's like releasing an albatross from around your neck.

For some people, forgiveness happens incrementally. Glenda, whose ex-husband controlled their relationship with his neediness and anger, recalls:

> For years, I've been working at forgiving my ex-husband, but I don't expect miracles. I'm pleased if I feel a little less resentment than I used to, a little more forgiving than I used to feel. It's like wearing one of those miner's hats. It only lights up the path a little way into the cave, but if you follow the light, it lights up more of the ground in front of you, and then you can take a few more steps. Forgiveness is like that for me.

Forgiveness as a Spiritual Gift

The counterpoint to the "you have to work at it" school of thought defines forgiveness as an emotion that cannot be generated, forced, or controlled, but which arises spontaneously from within. Supporters of this perspective often compare forgiveness to love.

Although love arises from the deepest part of us, we cannot *make* ourselves feel love; we cannot *will* our hearts to open. People who view forgiveness as a spiritual gift say it works much the same way, that when the conditions are right, the blessings of forgiveness will spontaneously appear.

Elizabeth Menkin, whose sister was killed by a drunk driver, believes "trying to forgive" can actually impede the healing process: "Forgiveness is a by-product of doing this work. It has to stay in your peripheral vision, because as soon as you focus on it, it's like a magnifying glass in the sunshine—it'll burn a hole right through the process."

Donna Jenson, who was raped by her father, believes forgiveness happens spontaneously when someone takes responsibility for his or her wrongdoing. She makes a distinction between forgiveness and acceptance—the place of compassion she reaches when she works hard to change her emotional landscape. Donna's line of demarcation has to do with effort.

> Coming to acceptance around my father was a mighty task that required blood, sweat, and tears. I had to open my mind to the fact I was an incest survivor because my father had been an abuse survivor. I had to allow myself to think about that; I had to consciously work at it.
>
> In my experience, forgiveness is very different. It's a palpable feeling I get when someone takes responsibility for the harm they've caused me—large or small. In their moment of contrition, forgiveness arises. A feeling of internal cleansing washes over me; I can feel it move through my body, taking with it any remaining anger or resentment. Everything lifts and I feel lighter, and that's not something I've ever had to work at.

In Donna's model, forgiveness and contrition go hand in hand. This leads us to a second dichotomy that exists around forgiveness: people who believe forgiveness must be earned and those who believe it can be granted unilaterally.

Forgiveness as Something That Requires Accountability

This school of thought inextricably links forgiveness with account-ability. The basic premise is this: You can't forgive someone who denies that you were injured or who fails to take responsibility for having hurt you. Until a wrong has been acknowledged, and there has been remorse and restitution on the part of the wrongdoer, forgiveness cannot be granted. In other words, forgiveness without accountability has no teeth.

Richard Hoffman, author of *Half the House*, expresses this point of view succinctly.

> There's this weird Hollywood idea that all relationships should have a happy ending—that everyone should forgive everyone in the final scene. But if a man burns down my house, I don't owe him forgiveness; he owes me a house. No one ever talks about what the person who perpetrated the crime owes. It's always the victim who owes forgiveness these days, and that's ridiculous.
>
> Real forgiveness restores the moral fabric of a community and a family. It says, "We are all accountable to each other. We owe each other a certain kind of treatment, and when someone violates those standards, the damage needs to be repaired."
>
> If someone cuts a net and I say, "There's a hole in the net," and the other person says, "Oh yeah, that's my fault. I'm sorry," that's great, but there's still a hole in the net. Who's going to take out the needle and thread and repair the hole? Everyone shrugging and saying, "That's okay, I forgive you," leaves us with a net full of holes, and it weakens us as a community.

When Elizabeth Menkin participated in the mediation with Susanna Cooper, the drunk driver who killed her sister, Elaine, she was asked to write a victim-impact statement clarifying how Elaine's death had affected her. In it, Elizabeth spelled out exactly what Susanna would have to do to "mend the net" and earn forgiveness.

> Forgiveness is not something which I believe is my obligation to bestow unilaterally, but it can be earned. The perpetrator must show the five R's: recognition, remorse, repentance, restitution, and reform. "Recognition" means admitting that what she did was wrong, and that she is responsible for the wrongdoing and all of the negative consequences that follow from it. (If she is in jail, she recognizes that it is because she drove drunk, rather than because the prosecutor or the judge was mean or unfair to her. If she is in pain, she recognizes it is because she drove drunk, not blaming it on the lack of pain medicine or a lack of medical science's ability to fix her as good as new.) "Remorse" means that each time she thinks of the wrong she did, she regrets that she did not make a better choice. It is a repeated rehearsal of how she wishes she had done it differently, how she would do it differently if given another chance. "Repentance" is when deep remorse leads to a firm resolve to do better in the future. "Restitution" cannot be direct in this case—there is no way that she can provide a wife for David or a sister for me. The only restitution she can make is a lifelong commitment to a daily effort toward making the world a better place. She is not required to complete the job of repairing the world, but she must not be excused from starting and continually working at the job. "Reform" means that she must create a new form of herself—to emerge as a sober person, a thoughtful and considerate person, a contributor. If she can do all of these, I can forgive.

This kind of active, ongoing accountability is at the core of the restorative justice movement. In restorative justice, it is the offender's acknowledgment, apology, and restitution that make forgiveness possible.

Rabbi Steven Fink: Responding Compassionately to Hate

We needed to give Tim and Mandy the chance to atone for their errors. If we didn't, it would be like saying that something at the core of Judaism was empty and meaningless.

—RABBI STEVEN FINK

On March 3, 1994, Rabbi Steven Fink and other members of Temple B'nai Jeshurun of Des Moines, Iowa, arrived at their synagogue only to find it desecrated with swastikas, neo-Nazi graffiti, and red spray paint. Outraged by this hate crime, the entire community rallied around the stricken congregation.

A week later, police acted on a tip and arrested Timothy Harris, age nineteen, and his seventeen-year-old girlfriend, "Mandy" (a pseudonym is being used here because she was a minor at the time the crime was committed). When confronted, Tim confessed to the crime and professed pride about what he had done. A runaway who had been taken in by members of the Aryan Nation, Timothy saw his act of hate-vandalism as a way to make a name for himself within the disparate white hate groups active in Des Moines at the time.

Once Tim and Mandy were arrested, Fred Gay, deputy district attorney for Polk County, approached Rabbi Fink and asked if he and his congregation would be willing to participate in a unique victim-offender mediation program, in which members of the congregation would meet directly with the perpetrators to express their outrage and feelings of violation, and to determine appropriate consequences for the crime.*

The decision to mediate was difficult for Temple members. The desecration of the Temple brought back painful memories of the Holocaust. More than one Temple member wanted to put

---

*The Polk County District Attorney's Office has an in-house Restorative Justice Center. The center facilitates one thousand meetings a year, for crimes ranging from simple misdemeanors to murder. Contact: Restorative Justice Center, 206 Sixth Avenue, Des Moines, IA 50309; (515) 286-2160.

Timothy Harris in jail and throw away the key. Others argued that sending him to jail would guarantee that he would become a hard-core Nazi, while meeting with him might give him the chance to turn his life around. Rabbi Fink recalls: "The mediation was the most difficult thing I've ever done because I had to overcome feelings of anger and hurt in order to see the perpetrators as human beings. Part of me wanted revenge. My spiritual home had been desecrated; that which I find to be most obscene had violated that which was most precious to me. Yet I wanted something positive to come out of it. We all did.

"In Judaism, we believe that in order to be forgiven, we have to ask for forgiveness, and in order for forgiveness to be granted, we have to atone for our sins. So in order to be true to our religious ideals, we needed to give Tim and Mandy the chance to atone for their errors. If we didn't, it would be like saying that something at the core of Judaism was empty and meaningless."

While Temple members were deciding whether to meet with Tim and Mandy, Tim and Mandy were deciding whether to meet with them. Once they pled guilty to a felony charge in adult court, they were told they could go before a judge for sentencing or participate in a mediation in which Temple members would determine their punishment. They opted for mediation.

Six weeks after the crime, Tim and Mandy and their attorney met for a facilitated dialogue with five members of the Temple B'nai Jeshurun congregation: two Holocaust survivors, a former Israeli paratrooper, the president of the congregation, and Rabbi Fink. Rabbi Fink says the four-hour session was excruciating but fruitful. "We heard from Tim and Mandy about why they had done this. We heard what they thought of Jews. Then we talked about how upset and angry we were. Several times Tim and Mandy had to leave the room because it was so hard for them to listen to us. Our expressions of outrage and hurt clearly got through to them."

For Rabbi Fink, seeing Tim and Mandy as human was at the heart of the mediation. "We'd built Timothy Harris up to be a monster, but as soon as we saw him, we realized that he was a pretty pathetic character. He spoke with a lisp and had tattoos all over his body. He had no self-esteem of any kind; he was a very sad person. Mandy was an easily influenced seventeen-year-old who had run away from her family and got in with a bad crowd. They were a couple of kids who'd been indoctrinated into neo-Nazi thought without really understanding what it meant."

After much debate, Temple members decided they did not want to see Tim and Mandy in jail. Instead, they came up with a rigorous restitution program. "They had to be tested regularly for drug and alcohol use because they were intoxicated at the time of the crime. They each had to get a GED. Timothy Harris had to get a hearing test because he had very poor hearing, and he had to wear a hearing aid, if possible. Both Tim and Mandy were required to go to counseling with a professional counselor, do one hundred hours of physical labor supervised by our custodian, and study for one hundred hours with me about Judaism and the Holocaust. If they did all of these things, all charges against them would be dropped."

Tim and Mandy agreed to these conditions and over the next six months met all of the requirements. They physically removed all of the paint from the building and learned about Judaism and the Holocaust. As they got to know real Jews, their anti-Semitism fell away.

In the half year he worked closely with the young couple, Rabbi Fink grew to care for them. "During that time, Tim and Mandy changed. They became more self-confident; their goals and aspirations became clearer. They developed a positive relationship with our custodian and me; I can honestly say we became friends. When Mandy turned eighteen and she and Tim decided to get married, they invited us to their wedding."

For Rabbi Fink and the entire congregation, this unique reconciliation process brought out the best in everyone. Seeing two aspiring Nazis turn their lives around was the most positive outcome anyone could have hoped for, and Rabbi Fink is extremely glad that he backed up his deepest beliefs with action. "Tim Harris is now a productive human being. The last time I saw him he was learning a skill, working as an apprentice for a plumbing company. I found him to be an exceedingly bright, talented person, who, with the right family background, would have gone to college and probably been an artist. I'm sorry that he didn't have that opportunity, but we gave him another chance. He's going to be better for it, and I think we're all going to be better for it. I feel in many ways that God worked through us to create healing. In the end, we could not help but grant Tim and Mandy forgiveness, because they earned it."

Forgiveness as Something That Happens Unilaterally

On the opposite side of the paradigm linking forgiveness to accountability is the belief that forgiveness should be granted unilaterally. In this belief system, the "victim" can forgive whether or not the wrongdoer takes responsibility for the wrong—or even acknowledges that it took place.

Winnie, a seventy-six-year-old Colorado woman, experienced this kind of forgiveness for her parents: the father who abused her and the mother who failed to protect her as a child. Both died without ever admitting what had happened.

Winnie's experience of forgiveness grew out of her friendship with a forty-year-old man named John, who had been coming to her house for ten years to do repairs. In the course of his visits, Winnie and John discovered that they were both in therapy and both valued spiritual growth. They enjoyed their camaraderie so much that John started scheduling his visits to Winnie's house at the end of the day so they could talk afterward.

One day, when John was fixing her plumbing, Winnie ran over and said, "I just have to tell you! I really think that I've been able to release my father and my mother." She explained that her father had sexually abused her and that her mother had failed to protect her, and that finally she had been able to forgive them.

John listened silently, emotion filling his face. Winnie remembers the moment well.

John's eyes searched my eyes. Tears were streaming down his face. Then haltingly, he began to tell his story: "I am a workaholic and a cocaine addict, and," he fought for courage, "I molested my stepdaughter!" He was really shaken. He told me, "I know I hurt her, and I've done everything I can think of to make up for it. I went into therapy and offered to pay for her therapy. I've made amends to her and begged for her forgiveness, but she has rejected all of my overtures." He sobbed quietly while I tried to absorb the enormity of what I had heard.

I stood there for a moment, stunned. Finally, I said, "This is just what I needed to hear." Then we just held each other. Clearly, John and I were meant to meet each other.

In that moment of forgiveness, Winnie, at seventy-six, symbolically became John's stepdaughter accepting his apology, and John, at forty, became her father, humbly accepting responsibility for what he had done.

In this instance, John and Winnie each had the benefit of a "stand-in" who enabled a deeper level of forgiveness to occur. But even when there is no "stand-in," people can still forgive unilaterally. Calvin did this with his sister, who had cheated him out of an inheritance.

When Dad was dying, Melanie was his main caregiver. In his final weeks, she talked him into signing a new will that left the disposition of his property in her hands. She saw to it that she got the bulk of his estate.

For years, I watched her live the good life on Dad's money. When she died ten years later, Melanie left the rest of it to her kids.

It gnawed at me. It interfered with my relationships with my nieces and nephews, and alienated me from other family members. I always had a chip on my shoulder. Finally, I realized that I was only hurting myself, so I decided to forgive her. When I did, I got to change the ending to the story. Instead of being "the brother who got cheated," I became "the brother who accepted his sister's failings." It was a tremendous relief not to hate her anymore.

In his description of forgiveness, Calvin expresses a widespread assumption—that people will be burdened with rage, grief, and a desire for vengeance unless they forgive. Although this was true in his case, it is not true for everyone. As author Ellen Bass once quipped, "Forgiveness is not required unless you want it to be."

The Trouble with Pseudo-Forgiveness

We live in a "feel-good" culture that encourages us to search for easy answers, speedy solutions, and the immediate cessation of pain. Because of this, in-depth healing from deep emotional wounds has fallen into disrepute. When people who are struggling to cope with the aftereffects of trauma or betrayal seek help, they are often told to take a pill, visualize their way into wholeness, "get well" in four to six sessions of therapy, and forgive, preferably as quickly as possible.

As a result, what passes as forgiveness in our culture today is often a kind of pseudo-forgiveness in which people gloss over their grief, anger, and pain in an attempt to generate a false sense of magnanimity. When forgiveness is seen as a litmus test for how healthy or spiritually evolved we are, a lot of pain is stuffed under its socially acceptable mantle.

Donna Jenson, who works extensively with trauma survivors, reports:

> People are walking around with the lid on a tremendous amount of unhealed material. When someone who's been severely hurt by a parent says to me, "I've forgiven my father" when there's been no acknowledgment, contrition, or making of amends, there's usually something between a brushfire and a tornado underneath.

The motivation to forgive prematurely often comes from a desire to avoid the pain of facing the harm that was done. Richard Hoffman, who "forgave" the coach who raped him, believes, in retrospect, that his stance of forgiveness was nothing more than a denial of his own vulnerability.

For years, I believed I'd forgiven Tom Feifel, but it wasn't forgiveness at all. It was denial that what he had done to me mattered. I responded to the rape in a very first-son-of-a-working-class-family kind of way. Forgiving Tom was my way of saying, "I'm a tough guy. Everybody has a few bites taken out of him on the way up. It's no big deal. Shake it off. Forgive and forget." I chose to think, "He was a good coach; we won a lot of games. Everybody has faults." Never once did it cross my mind that he might be raping other boys.

My forgiveness of Tom was a shrug, and when the story finally broke and more than four hundred men called to say that he'd abused them too, I could see that it was a moral shrug as well. It was my way of walking away from something that should have been confronted.

In *Forgiving and Not Forgiving*, psychotherapist Jeanne Safer devotes a whole chapter to the topic of pseudo-forgiveness. In it, she writes,

> Politicians and celebrities caught in compromising positions routinely ask to be pardoned when they don't mean it; people oblige even when they don't believe it. This ritual, though commonplace, is not innocuous. Colluding with insincerity breeds insincerity, until no one can recognize or experience genuine emotions. . . . [Pseudo-forgiveness] has about as much connection to the real thing as fruit-flavored LifeSavers do to fruit. Deep and important transactions are cheapened and rendered empty, robbed of their passion and their pain by the way they are reflexively invoked. . . .
>
> . . . Forgiveness comes in authentic and ersatz varieties. The instant type obstructs the difficult route to self-knowledge that alone can be liberating. In a society that places so high a premium on forgiveness at any cost, the imitations are often encouraged, applauded, and mistaken for the real thing.*

Forgiving and Not Forgiving, pp. 131, 141.

Resolution Is Possible Without Forgiveness

Pam Leeds's parents sexually abused her when she was a child, and then when she had children, they sexually abused them as well. Pam wanted nothing to do with her parents, and for years was consumed with rage. After a long and active healing process, Pam had a dream.

> I dreamed I was visiting my parents. I saw them through my adult eyes as sad, old, damaged people and also as lying, manipulative people. There was something I wanted to communicate to my father, but I didn't know how to do it without getting involved in our old dominance game. We were standing on the stairs, and I put my arms around him; he felt skinny, old, and familiar. He was very surprised, and I could feel his heart open for a moment; I knew I had only that moment in which to speak. I said, "I want you to know that I love you. I remember the good things that you did and I value them, but you also hurt all of us a lot. Because of that, we don't want you in our lives." Then I hugged him and walked away.
>
> The religiously oriented person I talked to about this dream says, "That's forgiveness," but it doesn't feel like forgiveness to me. To me, forgiveness would mean saying, "It's okay. I'm willing to act as if it never happened," and that is definitely *not* the case for me.
>
> For me, the dream was about being able to love and at the same time hold a realistic assessment of two extremely damaged and damaging people. I feel very clear about my boundaries with the people who offended me and mine. I don't want them in my life, but to stay in a place of rage and hatred is hurtful to me, and to see them only as monsters is to be less than fully human myself.

In Pam's case, relinquishing the right to hate led to neither forgiveness nor reconciliation—but it did lead to a place of greater peace. Miriam Gladys, who works extensively with abuse and alcoholism in Jewish families, found a word for this.

> When I started doing this work, I thought forgiveness meant that everything was better and everyone could go back to the

way things should have been. But the more I've worked around these issues, the less I believe it's possible to forgive some of the horrible things people do to each other. I realized I was looking for a word that said, "Yes, I understand that this happened. Now I am prepared to move on with my life." In Hebrew, there's a word "*shlemut*," and it means wholeness. To me, that's what forgiveness is about.

Like Pam Leeds, Vicki Malloy had to heal from incest. Unlike Pam, Vicki was blessed to have a father who owned up to what he did. As a result, Vicki and her father have achieved a remarkable level of reconciliation, yet forgiveness has never been part of the equation.

Vicki Malloy: Rebuilding a Relationship with My Perpetrator

For a number of years, my father and I struggled to have some kind of relationship. I kept trying because I'd always felt close to my father and I wasn't ready to say good-bye to him. I wanted to give him the chance to do right by me; I offered that to him, and he took it. He must have really loved me to put himself through that kind of agony.

—VICKI MALLOY, INCEST SURVIVOR

In 1985, when Ellen Bass and I were writing *The Courage to Heal*, I interviewed Vicki Malloy, whose father molested her once, because we wanted to demonstrate that sexual abuse did not have to be severe or protracted to have a profound impact on a child's life. At the time of that interview, Vicki was thirty years old and completely estranged from her father.

She recalls: "My father and I were always very close. We had a strong bond, but there was always something inappropriate about the way he was with me. He was too affectionate. His kisses would last too long. Things just didn't feel right.

"When I was twelve, I was asleep in bed. My father came into my room, put his hand down my pajamas, and started playing with my vagina. It woke me up. I pretended I was turning over in my sleep and turned away from him. He got frightened that I would wake up, and left. He never did it again.

"Before he molested me, I felt very free in my body. I was outgoing and friendly. I had boyfriends. Everything was awakening. And my first intimate sexual experience was with my father.

"I never told anyone about it, but afterward, I shied away from any physical contact with my father. I felt really icky if he hugged me. I went through my teens very depressed. It was as if all the vitality had been sucked out of me.

"In my early twenties, the incest came up periodically, usually around sexuality. I'd start to have trouble, and then the relationship would end."

In 1982, Vicki met her current partner, Gayle. "A couple of years into our relationship, I started struggling with intimacy. I knew it traced back to what my father had done, and I resented it. I decided to confront him, something I'd never done before.

"Part of what motivated me was that I was pregnant. I felt a very strong internal push to deal with my father before I became a parent."

At that point, Vicki hadn't spoken to her father in six years. That period of estrangement, Vicki says, was not planned or premeditated—it just happened. "My parents divorced. I grew up and didn't need my father anymore. I never called him, and he never called me. I realize now I couldn't get back in touch with him until I dealt with what had happened."

It Was Like a Poison Inside His Soul

Vicki called her father and said she wanted to see him. "He flew into town, and I confronted him. I said, 'You molested me.' He didn't say he didn't do it; he said, 'I don't remember that.' He had amnesia about the whole thing. Then he left and went home. It was very tense and sad and painful. But I think my father realized that he was going to lose me if he didn't pull it together. Once I gave him the information about why we were estranged, it was like a poison inside his soul. So he woke up and decided to face it.

"Several months after our confrontation, my father called and said, 'I did do that.' He also told me he had started some counseling.

"From that point on, we struggled to have a relationship, but our attempts to reconcile didn't go very well. We wrote letters back and forth, and he repeatedly asked for forgiveness. He was full of guilt, and it was extremely important to him that I forgive him. I said, 'I'm not ready to forgive you, and I don't know if I ever will be.' I didn't say it in a mean way. I just wanted him to know.

"He wrote back and said, 'My father was cruel to me, and I forgave him. Why can't you forgive me?' We went back and forth like that for quite a while. Finally, I said, 'This is not going anywhere. Would you be willing to see my counselor with me?' and he said yes."

My Father Was Open and Vulnerable

In 1987, Vicki's father flew into town so they could do several marathon therapy sessions together. He stayed in a hotel and met Vicki each day at her therapist's office. "Those sessions really opened things up between us. My father was as vulnerable as he could possibly be, and that's what led to us being able to have the relationship we have today."

The first thing Vicki and her father worked on was boundaries. "The critical thing about incest is boundaries, and I'd never set any with my father. So I had to figure out what I needed to feel comfortable and safe with him. The first thing was, 'If you want to have a relationship with me, you're not allowed to touch me. When you see me, you can't hug me until I say it's okay.' He hated that and said it was ridiculous, but I needed the control to be able to say, 'Okay, now you can touch me.'

"Slowly, he understood. He didn't like it, but he agreed to do it for me. It was extremely difficult for him, but for a couple of years, every time I saw him, I'd say, 'Hi, Dad,' and he'd say, 'Hi,' and we wouldn't touch.

"I also told him that he wasn't allowed to talk about my appearance. He couldn't say, 'You look really good' or 'You've gained a little weight,' because it felt to me like he was checking me out, and I did not like it."

The third thing Vicki wanted was to be able to talk to her father about the incest whenever she needed to. "I wanted him to know that it wasn't a done deal just because we'd talked about it in therapy. I needed permission to explore it further. He didn't like that either. He really wanted us to put this behind us, but he accepted my terms.

"I didn't take advantage of that. I knew how hard it was for him, and it wasn't easy for me either, so I didn't go out of my way to bring things up. But once in a while, I needed to. Once I asked, 'Dad, what was going on in your life that you would do something like that?' I remember worrying that he might tell me about his sex life with my mother, but he responded in a mature, respectful way."

I'm Concerned About Ethan's Safety

Several years into their reconciliation, an extremely troubling issue came up: the safety of Vicki's son, Ethan. "Ethan was two at the time, and Gayle was fierce in insisting that he not be alone with my father. I was devastated when she said that. I defended my father, saying, 'How dare you think he's going to do something to Ethan!'

"And Gayle said, 'What makes you think he wouldn't?'

"I looked at her in absolute disbelief, and said, 'Because my father was interested in *me*.' She gave me that look that said, 'You're in total denial. You are not in touch with reality.'

"I couldn't accept what Gayle was saying, so we had to go to counseling around it, and the worst part was that the counselor agreed with her. So Gayle and I had to talk to my father and his wife about it. Having his wife there was good because my dad had an ally, but it was terrible to see him so exposed.

"We sat down. I forced myself to look at my father, and I said, 'I'm concerned about Ethan's safety around you.' The look in his eyes made me want to die. It was, 'How can you think I would do that?' and also, 'I know I need to answer this.' Both were right there in his eyes.

"He said, 'I don't know what to say to convince you, but I don't lust after children. I'm not a pedophile.' Gayle and I believed him, and that cleared the way for him and Ethan to have a relationship.

"It was an incredibly intense conversation, but we had to talk about it. When it was over, we all took a huge sigh of relief. We had gotten through that terrible discussion with our relationship still intact."

My Father's Been Able to Come Through for Me

In the decade since then, Vicki's relationship with her father has continued to evolve. "Things have gotten increasingly comfortable. I no longer worry about my father being inappropriate. I can relax and be open around him now.

"My father isn't a phone person, so we don't talk much on the phone. I try to go see him every six weeks, but he lives four hours away and I work full-time, so it isn't easy. But I make it a priority to see him. Usually I take Ethan with me. Occasionally, Gayle comes along.

"I stay at my father's house now. There's a spare room, and Ethan and I sleep there. Often, the three of us watch sports together. My father and Ethan throw a ball around, shoot pool, and play miniature golf. Ethan is always eager to see his grandfather. It's clear they love each other.

"As my father gets older, he's started to depend on me more—

he's asked me to call him, and he's sought my advice about health-related decisions. He's also come through for me more. I asked him to tell me he loved me and to show more emotion, and he's done both those things. He expresses more love for me now than he ever did when I was a kid.

"My father still yields to my cues physically. He holds back until I initiate contact. I hug him now, but we're really not too physical, and I think that's okay. My relationship with my father is forever damaged on some level. We've patched it the best we can, but it is patched."

The Question of Forgiveness

Vicki's reconciliation with her father has taught her a tremendous amount. "I've learned about the strength of the bond between a parent and a child. I've learned that people make mistakes and it doesn't mean they're evil. I've learned that it's important to give people the chance to make right what they've screwed up, and that reconciliation is ongoing. Even though the big secret is out, I'm still processing my relationship with my father."

Although questions remain, Vicki is choosing not to broach the subject of incest with her father anymore. "My father is seventy-nine. He's declining, and I'm not interested in confronting him now. Even though there are times I'd like to talk about it, I'm choosing not to. Part of it is not knowing how much I'd get out of it, and part of it is not wanting to put him through it again. He's old, and I want to love him for the remaining time he has. I'm acutely aware that he's going to die soon, and I'm not the kind of person that needs to keep pushing at things. I'm ready to let it go."

Despite her willingness to let things go, Vicki has not forgiven her father. "I knew I didn't want forgiveness to be part of our reconciliation. If I didn't forgive, it felt like I still had some power in the situation, and I was so completely powerless as a child.

"My intensity around it has faded over the years, and it's been a long time since my father asked if I'd forgive him, but if he did, I'd say, 'No. I see you as a human being who has problems like everyone else, but I don't forgive you for molesting me.' I wouldn't say it to be mean or to punish him, but simply because it's the truth.

"I forgive my father for other mistakes he's made, but I believe there are some mistakes you don't get to wash your hands of. Incest is one. It's the absolute worst thing you can do to your child, and he did that to me."

The Turning of the Tides

In 1999, Vicki's father had a stroke that left him blind. He also has serious vascular problems that prevent him from walking much. The combination of those two things has narrowed his world considerably. "Now when we visit, we stay indoors and listen to music or watch TV. Increasingly, my father talks about his health problems."

Her father's mortality is shaking things up for Vicki. She knows her time with her father is running out. "It's a real time of change for us. I can feel him depending on me and needing me more; I'm entering the world of having an aging, ill father. I feel sad, and I'm wondering what his last years are going to be like and what role I'm going to play in his life. I feel a real pull to see him more, and I want Ethan to see him as much as possible. I'm really trying to make that a priority now."

Despite the uncertainty around her father's health, Vicki feels at peace with the man who once molested her. She is also deeply grateful for the reconciliation they have achieved. "My father defied all the odds. The percentage of fathers who are willing to admit what they did and go through what I made him go through is very, very low. He was willing to go through hell to save his relationship with me, and I really admire him for that. I know I'm really lucky."

Are Some Things Unforgivable?

There is a continuum of ways human beings can hurt each other. Like Vicki, many people believe the offenses at the far end of the continuum are unforgivable. Former batterer Franklin Carter, who has sincerely practiced the five R's, believes it is not only unnecessary but inappropriate for his ex-wife to forgive him. "I don't expect Natalie to forgive me. I expect her, for the duration, to be cautious around me, knowing what I can do. Expecting her to forgive me for unethical, abusive treatment is one of the fallacious niceties in our culture, and I think it does a lot of damage to people who don't have any power."

Franklin takes this thinking a step further. "Do I forgive myself? No, I don't. These were conscious choices I made. They had intent. It serves no purpose for me to forgive myself."

Photojournalist Dith Pran, who survived the genocide of the Khmer Rouge in Cambodia, also believes that it is the intent of the perpetrators and their relative power that differentiates those he can forgive from those he cannot.

> As a witness and survivor of the Cambodian killing fields, I could never forgive or forget what the top leadership of the Khmer Rouge has done to me, my family, or friends. It's impossible. I blame the dozen leaders, the brains behind a sadistic plot, who ordered the death of millions of people, including the disabled, children, religious people, the educated, and anyone they thought was a threat to their ideas. My father died of starvation, my three brothers and sister were killed, along with many nieces, nephews, and cousins. Friends I had known all my life and who worked beside me in the fields were taken away and killed. We lived in constant fear in the labor camps. There was no sympathy for us. We were in a cage with tigers and there was no way out. All we could do was pray to God. . . .
>
> Pulling away from the Khmer Rouge leadership, I can forgive the soldiers of the Khmer Rouge, those who actually did the killing, although I can never forgive what they did. . . . I have always felt that most of the soldiers were trapped. Most of them came from the jungle, were uneducated and very poor. They were taught to kill. They were brainwashed. More importantly,

they were forced to kill. If they didn't follow the orders of the Khmer Rouge leadership, not only would they have been killed, their entire families would have been killed. . . .

We need to separate the true culprits from the pawns, the evil masterminds from the brainwashed. We cannot label everyone the same. There is a world of difference between the leadership of the Khmer Rouge and the individuals who followed their orders.*

Dith Pran raises two critical questions: "Who is responsible when evil occurs?" and "Under what circumstances does a wrongdoer deserve forgiveness?" These questions, as well as a third, "Whose job is it to grant forgiveness?" are explored extensively in Simon Wiesenthal's classic book, *The Sunflower: On the Possibilities and Limits of Forgiveness.*

Wiesenthal, a Nazi hunter, opens his book with a narrative about his internment in a German concentration camp; he describes living in subhuman conditions under the constant threat of death, witnessing countless murders, sadistic assaults, and atrocities. At one point, a half-starved Wiesenthal is sent on a work detail outside of the camp; while there, he is brought to the room of a dying Nazi, who has asked that a Jew, any Jew, be sent to his room.

The dying Nazi wants to confess to a Jew; he is looking for absolution. He tells Wiesenthal of a barbaric act he participated in two years earlier—forcing two hundred Jews, mostly women, children, and old people, into a three-story house, which was then sealed and set on fire, incinerating everyone inside. It is the memory of this event—the screams, the stench, the sight of a father and son leaping to their deaths—that is tormenting the young soldier as he lies dying, and he wants Wiesenthal to grant him forgiveness. Wiesenthal stays and listens to the young man's horrific story, but ultimately walks out of the room, silent, unable to forgive the dying man.

---

*This quote appears in Dith Pran's essay in Simon Wiesenthal, *The Sunflower: On the Possibilities and Limits of Forgiveness* (New York: Schocken Books, 1996), p. 230. Copyright © 1969, 1970 by Opera Mundi, Paris. Copyright © renewed 1997 by Simon Wiesenthal. Used by permission of Schocken Books, a division of Random House, Inc.

For years, this exchange haunted Wiesenthal. Eventually, he wrote up the story of this encounter and sent it out to an international array of prominent thinkers: Christian, Jewish, and Buddhist theologians, professors, statesmen, philosophers, journalists, Holocaust survivors, victims of other totalitarian regimes, and even a Nazi war criminal. He asked each of them to imagine being in his place, in that room with that dying Nazi, and then invited them to answer the question "What would you have done?"

The resulting collection of essays, which make up the bulk of *The Sunflower*, is a fascinating study of forgiveness.* When faced with the most horrible crime imaginable, Wiesenthal's respondents give a tremendous diversity of answers. Most of those who answered began their essays by stating that they couldn't imagine being in Wiesenthal's shoes, and that no matter what theological or moral argument they were about to put forth, judging his choice, considering the nightmare he was living in at the time, was wholly inappropriate. Yet many went on to answer according to their conscience and beliefs.

The majority of Christians who answered maintained that since God forgives all those who repent, Simon should have forgiven the young Nazi, who was asking for absolution in his final hours. Former Notre Dame president Theodore M. Hesburgh epitomized this point of view: "My whole instinct is to forgive. Perhaps that is because I am a Catholic priest. In a sense, I am in the forgiving business. I sit in a confessional for hours and forgive everyone who comes in, confesses, and is sorry. . . . Of course, the sin here is monumental. [But] it is still finite and God's mercy in infinite."†

British author and former member of Parliament Christopher Hollis shared Hesburgh's perspective: "The law of God is the law of love. We are created in order to love one another, and, when the law of love is broken, God's nature is frustrated. Such bonds when broken should be reforged as soon as possible. We are under obligation to forgive our neighbor even though he has offended against us seventy times seven."‡

The Sunflower was first published in English in 1976 and revised in 1996 with a new generation of respondents.

---

†Ibid., p. 169.

---

‡Ibid., p. 177.

Most of the Jewish respondents strongly disagreed with this point of view, stating emphatically that, according to Jewish law, Wiesenthal not only shouldn't have forgiven, but *couldn't* have. Forgiveness by proxy is forbidden in Judaism. Therefore, only the murdered Jews could have forgiven the dying man, and of course that was impossible.

Rabbi laureate and author Harold Kushner approached the question differently, exploring how forgiveness might actually benefit the Jew who granted it.

Forgiving is not something we do for another person, as the Nazi asked Wiesenthal to do for him. Forgiving happens inside us. It represents a letting go of the sense of grievance, and perhaps most importantly a letting go of the role of victim. For a Jew to forgive the Nazis would not mean, God forbid, saying to them, "What you did was understandable, I can understand what led you to do it, and I don't hate you for it." It would mean saying, "What you did was thoroughly despicable and puts you outside the category of decent human beings. But I refuse to give you the power to define me as a victim. I refuse to let your blind hatred define the shape and content of my Jewishness. I don't hate you; I reject you." And then the Nazi would remain chained to his past and to his conscience, but the Jew would be free.*

In the Buddhist tradition, it is believed that each soul continues to evolve through many lifetimes. Therefore, even the most horrible criminal can better himself—if not in this lifetime, in lifetimes to come. Monk Matthieu Ricard expressed the Buddhist idea that forgiveness is always possible and that one should always forgive.

No matter how bad someone is, we believe that the basic goodness remains. . . . "The only good thing about evil," goes the Buddhist saying, "is that it can be purified." In Buddhism, forgiveness does not mean absolution, but an opportunity for the inner transformation of both victim and perpetrator. The

---

*Ibid., p. 186.

perpetrator of evil will suffer over many lifetimes to a degree determined by his actions, until he is ready for inner transformation. For the victim, forgiveness is a way of transforming his own grief, resentment, or hatred into good. To grant forgiveness to someone who has truly changed is not a way of condoning or forgetting his or her past crimes, but of acknowledging whom he or she has become.*

Yet in the case Simon Wiesenthal sets before us, had the young Nazi really changed? This question was raised repeatedly; many of the respondents doubted the sincerity of his repentance, speculating that he may very well have continued his butchery had he not been on his deathbed. Rabbi Joseph Telushkin elucidated this perspective: "We can only know the full truth of a person's repentance if the penitent encounters the same situation in which he first sinned, and then refrains from sinning. But, of course, no such opportunity could be granted this young man. We know that he *voiced* regret over his murderous deeds; unfortunately, that is all we know."[†]

Others held that if the young Nazi had been truly penitent, he should have asked to speak not to an anonymous Jewish prisoner, whom he hoped would assuage his guilt, but rather to his superiors in the SS—urging them to stop the genocide.

A number of respondents deemed the question of the young man's repentance irrelevant; they maintained that the monstrosity of the crime simply put it beyond the pale of forgivable offenses. Psychotherapist André Stein expressed this point of view.

Can we, indeed, advocate forgiveness toward those who have committed crimes against humanity? Should we not warn those who contemplate evil acts that there will be no mercy even on their deathbeds should they give in to the seduction of killing? The consequences of participating in genocidal acts must include dying with a guilty conscience.[‡]

---

*Ibid., p. 325.

†Ibid., p. 263.

‡Ibid., p. 253.

And retired U.S. major general Sidney Shachnow wrote:

> Simon Wiesenthal was right in not granting forgiveness, for two reasons. First, he did not have the moral right to do so, and second, this savage did not deserve it. He stepped over the boundary where forgiveness is possible. That SS officer should take up his case with God. I personally think he should go to hell and rot there. I doubt very much that my God would grant him forgiveness. After all, what does it take to serve in hell?*

I found *The Sunflower* to be a haunting, provocative book. Throughout its pages I was reminded again and again that forgiveness is a highly personal decision, based as it is on religious beliefs (and differing interpretations of those religious beliefs), moral precepts, life history, and personal experience. It is clear from reading these profoundly moving essays that there is no single answer to the question "Are some things unforgivable?"

A Personal Decision

When opinions about a highly subjective subject are this diverse, allowing for personal differences is essential. Saying, "*You* must forgive" is very different from saying, "*I* must forgive."

The biggest problem with forgiveness is how often it is foisted on people. People who have suffered grave injuries are urged to forgive, and when they don't, they are often accused of being vindictive. These judgments are based on the erroneous assumption that forgiveness is simply a matter of changing your mind, and that stubbornness is the only reason someone does not forgive. This way of thinking leads to a further indictment of the victim.

Telling an injured person that she's being vengeful because she won't forgive is as unfair as telling someone he's being callous when he fails to fall in love. When people are told they must forgive, it sets them up to feel inadequate if they don't *feel* forgiving. Convinced that they

---

*Ibid., p. 243.

cannot find peace without forgiveness, they sometimes get stuck in feelings of despair that keep them from exploring other avenues that might help them progress toward wholeness.

There is wisdom in giving each other the space to formulate our own beliefs, have our own experiences, and draw our own conclusions. Let those who believe in working toward forgiveness strive to achieve it. Let those who believe it arrives through serendipity wait for its appearance from within. Let those of us who find certain things unforgivable seek other paths to peace. And let us all find wholeness—*shlemut*.

PART FIVE

Finding Peace

CHAPTER 10

When Reconciliation Is Impossible: The Task of Letting Go

A "no" uttered from the deepest conviction is better and greater than a "yes" merely uttered to please, or what is worse, to avoid trouble.

—MAHATMA GANDHI

No matter how much we desire it, work for it, or pray for it, reconciliation is not always possible. People refuse contact, hold on to grudges, leave no forwarding address, or die. They can be too drunk, mentally ill, or hostile to make reconciliation a possibility. Yet even if we never speak another word to the other person, we can still find a place of peace inside ourselves.

Accepting That the Relationship Is Over

To let go of an estranged relationship, we must first acknowledge that it is over. Until we give up hope that things might change, we will not be free to move on. Yet when relationships are significant, it is very difficult to face the reality that they are irreconcilable. Jacqueline, who was in an ongoing conflict with a friend, recalls:

I hurt Cindy and wrote her a letter of apology. Cindy wrote a nasty letter back, and then we sent a few more letters back and forth. Then it felt like the ball was in my court; she had written to me, and it was my turn to say something back.

I believed that as long as Cindy requested a response, I had to give one. It was hard for me to see *not* responding as an option, but it was not only an option, it was the *appropriate* option. Writing to her kept refueling this conflict, and I needed to let her go.

That realization freed me. I'd always expected the relationship to go in a particular direction. When I realized it wasn't going to be that kind of friendship anymore, I felt grief, but also a deep sense of relief.

Because Jacqueline *chose* to end the relationship, she felt sad *and* empowered by her decision. She was relinquishing a friendship, but the fact that she was doing so voluntarily meant that she was still maintaining a sense of control. But when someone closes the door in *our* face, the dynamic is quite different.

Diane DeVito was in her late thirties when she began to have memories of incest with her father. When she told her mother about it over lunch one day, it sent shock waves through the DeVito family. Diane began getting angry letters and threatening calls and was ultimately cast out of her family.

Two years after her exile began, Diane decided to reach out to her mother.

I was so distraught over an unsuccessful in vitro fertilization that I sent my mother a note, which said, "I'd like to see you. I've been going through some very difficult times." She said, "Okay, let's meet for lunch." My father dropped her off at the restaurant because my mother doesn't drive, but he didn't come in.

My mother and I had a tearful lunch. We cried and hugged and said how sorry we were that things turned out the way they did. We didn't discuss the incest, but we both expressed how sad we were that we couldn't be together. I started feeling very close to her. We were in the middle of Bloomingdale's saying good-bye, and I didn't know if I was ever going to see her again. I started crying hysterically. The woman spritzing perfume was staring at us, but we just kept hugging each other and crying. Then my mother disentangled herself and said, "Well, I'll talk to you soon," and we went our separate ways.

Diane and her mother got together for lunch a few more times, but then her mother started to withdraw. Diane remembers quite clearly the last time they met. It was three years ago.

My mother had walked a mile in extremely cold weather to meet me because my father refused to drive her if she was coming to see me. I remember thinking, "My mother must really love me to have walked all this way." But as soon as we got to the restaurant, she told me that my father and brother had told her she couldn't see me anymore.

Her mother's choice to comply with her father's wishes still astounds Diane. "It's incomprehensible to me that my mother would choose my father over me, but that's exactly what she did."

At the time, Diane wasn't ready to accept that their estrangement was permanent.

I firmly believed that we were going to reconcile because things usually worked out for me at that point in my life. Ultimately, I believed that my family would see that I was right, life would be fair, and we'd get back together.

I fantasized that it would all happen when I had a baby. I thought it might take a death as well, but I wanted it to be a baby. Well, I didn't get pregnant, but my sister did, so I thought, "Now it'll happen, because she's having a baby." So I tried to get back into the family. I sent cards and gifts, but they were ignored. And this awful silence has continued to grow. I see my relatives in church, and they turn the other way. I see my father at the racquet club, and we ignore each other. I've been shunned like this for years, and I've reached the point where I no longer expect things to change.

After years of infertility, I've had to face the fact that I'm not going to have a biological child, and that has taught me that sometimes life does lead to dead ends. I believe that's what's going to happen with my family.

Although the estrangement still grieves her, Diane is slowly regaining her equilibrium. "I have to remind myself that my life is bigger than the fact that my family won't speak to me. Deep down in my center, I know I'm not the terrible person my family tells me I am. More than anything, that allows me to continue."

Letting Go When You Don't Know Why the Relationship Ended

In Diane's case, it was clear to everyone involved what the estrangement was about. But sometimes the person who is being cut off does not know why the relationship is over. That's what happened to Peggy O'Neill, who grew up in a large Irish-Catholic family. Peggy was always close to her youngest sister, but five years ago, seemingly out of the blue, Teresa stopped speaking to her.

Peggy O'Neill: It's in Her Hands Now

You know when you've wronged somebody. There's an inner sense: "I blew it. I deceived you. I was insensitive." But I don't have that with Teresa. Inside myself, I can't find anything to apologize for.

—PEGGY O'NEILL

By the time her youngest sister, Teresa, was born, Peggy O'Neill was nearly eleven, her parents were worn out, and the job of raising the youngest O'Neill fell most heavily on Peggy and her older sister. Although Peggy's capacity to mother was limited at eleven, she adored Teresa and doted on her.

As they grew up, the sisters remained close. Teresa came out as a lesbian and partnered with Anne, who had a son, Riley. Peggy married and had her first child, Brian, when Riley was three. The two sisters and their families saw each other frequently; they spent holidays, weekends, birthdays, and vacations together. The two young cousins adored each other. By all appearances, the O'Neill sisters had an intimate and loving bond.

But shortly after the birth of Peggy's daughter, Katie, Teresa began to distance herself. At first, Peggy chalked it up to the promotion Teresa had gotten at work, assuming her sister was busy with her new responsibilities. But eventually, she realized something else was going on. "It was at Katie's first birthday party that I couldn't ignore the edge. All contact from Teresa stopped after that birthday. I thought something might have happened at the party—perhaps I'd spent too much time with my friends, and Teresa felt slighted. I checked that out with her the next time I saw her at my mom's house. She insisted that everything was fine, but she still wouldn't return my calls. Brian would call Riley, and Riley wouldn't call back. My birthday came and went, and she made no contact whatsoever. I had a terrible gut feeling about it.

"Several months later, we were up where Teresa and Anne live, and we called to ask if we could use their pool, something we'd done many times before. Teresa said yes, but when we got there, she and Anne were very cold to us. I went to Teresa privately and asked, 'What's going on? You don't call us. You're not coming down. We're not talking. We miss you.'

"She said, 'Nothing's wrong. I'm just busy with work.' But I didn't believe her."

Try, Try, Try Again

A year into their estrangement, Peggy approached her sister at a family reunion. "I asked, 'What's wrong? What's going on?'

"Once again, she said, 'Nothing.' She gave me a completely cold shoulder.

"That fall, at another gathering, I approached her again. I said, 'You've got to tell me what this is about.'

"She said, 'I don't want to talk about it.'

"I said, 'Teresa, whatever I've done, I'm sorry. But if you don't tell me, I can't make it right.'

"She repeated, 'I'm not ready to talk about it.'

"I said, 'Can you tell me when you will be ready to talk about it?'

"She said, 'Maybe sometime.'

"That November, we had Thanksgiving at my mom's, and I went to Teresa and Anne, crying, and made an appeal. I said, 'Do you have so much love in your life that you can afford to cut off someone who loves you as much as I do?'

"Teresa just looked at me as if I wasn't there. I turned to Anne and said, 'Somebody's got to tell me what's going on.'

"Anne said, 'That's up to Teresa.'

But Peggy still didn't give up. Later that same day, she found Teresa alone and tried to talk to her again. "I said I was willing to listen to anything she had to tell me without defense. I told her I'd apologize. I gave her carte blanche. Basically, I said, 'Lay it on me! I'll accept it.' I said, 'Not knowing is torture. This alienation is killing me.'

"Basically all I got was a big egg. Teresa just repeated, 'I'm not ready to talk to you.' "

What Could I Possibly Have Done?

A year and a half into their estrangement, Peggy was heartsick. "It would usually hit me around three in the morning. I'd wake up with a fist in my gut, feeling this horrible despair and helplessness. I'd lie there for hours, wracking my brain trying to figure out what I might have done. I thought about every little insensitivity I might have shown her. I wondered, 'Was it about her being gay? Could I have offended her in some way?' Then I thought it might have had to do with my father. My sister had always idealized our father, and I had told her some negative stories about him. Was she mad at me because I'd burst her bubble? Or was she upset about differences in our parenting styles? Was this all because I hadn't been strict enough with Brian when he was two?

"I kept trying to figure out what I could have possibly done that was so egregious that I didn't deserve forgiveness, and I couldn't come up with anything. I had never intentionally hurt Teresa. I'd never said anything behind her back. I hadn't done anything I could see to cause her to walk out of our lives the way she did.

"That's when I got angry. I could see that whatever I had done, I wasn't going to be forgiven by my sister. I wondered if Teresa was on a power trip. What pissed me off the most was the way she had cut off my kids. They missed Katie's birthday and Brian's birthday; we weren't even invited to Riley's birthday. We should have been together for all of these occasions. Instead, we'd become strangers."

I Told Her I Was Done

Months passed with no contact between the sisters. Peggy's marriage ended: she was evicted from her house and forced to live with her kids at a friend's house while she looked for a place to live. "It was a terrible time for me. I wanted my family to rally around me, and my sister wasn't there: no phone calls, no cards, nothing. I felt betrayed and abandoned." The hurt magnified.

A few months later, a close cousin Peggy and Teresa had grown up with died unexpectedly. Her death sent shockwaves through the family. At her funeral, Peggy approached Teresa in church. "I said, 'That could have been you or me. Death is as final as it gets. Do you want us to die like this? Doesn't this melt the ice at all?'

"She said, 'It makes me think,' but that was it. We went through the rest of the funeral not speaking to each other.

"When I saw that Teresa was able to do that and when six more months went by with no contact from her, I started to harden. We were in the third year of our estrangement, and I'd done everything I possibly could, and I had hit a wall every single time. There was nothing else I could do.

"The next time I saw Teresa at a family gathering, I said, 'I've tried everything to get you to talk to me, and I'm not going to approach you again. I'm done. If there's going to be any more contact between us, it's going to have to be up to you.' Saying that to my sister was one of the most liberating things I've ever done."

It's Not Over Till It's Over

Although Peggy stopped approaching her sister, they still ran into each other at family functions. For a long time, they ignored each other. Eventually, they began exchanging pleasantries, but nothing more.

Five years into their estrangement, one of Peggy's uncles died. At the funeral, Peggy noticed a change in her sister right away. "Teresa seemed a lot more friendly, so when she was leaving, I followed her to her car. I said, 'I told you I was never going to do this again, but you seem receptive. Are you at a point where you want to put this aside and be friends again?'

"She said, 'Yes, I am.'

"I said, 'I have a lot of deep hurt, and a lot of healing has to be done. I think what you did was really wrong, and I've got a lot of anger. But I miss you, and if you're willing to listen to me, maybe we can find a way to heal this and start over.'

"She said, 'I'd like to do that.'

"We talked for a half hour. I told her that Brian had been really hurt. I said, 'He doesn't even know you anymore. And you're a complete stranger to Katie.'

"She replied, 'I know. How about if I come down and see if we can start picking up the pieces.'

"I said, 'Let's do that.' Then we hugged each other, and she drove away."

Peggy felt open to her sister's overtures, but she wasn't as receptive as she might have been earlier. "I don't trust Teresa, and it's going to take time to rebuild that trust. I'm going to have to see some insight and self-awareness on her part so I can feel confident that she won't do this again. Once we start talking, my anger is going to rise, and Teresa may not be able to accept what I have to say. We might have a disagreement and conclude, 'We can't resolve this,' but at least the reason will finally be out on the table.

"I'm willing to see Teresa, but I'm going to wait until she calls to make arrangements. I hope she does, but if she doesn't, that would be okay, too. At this point, if we never went any further than we have, I could run into her at a family event and exchange pleasantries and be fine with that. It would be nice to reconnect, but I've lived this long without her, and I can continue to do so."

P.S. More than a year has passed since Peggy talked to her sister at the funeral. She has not heard from her again.

Letting Go Is a Process

Letting go means doing all we can from our end of the relationship, then gradually accepting the reality of our circumstances. Letting go happens naturally as we discern the truth.

Vicki Shook believes it is impossible to "make yourself" let go of a relationship.

You can feel the pain and acknowledge the frustration. As you do that, things change. You'll either let go, or you won't. If you're still holding on to the relationship, the next thing to investigate is "Why am I still holding on? Maybe I haven't experienced my sadness about letting go of the ideals I once held about this person. Maybe I need to grieve more." Perhaps after that, you'll feel a loosening, more of a capacity to let go.

The closer and more important the relationship, the longer it takes to give up hope that things might change someday. It took twenty years for Amanda to make peace with the father who abandoned her when she was nineteen.

> I've finally realized that resolution isn't always what you think it's going to be. It's not always somebody telling you what you want to hear or even getting a chance to say what you want to say. Sometimes resolution is coming to terms with the fact that you're always going to feel sad about not having that person in your life.

Permanent estrangements between parents and children are among the most difficult to accept. Helen Meyers is a mother who has had to come to terms with her son's rejection.

Helen Meyers: I Can't Force Him to Open the Door

> *People always said to me, "Things will change. Something will happen and he'll wake up one day and remember you." I used to believe that, but our estrangement has been going on for so long that I don't believe it anymore.*
>
> —HELEN MEYERS

Helen Meyers and her husband, Jake, have been estranged from their only son, Philip, for seven years. During this time, there have been periods of no contact, sporadic explosions, and many angry words. Philip, who is a successful doctor in his early thirties, has cut off most of his extended family as well.

Helen and Jake have never been told exactly what they did to be cast out of their son's life, but around the time he met his future wife, he began to distance himself from them. In the intervening years, Philip has accused them of insulting his wife, not being as generous as his in-laws, and various other affronts.

Helen and Jake have done their best to work things out with their son, but to no avail. Last year, they threatened legal action in order to see their grandchildren. Helen describes her relationship with her son as "extremely strained and volatile. I don't know when the next explosion will come."

When Philip withdrew initially, Helen was brokenhearted. "I felt defeated. I had given my life and breath to this child, and he turned around and forgot he had a mother. I've always been a very up, friendly person, but when this happened, I was devastated. Being a good mother had always been very important to me, but when Philip rejected us, I started to feel like I'd failed. I had so many unanswered questions: 'How did we turn into bad people overnight?' 'Why did he reject us and his whole family?' 'Where did we go wrong?' 'What could I have done differently?' I finally realized that some of my questions were never going to be answered.

"After a lot of counseling and soul-searching, I came to the conclusion that I hadn't been a bad mother. Philip was never beaten or neglected. My husband was a coach on his teams. I was always proud of Philip. I know I made mistakes, but I did the best I knew how.

"Ultimately, I recognized that I had a choice: I could fall into a sinkhole and feel sorry for myself for the rest of my life, or I could move on and make something out of my life. That's what I decided to do.

"I'd been an executive secretary for twenty-five years. I quit my job so I could do something different. I went to a career center and took an aptitude test. They said I'd make a good counselor. So I went back to school, and I've done really well. I'm in four honor societies, and I love school; it's given me a way to feel good about myself again. My son may hate me, but I'm making something out of myself.

"Ultimately, what's helped me most is realizing I couldn't change Philip. All I could change was my attitude—and I have. I'm moving on with my life, with or without Philip in it. Of course, I want him and his family in my life, but that's not something I get to control. I believe Philip still cares about us, but he's shut the door and I can't force him to open it. Until he decides to reach out to us, there's nothing my husband or I can do. So we're moving on despite Philip, and it's a tremendous relief to finally do so."

Leaving the Porch Light On

Although Helen has moved on with her life, she makes it clear that she would be receptive if circumstances changed. This kind of mature receptivity is very different from putting your life on hold and longing for an outcome that is improbable at best. I like to think of it as leaving the porch light on; you are in your home, puttering and content, focused on what you need to do in your own life, but you still keep a warm place in your heart for the person who is gone.

Susan Frankel is a therapist in San Francisco. Even when she works with people from the most troubled of families, she always tries to help her clients find some way—no matter how minimal—to sustain a thread of connection. Whether it is sending a yearly holiday card or exchanging an occasional e-mail, Frankel believes maintaining some bond is preferable to severing all ties.

> There are ways to stay connected without going into the lion's den all the time. If someone is constantly being exposed to a situation that overwhelms her, maybe the way to stay connected is not through visiting or returning to her childhood home. I always look to see if there's a way to embrace something positive in the relationship so that people don't lose all connection to their family. Otherwise, they're untethered, and I don't think that's healthy for anyone. Sometimes the connection is only in spirit, but still the intention is to connect. I've seen that attitude alone—even when nothing more is possible—make a big difference in people's lives.

Pam Leeds grew up with parents who remain so abusive that the only connection she *can* have with them is in spirit. Pam's story illustrates that it's possible to feel deep compassion for people and still choose not to have a relationship with them.

Pam Leeds: Compassion from Afar

We all long for that moment where the people who have harmed us say, "I'm sorry," and we say, "I'm sorry for the harm I've done you," and everyone comes together in a big group hug, but that hasn't been an option for me. My parents were simply incapable of doing that kind of work.

—PAM LEEDS

Pam Leeds was severely sexually abused by both of her parents. Her mother and father were poisoned, rigid people who were never going to acknowledge what they had done. Being with them in the present was untenable. So eight years ago, Pam broke off all direct contact with her parents. From the beginning Pam's reconciliation journey has been an inside job. "I went to therapy for a long time. I did a lot of spiritual work. I had to forgive myself for what happened. I needed to get away from my parents to see them for who they were—damaged people rather than horrible monsters controlling my life.

"From an adult perspective, I could see that their lives were limited by the choices they had made, and they made some terrible choices. Instead of nurturing their children, they exploited us.

"My parents operated from such a sad and damaged place. They were surrounded by potentially loving relationships, and they missed out on them. I wish they could have experienced a tenth of the happiness I have in my life today.

"My life is rich with people. I have a strong and loving bond with my partner, mutually supportive relationships with my young-adult children, and a community of good friends. These are all things my parents never had. I began to see this huge gap between the kind of life I was leading and the impoverished lives they had led. I began to feel a great sadness that they had experienced so few of the things that make life rich and give it meaning. But I also knew it was unhealthy and unsafe for me to have them in my life."

May You Be at Peace

Despite her separation from her parents, Pam has continued to heal and open doors to even greater compassion. "I found that I sincerely desired healing for my family. I consciously thought of each of them and what they had done. I described the sadness I felt about their separation from the most important things in life—connection and love. I prayed that the damage that they had done not be continued or passed on, and that they be healed.

"A friend taught me a wonderful meditation I sometimes use. It goes, 'May you be free of suffering. May you be healed deep inside. May you dwell in open heart. May you be at peace.' When I say that for the people who have hurt me, it puts me in an openhearted place in the world.

"Praying for them allowed me to step back and see my parents as people who needed greater help than I could give them. Prayerful meditation has helped me feel connected to a much larger network of compassionate beings, and I laid my parents in their hands."

I Had No Desire to See Her

Three years ago, Pam learned that her mother was dying, but she had no desire to see her. "During the time she was dying, my own children were healing from sexual abuse my parents had inflicted on them years earlier. I had to put my children first. Seeing my mother just wasn't possible. But while she was dying, I worked hard on my issues with her—just not in person. I wrote poetry. I drew pictures. I looked at the mothering I received and the mothering I didn't receive.

"One morning I had a dream. In the dream, I was on a journey with my husband and my children, and I saw my mother. She and I went off together to talk for a few minutes. She wanted me to eat with her, and she held out this really disgusting food. I said, 'No, I'm not interested.' She insisted and was very manipulative. I said, 'No, that's your choice, but that's not what I want to eat. If we're going to eat together, we need to pick out a restaurant where everyone can make their own choices.' But my mother didn't want to do that. Then I noticed that she was poking at her face, and it turned out that she was wearing a mask. I thought, 'Why hasn't anyone ever realized that she was wearing a mask before?' Then she poked her fingers inside her brain, and went into a seizure. I carried her over to a bed and laid her down and said, 'This is more than I can handle. She's too sick for me to help her.' There was a secret service man standing nearby, and I said, 'This woman's sick. She needs help.' He said, 'Oh, her condition is known. Her Personal Physician knows how to help her.' So I said good-bye and left her there. That was the end of the dream. That night my brother called to tell me that my mother had died.

"It was quite a dream, and I would like to believe that her Personal Physician came to take care of her, because I knew that I couldn't.

"When my brother told me that my mother died, the first thing I did was light a candle. I prayed that her soul be taken straight to heaven and that the evil she had done would be gone with her death.

"A month later, I visited her grave. I spent some time in prayer, acknowledging that she was really dead. Then I let her go, and it felt to me like it was over. The question that came into my mind was 'What can I do about it?' and the answer that rose up was 'Be in the world in a way that contributes. Help make this world a place where it's less likely for people to grow up as damaged as she was.'

"For me, being active in the world has taken a lot of different forms. I speak up as a survivor of sexual abuse. I've tried to make my professional colleagues more aware of issues around abuse and trauma. I donate to survivor and child help organizations. A friend and I plan to volunteer for a group that gives social support to teen mothers. Though each of these things is small, they increase healing in the world, and I believe they make a difference."

The Opposite of Estrangement

However we do the work of letting go, whether through prayer, meditation, activism, or symbolic rituals, it is possible to achieve a sense of inner resolution even though a relationship is outwardly irreconcilable.

When I began this book, I believed that the opposite of estrangement was reconciliation, but I've come to realize that the opposite of estrangement is peace.

None of us gets to control the level of reconciliation we achieve, but we do get to determine what we do with the hand life deals us. And sometimes the wisest course of action is to let a relationship go. As Alexander Graham Bell once said, "When one door closes, another opens; but we often look so long and so regretfully upon the closed door that we do not see the one which has opened for us."

Even a failed reconciliation can open a new door, bringing deeper self-knowledge, unexpected opportunities, new chances to love, and ultimately a sense of peace.

CHAPTER 11

When We Meet Again:
The Benefits of Reconciliation

I've learned that it is possible to go through the most intense amount of
hell and come out of it accepting things you never thought you could
accept and loving people that you never thought you could love.

—PATRICIA ROBINSON

Reconciling after an estrangement is one of the most gratifying things
we can do. Reestablishing trust after it has been broken is a gutsy, difficult challenge, and those who accomplish it are rewarded with a deeper
sense of compassion, restored faith in human decency, and renewed
bonds of love. Many people who successfully reconcile report that their
new relationships are healthier and more enjoyable than the relationships they had before. When two people make an effort to listen to each
other and learn to work with their differences, a sense of cooperation
and accomplishment pervades their relationship. Understanding the
fragility of love, they no longer take each other for granted and cherish
each other instead. Relationships soften, strengthen, and deepen, and
optimism returns.

Enjoying the Pleasures of Recovered Love

Renewed bonds bring a wealth of gifts: companionship, intimacy, shared pleasures, a sounding board in times of trouble. That's why I treasure my reconciliation with my friend Nona. She's one of those people I may not talk to for months at a time, but when I finally do, it feels like we pick up our conversation right where we left off. Nona is part of my family. I love her. I love her kids. I love our wacky stories. If I'd lost Nona, I would have lost so much of my history.

This theme of continuity comes up in many reconciliation stories. Molly Fisk, who reconciled with her mother, recalls: "The historical connection between us is really important to me. My mother laughs at jokes no one else in the world would laugh at because she knows the stories behind them. It's wonderful to feel that kind of camaraderie again."

Renewed closeness is one of the greatest benefits of reconciliation. Ed, estranged from his son for years, savors the intimacy they can now experience: "Now that I'm comfortable visiting my son, I'm getting to know my grandchildren. I can share in my son's life and accomplishments. It's great to feel like a family again."

Reweaving the Web of Community

Reconciliation allows people to reestablish bonds of support that were previously severed. In families, where people traditionally care for each other, establishing this kind of safety net can provide comfort, assistance, and solace in facing life's most challenging passages.

Elizabeth, who has reconciled with her brother, is grateful to have an ally in her mother's declining years. "Now that my mother is becoming more dependent, my brother and I are able to work as a team to figure out what to do."

Being able to care for aging parents without resentment is a common benefit of reconciliation. Marni, who made peace with her father, is glad to be there for him in his declining years. "My father and I are on solid ground. He's not gravely ill, but between arthritis, high blood pressure, and being extremely overweight, he's got one problem after another. In his decline, he doesn't have to worry that he's going to be abandoned. He knows he can depend on me."

Yet it's not just in times of need that it's good to have family around. Renewed bonds bring rewards in joyful times as well. Anne, who reconciled with her daughter, recalls: "When my granddaughter was born, I came for a week and cooked the meals and kept the household running. That might seem like a pretty normal thing for a grandmother to do, but five years ago, it would have been inconceivable for me to be welcomed into my daughter's home like that."

My mother and I have also experienced many gifts because of our reconciliation. She recalls one of them: "My children threw me a big surprise birthday party. I was in a real funk about getting older. Everything seemed to be going wrong in my life: one of my close friends had just died, I was involved with a man and it fell apart, and on top of that, I was having dental problems. But then my daughter and my best friend, Audrey, dreamed up this surprise party for me.

"I knew Audrey was planning to invite a few of my friends over, but I had no idea that all of my siblings were coming or that my children and grandchildren would be flying in. They kept it a big secret, and when I opened the door, there they all were.

"My daughter had asked everyone to bring a bead that symbolized their relationship to me. As each person handed me the bead, they talked about how we met and the significance of our relationship. Hearing those stories was like seeing my whole life pass before my eyes. Then my granddaughter strung the beads into a necklace and gave it to me.

"It was one of the most gratifying, loving experiences of my life, and it never would have happened if I hadn't reconciled with my daughter."

Reconciliation Leads to Peace

As reconciliations deepen, old anger, hurt, and resentment lose their grip. Wounds that once seemed central recede into history. Preoccupation with the other person's mistakes and failings subside. Vicki Shook experiences this whenever she resolves a major conflict with someone.

When I have a deep reconciliation, I can always tell because I have no interest in talking about the problem anymore. When something remains unresolved, I feel like a dog with a bone; I keep returning to it and gnawing on it. But when something is really taken care of, the problem loses its charge, and I lose interest; I don't want to stir the pot anymore.

As old pockets of pain diminish, feelings of resolution increase. Mia, who had a falling out with her best friend over a house they bought and lived in together, watched this emotional shift take place in her dreams.

> During the first year we were estranged, I had all these dreams about us and this big house. Sari and her husband would be inside the house, and I'd be outside feeling excluded, trying to find a way in. Other times, I'd dream that I'd take half the house and Sari would take the other half. I always woke up feeling hurt and betrayed. But once we reconciled, the dream changed. In the last one, Sari and I were living together again. We'd finally figured out who was going to live where, and the sunlight was coming through the windows in just the right way. We were living together in peace.

Even when reconciliation doesn't lead to closeness, it can still bring about feelings of resolution. Barbara Newman, who e-mailed her brother after thirty years of silence, recalls, "It felt good to do it, but it wasn't a tremendous relief. It didn't lift a heavy burden or change my life. A screwed-up piece of my past life fell into place. Now I feel more grown up."

Increased fulfillment and confidence are themes that echo through many reconciliation stories. Carol, who reconciled with her son, feels much less of a need to be vigilant around him now: "There's more love and less apprehension. I have less fear of saying the wrong thing; if I make a mistake, I no longer worry about being judged harshly. I don't have to be anybody but myself."

As we achieve this kind of security in a relationship, we become more able to handle the unexpected twists of fate that life sometimes brings. Molly Fisk, whose mother was diagnosed with cancer shortly after they reconciled, is grateful that she was able to resolve her feelings about her mother before she got sick.

I love my mother and don't want her to die, but I know if I were standing around her coffin with all my brothers and sisters, I'd be crying, but it wouldn't be with the kind of desperation my siblings would be crying with. When my mother dies, I'm not going to have all that unresolved loss, abandonment, and betrayal rolling around underneath my grief. I've already dealt with those feelings. I feel at peace with my mother now.

Reconciliation Rekindles Optimism

Reconciliation often rekindles people's faith in themselves and in the people around them. Patrice, who reconciled with her mother, put it this way: "Getting my mother back gave me tremendous faith in the possibility that things can turn around when you least expect them to. I gained a deep conviction that things do work out and that there can be justice in the world. I know things don't always turn out that way, but I now know for me that they can."

Richard Hoffman also developed faith in his ability to solve seemingly intractable problems.

> I've become an amazing optimist. Working through this with my father makes me committed to relationships in a whole new way. There's hardly anything that comes up in my marriage that my wife and I can't deal with; the same is true for my friendships. I've learned that you can sit down with someone and have an incredibly difficult conversation and not die from it, and no one has to get hurt in the process.

Knowing that you have beaten the odds and ended an estrangement can be incredibly gratifying. As Pete Salmansohn put it, "We made a quantum leap in a situation that I believed would never change, and it opened up the world for me."

A Deep Sense of Peace

It is a week before the end of my mother's extended stay in Santa Cruz. My brother, Darren, and I have organized a family reunion for all the West Coast members of our family. Everyone converges at my house. All four members of our original nuclear family show up—a rare occurrence in a divorced family like ours—along with my niece from Port Townsend, my cousin from New York, his daughter, and a number of other cousins.

It's a fabulous weekend. We feast and talk, Darren serenades us with vintage rock and roll on his guitar, and Karyn shows off her garden. Eli and Lizzy, the only little kids, bask in an abundance of attention. I hire my friend Evelyn to come give everyone massages. On Saturday, we celebrate two birthdays: Eli's seventh and my father's eighty-first. We all sense that this will be our last birthday with Abe.

After dinner, a bunch of us walk down to the ocean just before it storms and have a great time reveling in the wild, windy weather. Back home, we relax with hot tubs, tea, and music. The younger generation camps out on my living room floor, swapping stories late into the night.

Sunday afternoon, after our guests leave, my brother, mother, and I eat leftovers and talk about the party. I say how wonderful it felt for me to be at the hub of this gathering, to be the person who brought everybody together. I talk with amazement about the fact that everyone converged at my house, ate at my table, and slept in my beds. It is evident to all of us that the influence of my parents' generation is waning, while that of my generation is on the rise.

That evening, the three of us spend several more uninterrupted hours together, something we haven't done in twenty-five years. Initially, we try to come up with an activity—a movie, dinner out, some kind of entertainment. But Karyn catches wind of our plans and asks, "Why are you so eager to go out? You three never see each other. Why don't you stay here and talk?"

Discerning the wisdom of her words, we ditch our plans and settle in on the couch instead. As we talk, I marvel at the feeling of intimacy we have achieved. After more than three decades of conflict, we have entered new territory. As adults who share a rich, complex, and checkered history, we can now sit together comfortably, cherishing each other and talking about our lives.

Basking in the pleasure of the moment, I realize that the chip I've carried on my shoulders for years is gone. Temme is no longer my enemy; she is a vulnerable, sincere human being who wants to love us and be loved in return. "That's what's happening here," I think to myself, "and that's probably all that ever really was happening." The simplicity of that truth takes my breath away.

For a while, our conversation rambles, but eventually we move on to the subject of my mother's visit. I thank her for taking the risk to spend her winter with us and say I hope she will come back next year. She tells me how much she appreciates my hospitality and how happy it makes her to see my life so rich with blessings. Darren asks her if she would ever consider moving here, and her face closes down a little. She hesitates, then says, "I don't know. I have so many roots in New Jersey. I don't think I could ever really leave there." Then she looks at me, "And I'm not sure Laura and I are ready for that."

What happens next is hard to describe, but something breaks open in my chest, and I feel a little bubble of words rise from my deepest core to the surface. I recognize that what I'm about to say will change things between us forever, but I also know that this truth, like all the others I have shared, needs to be told. "Mom," I say, "I want you to move here. I want to take care of you when you get old."

For a moment, it is quiet in the room. The next moment, all three of us are crying. For years, my mother's deepest fear has been that she would grow old away from her children. Tonight, feeling with certainty that I am an adult and no longer a child, I realize that I don't want her to have to worry any-more.

"Wow," Temme finally manages to say. "I never thought I would hear you say that."

"I love you, Mom," I say. "I don't want you to worry. I want to be there for you."

"I love you, too," she says. Then it is quiet again.

Darren sits silently, his heart wide open, bearing witness to our miracle.

Finally, Temme speaks again, "It's going to take a while for me to absorb this."

"Me, too," I say.

After that, there is not much more to say, but we chat a while longer. Finally, we all get sleepy. Temme drives back to her condo, Darren heads to our guest room, and I fall into bed happy, treasuring the bond that has been restored.

FREE RECONCILIATION NEWSLETTER

If you are seeking inspiration and practical support on your path to reconciliation, Laura Davis offers a free reconciliation newsletter, available via e-mail. The newsletter features inspiring quotes and suggestions, tips on reconciliation, and will let you know when Laura is coming to your area. If you want ongoing support as you heal the relationships in your life, you can subscribe for free at www.lauradavis.net.

Laura also offers a variety of information products to support you on your path to reconciliation. To learn about her tapes, videos, lectures, and seminars, or to book her for a speaking engagement, visit her at www.lauradavis.net.

Laura welcomes feedback or responses to *I Thought We'd Never Speak Again*, but regrets that she is unable to answer individual letters. If you have a reconciliation story that you would like her to consider for possible publication in a future book, please e-mail her or send a one-page summary and a self-addressed, stamped envelope to:

> Laura Davis
> *I Thought We'd Never Speak Again*
> P.O. Box 5296
> Santa Cruz, CA 95063-5296
> e-mail: lauradavis@lauradavis.net
> Web site: www.lauradavis.net

APPENDIX A: ARE YOU READY FOR RECONCILIATION?

Reconciliation is possible only when we become larger than the people who have hurt us and the things that have caused us pain. This questionnaire will help you determine whether you are ready to pursue reconciliation at this time.

Circle the number beneath each question that indicates your current feelings. If your response is a strong "no" or "yes," circle the numbers at either end of the scale. If your answer is more mixed, choose a number in the middle that most accurately reflects where you are today.

1. Has a relationship with someone you once cared about ended because of anger, betrayal, or miscommunication?

1	2	3	4	5	6	7	8	9	10
no									*yes*

2. Do you miss the other person and wish he or she could still be in your life?

1	2	3	4	5	6	7	8	9	10
no									*yes*

3. Have you worked through your own feelings enough to approach this person in a new way?

1	2	3	4	5	6	7	8	9	10
no									*yes*

4. Are you ready to take responsibility for your role in what happened?

1	2	3	4	5	6	7	8	9	10
no									*yes*

5. Have you developed a sense of compassion for the other person?

1	2	3	4	5	6	7	8	9	10
no									*yes*

6. Have you moved beyond fantasies of revenge and retaliation?

1	2	3	4	5	6	7	8	9	10
no									*yes*

7. Could you move forward even if you receive no apology or acknowledgment that you were wronged?

1	2	3	4	5	6	7	8	9	10
no									*yes*

8. Are you being realistic about the other person? Have you stopped pinning your hopes on a fantasy?

1	2	3	4	5	6	7	8	9	10
no									*yes*

9. If a limited relationship is all that is possible, would that be acceptable to you?

1	2	3	4	5	6	7	8	9	10
no									*yes*

10. Can you be in this relationship and still feel good about yourself?

1	2	3	4	5	6	7	8	9	10
no									*yes*

11. Given the risks involved in reaching out, are you willing to face the worst possible scenario?

1	2	3	4	5	6	7	8	9	10
no									*yes*

12. Do you have what it takes to rebuild this relationship?

1	2	3	4	5	6	7	8	9	10
no									*yes*

If the majority of your answers cluster around the "yes" end of the scale, it's a good indicator that you are ready to pursue reconciliation. Answers that cluster around the "no" end of the scale point out issues you may need to resolve before you will be ready to reach out to the other person.

APPENDIX B: IDEAS FOR REFLECTION AND DISCUSSION

When you are working on issues of reconciliation, it can sometimes be useful to talk to other people who are trying to heal damaged relationships. This can be done informally with one other person or in a more structured group setting with peers. You may even decide to find someone to facilitate an ongoing discussion group.

The questions below can be used to stimulate discussion. They can also be used as prompts for journal writing or self-reflection.

Basic Guidelines for Sharing with Others:

Discussing personal issues with other people requires an atmosphere of trust and safety. Whether you are talking with one other person or ten, the following guidelines can help create an environment conducive to support and personal sharing:

- **A discussion group is not a substitute for therapy.** When relationships are damaged to the point of estrangement, deep issues often must be worked through before reconciliation can be considered. Such work should be done in a safe context with a therapist or qualified counselor. A peer discussion group is not a place to work through the traumas we have suffered. Rather, it is designed for people who have *already* resolved much of the pain, grief, and anger associated with their initial injuries.

- **Whatever is said must remain confidential.** People's struggles with relationships are extremely personal. When people choose to discuss such matters, it is critical that what they say not be repeated or discussed outside of the group, even if you think you're disguising their identity. Agreeing to confidentiality, and honoring that agreement, is essential.

- **Be aware of giving everyone an equal chance to participate.** In order for a group to succeed, time must be shared equitably. When one person monopolizes the group's time or resources, people feel used and left out, and rapidly lose interest in participating. Consider having one person serve as timekeeper as a way to allocate the time fairly.

- **Remind each other that the goal of talking is to help people move toward reconciliation, rather than provide a forum for rehashing old injuries.** When we talk about estranged relationships, it can be tempting to go over all the ways we were wronged and all the terrible things the other person did to us. Although it is necessary to come to terms with what happened in the past, a group focusing on reconciliation is not the appropriate place to focus on what went wrong. A brief summary of the circumstances that led to the estrangement can be useful as part of an initial introduction, but talking in detail about "who said what to whom" will only reinforce negative feelings. When your goal is to reconcile, it is best to focus on what you want to do now and how best to achieve it.

- **Respect individual differences.** Not everyone approaches reconciliation in the same way. A successful outcome for one person might be wrong for someone else. One person might explore her situation and decide not to pursue a face-to-face reconciliation, after all; another might be willing to make compromises that wouldn't be acceptable to someone else. A cornerstone of any discussion of reconciliation must be an underlying sense of respect for people's individual feelings, responses, and choices.

- **The focus of the group should be on sharing and listening, rather than on giving advice.** None of us knows what is best for another person. Listen to each other and encourage each other, but don't tell other people what to do.

Discussion Questions

The following questions correspond to the chapters of *I Thought We'd Never Speak Again*. When working in a group, you may find that your dialogue is more fruitful when everyone has recently read the chapter being discussed.

Chapter 1: Growing Through the Pain: Estrangement, Time and Maturity

1. What circumstances in your life have made you ready to consider reconciliation?

2. How have you been hurt by the estrangements in your life? How have you benefited from them?

3. People are complex and multifaceted, and so are their relationships. What paradoxes, if any, exist in the relationship you want to reconcile?

4. Discuss the idea expressed on page 28, "Mature people learn to embrace relationships that aren't perfect."

Chapter 2: Building a Self: The Importance of Autonomy

1. Read "The Importance of Boundaries" (page 30). What does the concept of boundaries mean to you? What limits have you had to set, or would you need to set, in order to renew the relationship you're considering?

2. Read "When Injuries Are Unforgivable" (page 33). What kind of healing have you had to do to "balance the scales" in your relationships?

3. On page 39, Davis writes, "Focusing on our pain is what enables us to move through it. Beyond a certain point, however, identifying with past injuries can be limiting. While it is often empowering to identify as 'a battered wife,' 'an abandoned husband,' or 'the mother of a drug addict,' in order to claim our legacy and heal from it, aligning ourselves with our injuries only benefits us for so long. Ultimately, a label that initially brought strength, solidarity, and understanding can become a prison from which we must free ourselves." How do you feel about this statement? Are there ways it has or hasn't been true in your life?

4. Discuss Kathleen Ryan's story (page 41). What does it mean to "agree to disagree"? Do you think you could do what Kathleen and her parents did? Why or why not?

5. What's the difference between reconciliation and capitulation (page 47)? If you can, give an example of each from your own life.

Chapter 3: Finding Clarity: The Task of Discernment

1. Take the time to individually respond to the questions outlined in "What's Happening Now?" (page 50). Discuss your answers, highlighting things you learned or things that surprised you.

2. What role did you play in the estrangement of the relationship you are currently exploring? How did your actions, insensitivity, lack of awareness, or miscommunication contribute to the failure of the relationship?

3. On page 55, Davis writes, "When we are embroiled in a conflict with another person, we typically see it from our own narrow perspective, thinking in terms of the dynamics in *our* family, *our* friendship, or *our* marriage, rather than considering the larger societal forces that may have contributed to the way the relationship played itself out." Discuss the broader context in which your particular estrangement took place.

4. When you move beyond fantasies of an ideal reconciliation and look at the other person objectively, how much do you think he or she will be able to respond to your needs and feelings? What changes, if any, can you realistically expect the other person to make?

5. Read Davis's description of her car ride to San Francisco with her mother (page 60). Describe a time you broke through your habitual responses and turned a negative situation around.

6. Read Sharon Tobin's story (page 65). What kind of person are you trying to be as you pursue this reconciliation?

7. Outside of the group, answer the questions on page 67, "Does This Relationship Warrant Reconciliation?" Then discuss the kind of reconciliation you are considering at this time.

8. Read Elizabeth Menkin's story (page 80). Discuss whether or not you think you'd be able to do what she and her family did. Talk about possible applications of restorative justice in your life and in your community.

Chapter 4: Taking the First Steps: Gathering Courage

1. What risks do you face in pursuing reconciliation at this time?

2. What's the worst thing that could happen? Are you prepared to face the worst possible scenario? Why or why not?

3. Read "Fear Doesn't Have to Stop You" (page 106). Describe a time you were scared but took action anyway. What helped you move beyond your fears?

4. Read "Taking the First Step" (page 108). What first step makes sense in your situation? Why do you think that would be the best approach?

5. On page 113, Davis writes, "When we reach out to someone from whom we've been estranged, we agree to a two-way dialogue in

which both people express feelings and have issues to resolve. This kind of active involvement is very different from only *thinking* about the relationship, where we hold all the cards and retain all of the control." If you pursue this reconciliation, what are some of the issues you may be called upon to face?

6. Read "The Courage to Change" (page 119). Are there habitual ways you deal with conflict? If so, what are they? How might these patterns need to change in order for you to develop healthier relationships?

Chapter 5: Persistence Over Time: The Importance of Determination

1. Read Miriam Gladys's story (page 130). What do you think about her level of persistence in pursuing reconciliation with her youngest daughter, Ruthie?

2. In "Don't Sweat the Small Stuff" (page 138), Davis writes, "When we're rebuilding a relationship, it is important to keep our sights on our higher objective. There may be times we need to sacrifice short-term comfort for the sake of attaining long-term goals. This might mean putting out more than our share of the energy in order to get the ball rolling, holding back on saying all of our 'truths' at once, going slower (or sometimes faster) than we might want to, or compromising on issues that are less important to us than others." In what ways might you need to adjust your approach in order to make your attempt at reconciliation more successful?

3. Read "Creating a New Future Together" (page 147) and "Establishing New Ways to Connect" (page 149) and "Bridging Distance, Getting Closer" (page 152). What steps could you take to build a more positive relationship in the present?

4. How committed are you to the reconciliation you're considering? Why?

Chapter 6: Communication That Furthers Closeness: The Role of Listening and Honesty

1. From your point of view, how much of a role should talking about the past play in reconciliation? How might that vary from situation to situation?

2. Read "The Relationship Between Honesty and Discernment" (page 168). Can you describe a time when talking about a conflict helped resolve things? A time when talking only made things worse?

3. Describe a time you listened deeply to someone you had a conflict with. What happened as a result? What gets in the way of you listening deeply more often?

4. Read "The Marriage of Authenticity and Kindness" (page 189). What do you think the relationship is between honesty and kindness? In your life, have you leaned more toward honesty or kindness? Why? What's been the result?

5. On page 201, Davis quotes Danish physicist Niels Bohr as saying, "The opposite of a correct statement is a false statement. But the opposite of a profound truth may well be another profound truth." What do you think of what Bohr said? How might it apply to your situation?

6. Read Melodye Feldman's story (page 202). What does her work with Israeli and Palestinian girls have to teach us about making peace with our "enemies"?

Chapter 7: Recognizing Our Shared Humanity: Finding Compassion

1. This chapter opens with a quote from Nisargadatta Maharaj: "The mind creates the abyss and the heart crosses it." Has there ever been a time when that has been true in your life? If so, describe what happened.

2. In the past, what has enabled you to feel compassion toward people you once judged or felt angry with?

3. On page 213, Davis writes, "Whenever I have reconciled with someone, I've had to go through an internal process of accepting things about the person that I don't like: it might be neediness, self-centeredness, or lack of responsibility around money. When someone does something I don't like, I remind myself, 'This is one of those foibles.' Rather than judge flaws, I strive to 'appreciate quirks' instead." Describe a time you were able to do this successfully.

4. Describe the relationship between the way you view your own mistakes and the way you view the mistakes of others.

5. Read "Sometimes Just a Little Is Enough" (page 219). What do you think of Colleen Carroll's approach? Would it work in your life? Why or why not?

6. Read Armand Volkas's story (page 226). If you were a child of a Holocaust survivor or the child of a Nazi, would you choose to participate in such a group? Why or why not? What do you think of Volkas's premise that we need to "recognize the perpetrator within" before we can make sense of human cruelty? Do you believe this idea could be relevant for us in dealing with our "enemies" today?

Chapter 8: Taking Responsibility: The Role of Humility and Accountability

1. Describe a time when pride got in the way of a relationship you cared about.

2. Read "Learning to Apologize" (page 249). What do you think constitutes a good apology? What gets in the way of your apologizing the way you'd like to?

3. Describe a time you backed up an apology with action.

4. What level of accountability would you need to offer (or receive) in order to reconcile the relationship you're considering? Why?

5. Describe a time you took responsibility for something harmful that you did. How hard was it for you to acknowledge what you had done? What was the outcome? Was it worth it to you to have admitted your mistakes? Why or why not?

Chapter 9: The Question of Forgiveness

1. What's your personal definition of forgiveness?

2. How do you think forgiveness happens?

3. Would someone need to take responsibility for his or her actions before you could forgive? Why or why not?

4. What's the difference between pseudo-forgiveness and genuine forgiveness?

5. Do you believe it's possible to find peace or achieve reconciliation without forgiveness? Why or why not?

6. Read "Are Some Things Unforgivable?" (page 286). When you think about extreme evil, like Hitler's Final Solution or the bombing of the World Trade Center and the Pentagon, how do you answer the question, "Are some things unforgivable?"

Chapter 10: When Reconciliation Is Impossible: The Task of Letting Go

1. Describe a relationship in which reconciliation was impossible. How did you feel at the time? How do you feel now?

2. Think about a relationship in which you were forced to find resolution on your own. What approaches did you take? Were those approaches successful in helping you find resolution? Why or why not?

3. Read Helen Meyers's story (page 304) and "Leaving the Porch Light On (page 306). What would it mean to you to "leave the light on" when a relationship is irreconcilable?

4. On page 310, Davis quotes Alexander Graham Bell as saying, "When one door closes, another opens; but we often look so long and so regretfully upon the closed door that we do not see the one which has opened for us." How has this statement been relevant in your life?

Chapter 11: When We Meet Again:
The Benefits of Reconciliation

1. Have you ever successfully reconciled a relationship? If so, how have you benefited?

2. How have your experiences with reconciliation, both positive and negative, influenced your approach to relationships? Your worldview?

INDEX